—— OTHER BOOKS BY CHRIS BROYHILL ——

THE COLIN PEARCE SERIES

THE VIPER CONTRACT

THE CABO CONTRACT

THE SATAN CONTRACT

THE SHADOW CONTRACT

THE BRONCO CONTRACT

THE ENTERON CONTRACT

BUSINESS AVIATION LEADERSHIP: FROM THE TRAITS TO THE TRENCHES

CHRISTOPHER M. BROYHILL, PH.D., CAM
AND
OVER 50 LEADERS FROM THE BUSINESS AVIATION INDUSTRY

Published by
Chris Broyhill Books, LLC
Arlington, TX
2022

ISBN-13: 979-8-9856676-1-5

Paperback

A portion of net proceeds from sales of this book
will be donated to the Scholarship Fund for the
NBAA Leadership Conference.

To Aviation Leaders:

Past, Present and Future

TABLE OF CONTENTS

FOREWORD

Leadership is both an art and a science, and in action, it is an individual endeavor, which can have different meanings for different people. It is as unique in its execution as the leaders who practice it. During my 34 plus years in the military and 20 in the world of civilian business, I have encountered more examples of leadership than I can remember. Many of those examples and leaders were outstanding, focused on the mission, concerned for their people, and selfless with their efforts. Some have been bosses, some of have been my contemporaries, and others my subordinates, but all have provided important lessons for me, both from their successes and their failures.

In the pages that follow, author Chris Broyhill, whom I served with in the United States Air Force and in business aviation, will present the examples and the lessons from a host of leaders in the business aviation industry and he will bring leadership to life. His research on pilots, technicians, and other personnel retention over the last few years has been ground-breaking, and his latest study has provided crucial data to illustrate the importance of the actions and attributes of leaders in the retention equation. Broyhill's research focuses on leadership traits, and he pairs the results of that research with compelling stories of leaders from across the industry who illustrate those traits in action. Broyhill also shares some of his own experiences with each trait that he considers. The combination of research and reality, of data and discussion, provides an unprecedented examination of the leadership in our industry and how it impacts the myriad issues that occur on a daily basis. The leaders who have lent their extraordinary experiences to this book were open and candid about both their victories and their mistakes, and the lessons from those experiences offer a rich collection of insight for present and future leaders.

True leaders never stop learning how to lead. They are always looking to increase their knowledge of their craft and typically have libraries of books and articles on the art and science of leadership. Dr. Broyhill's work is a worthwhile addition that will be added to my library and I highly recommend it for yours as well. While his book focuses on the unique environment of business aviation, it also shows that the art of leadership crosses many boundaries, and the concepts that underlie it are timeless.

Lloyd W. "Fig" Newton
General, USAF (Retired)
Former Chairman, NBAA Board of Directors

ACKNOWLEDGMENTS

It's been two years since the first edition of this book was published. It was released during the NBAA Leadership Conference in February 2020, probably the last large business aviation gathering that wasn't affected by the COVID-19 pandemic.

In the weeks that followed, the pandemic set in, cities and states began locking down, and travel, the lifeblood of our industry, essentially stopped. While some business aviation operators continued to work, many ceased operations as corporations throughout the United States and the world tried to envision the future. The instantaneous cessation of travel devastated the passenger-carrying airlines, and their leaders hastily implemented the same game plans they had utilized in the past, parking jets, furloughing crew, and crossing their fingers for a return to normal operations. But this time, they added a new option to their playbook. Convinced that the return to normal operations would take years, they offered early retirements to thousands of pilots and other employees.

They were wrong.

The travel industry rebounded in months, not years and business aviation, offering more predictable and controllable environments than the airlines for COVID, led the way. As the airlines struggled to meet the rapidly growing demand for flights, they recalled their furloughed pilots, cleared out their hiring pipelines, and went in search of more personnel to replace those who had been offered early retirement. In approximately a year from the date of the first national lockdowns, the airlines were back in full hiring mode. Meanwhile, business aviation was booming. The inventory of pre-owned aircraft dwindled to historic lows and deliveries for new aircraft continued to get pushed to the right as demand grew. The combined effects of airline hiring and business aviation expansion have created a demand for aviation personnel that is unlike anything I've seen in my lifetime.

Hence the reason for the second edition of this book.

As business aviation leaders struggle to retain their employees in this unprecedented era, perhaps the research in this book and the stories of what other leaders did "in the trenches" will add something to their leadership toolkits that will assist their efforts. For aspiring leaders, this book might provide the opportunity to learn from both the triumphs and failures of those who have led before you and spare you a mistake or two as you make your own way.

A second edition of an existing work implies there is fresh material in the new volume. If a reader compares the two books, he or she will see that there are some leadership stories that have been added and others have been removed. The additions were largely an effort to add more diversity to the group of leaders in the book. For this edition, I interviewed five additional people, two of whom are female, and two of whom are men of color. The push for increased diversity in our industry is critically important, not only because it's the right thing to do, but also because diversity in areas like gender and race can often bring diversity in viewpoint and perspective, something that is highly desirable in a leadership context. The stories that were removed were largely a function of redundancy and space.

Once again, I am deeply grateful to the men and women whom I interviewed for this book and whose names appear on the pages that follow. Some of them would allow me to use their company names, others preferred to have their companies remain anonymous, but all were gracious with their time and energy to support the book. It should be noted that all the views and opinions of the leaders quoted in this book are their own views and not necessarily those of their companies. I tried to capture their words as accurately as possible, but any errors, omissions, or inaccuracies are mine alone.

As always, to my friends and loved ones who supported me throughout this process, thank you for your belief, your friendship, and your love. Without you, my life would be a poorer place.

INTRODUCTION

Leadership is easy to recognize, but it can be challenging to define. It's one of those things that we know when we see it, but if asked to precisely describe it, words would come up short. If you perform an internet search on "definition of leadership," you will receive hundreds of millions of returns. Some of the sites will try to provide a precise definition. Others will lead you into discussions of leadership styles. Still, others will discuss leadership traits. There will be agreement between some sites, and radical disagreement between others. But the fact that there are so many attempts to capture the definition of leadership begs the natural question: if we all recognize leadership when we see it, why is it so difficult to nail down?

One of my favorite quotes about leadership comes from Dwight David Eisenhower, who commanded what is arguably the largest military force in history and went on to be the 34th President of the United States. He captured leadership this way:

"Now I think, speaking roughly, by leadership we mean the art of getting someone else to do something that you want done because he wants to do it, not because your position of power can compel him to do it..."

General/President Dwight D. Eisenhower,
May 12, 1954

Craig Olson, a Fortune 500 Vice President of Aviation and former Blue Angel pilot, summarized leadership in one of the best and most straightforward explanations I've heard. "Leadership," he says, "is uniting and motivating a group for a common cause and articulating the reason for the cause" (Olson, 2019).

So, what does that look like in action? Possibly the most inspiring leader I've ever met was one of my squadron commanders when I was flying the A-10 at RAF Bentwaters/Woodbridge during the late 1980s. His name was Lieutenant Colonel Al "Mud" Moore. His nickname had come from an incident in Southeast Asia when his A-37 was shot down, and he had to wade through the mud of the rice paddies to be rescued. He later led the development of the tactics for the then-new A-10 Thunderbolt II. Mud was a product of his time. He was irascible and hard to predict. His line of choice was: "Do this or I'll kill you." (Certainly not a leadership technique you could use in today's politically correct world!) But Mud Moore could have commanded me into battle against the Soviet horde and certain death, and I would have gone without hesitation. Yet, even now, with many leadership positions behind me, many leadership books read, and a Ph.D. dissertation that focused on leadership performance in regard to safety culture, I'm not sure I could tell you how Mud Moore inspired that response in me.

Hence, this book is not about definitions of leadership. Instead, it's about leadership in action.

In the pages to come, we'll examine leadership in the form of fifteen traits as manifested by over 50 leaders in the business aviation industry. Each chapter will provide some definitions and discussions of the particular trait for explanation and provide some research results for context. But the majority of each chapter will discuss the trait as visualized and utilized by the men and women who have been gracious enough to share their stories. There is considerable diversity in this group. There is diversity of position; some of these leaders are CEOs, some are Directors of Aviation for large departments, and others are Aviation Managers for single-aircraft operations. There is diversity of background; some of the leaders in this book started life in the military like I did, while others came up through the civilian ranks, and a few have an airline background. There is diversity of gender; nearly a third of the leaders in the book are female. And there is diversity of vocation; many of the leaders in this book are not pilots.

I should probably mention that I'm not a big fan of leadership books written by people who haven't been in the trenches. No one would tell you how to fly a jet or turn a wrench unless they had done it, yet there are many leadership books promulgated by academics and researchers. As one who has been in aviation leadership positions for the majority of his adult life, all of them at the tactical/operational level, I've had my fair share of both successes and failures. Those experiences have allowed me to appreciate and contextualize the inspiring stories of the men and women whom I discuss in this book. If my own leadership journey has been about nothing more than the ability to understand and appreciate the stories here, it's been worth every step and every moment.

In the pages that follow, we'll review the research I conducted about the impact of leadership on personnel retention in 2019. Then we'll examine leadership from the perspective of fifteen traits leaders manifest in that act. We'll define each trait, touch upon the research about it, then delve into the stories of leaders from our industry and read about how they used that trait to lead others. Each chapter will also feature some thoughts for leaders to consider about that trait in their own leadership journey. Finally, each chapter will end with a reflection of my own on that particular trait.

This book is about life in the trenches of leadership. While the scholarly and academic perspective is useful, the focus of each chapter will be the views, the works, and even the emotions of leaders in action, doing what they had to do, to accomplish what had to be done. And how, along the way, they inspired others to follow.

Business aviation leaders, current and prospective, read on!

Christopher M. Broyhill, Ph.D., CAM
Arlington, Texas
January 2020

---------------- **THE RESEARCH** ----------------

LEADERSHIP AND RETENTION

A STUDY OF THE IMPACT OF LEADERSHIP ON PERSONNEL RETENTION

While leadership is as much an art as it is a science, data can provide some useful explanation and context for the activities of leadership. During the time that I was conducting interviews for this book, I also performed survey research that involved the impact of leadership upon personnel retention. The survey was a team effort. It was built in cooperation with my fellow members of the Business Aviation Management Committee (BAMC), and it was administered by the staff of the National Business Aviation Association (NBAA). This year's survey was a culmination of three years of research.

THE RETENTION PROBLEM

Personnel retention is a significant issue for the business aviation industry. According to the latest Boeing study, 804,000 pilots will be required to fill cockpits over the next twenty years, 212,000 in North America alone (2019). Of those pilots, 645,000 will be needed for the airlines and only 98,000 for business aviation (Boeing, 2019). This demand has been exacerbated by a recently mandated increase in the flying hours required for commercial pilots, an aging pilot workforce leading to more retirements, fewer new pilots coming out of the military, and a general decline of interest in the career field in general (Premack, 2018). Whether an actual pilot 'shortage' exists may be a subject for debate, but the demand is real and has led to an exodus of business aviation pilots to the airlines.

The situation is perhaps more critical for technicians in business aviation. The Boeing study predicts that 769,000 technicians will be required over the next twenty years, 193,000 in North America (2019). The same research predicts a similar lopsided demand of commercial versus aviation personnel as the pilot force; 632,000 technicians will be needed in commercial aviation and 93,000 in business aviation (Boeing, 2019). There seems to be no doubt about a personnel shortage where technicians are concerned. The Aeronautical Repair Station Association (ARSA) believes the industry is facing a technician shortage of crisis proportions (AVM, 2019).

How do we keep people in business aviation?

Personnel retention is a multifaceted issue. I liken it to a three-legged stool, which will topple if any one of the three legs are either absent or not given equal emphasis.

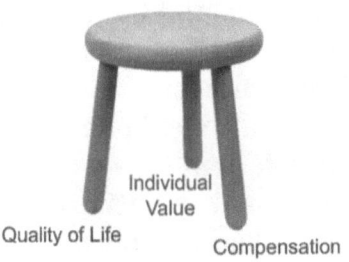

Figure 1. The Three-Legged Retention Stool.

Quality of life is about predictability of life, i.e., can an employee plan to be somewhere on a specific date, at a particular time, and not have his/her job interfere? Compensation is relatively straightforward; it is merely about whether an employee is paid fairly. The last leg, individual value, can be summed up easily: does the employee enjoy coming to work? Does he or she like their job?

PREVIOUS RESEARCH

In 2017, we took a qualitative approach to the retention problem and focused on the reasons why pilots were leaving business aviation for the airlines. The results were interesting, to say the least. We discovered that pilots who had considered or

3

were considering leaving business aviation for the airlines were a statistically different group than their counterparts who hadn't or weren't deliberating the same decision. These "pro-airlines" pilots were more likely to think they weren't compensated fairly, didn't have a predictable life, and the company didn't care about their quality of life than their "anti-airlines" counterparts. The desire for a better quality of life was the top reason "pro-airlines" pilots were considering leaving business aviation.

In 2018, we took a quantitative approach. We knew the industry had a problem, and we wanted to understand how extensive the problem was. We focused on personnel turnover in business aviation organizations over the three previous years, since 2015. The results were startling. In the last three years, 63% of the operators surveyed had lost at least one pilot to a position elsewhere, and nearly a third of the pilot force, 29%, had changed jobs. During that same period, 33% of the operators had lost at least one technician to a position elsewhere, and 22% of the technician force had changed jobs. The majority of operators surveyed believed that the personnel landscape had changed significantly since 2015. The operators also thought that both pilots and technicians were more challenging to retain and that filling open positions was more difficult over the same period than it had been previously. In contrast to the previous year, better compensation was the number one reason given for departure. Interestingly, when we constructed graphs of notional business aviation compensation levels versus airline compensation expectations, we showed that somewhat moderate increases in compensation rates could generate levels of uncertainty that would dissuade business aviation personnel from making the transition.

THE 2019 STUDY

Since we had addressed two legs of the retention stool in 2017 and 2018, we decided to tackle the third leg, the individual value leg, in 2019. The degree to which an employee enjoys their job is typically a function of organizational culture[1], and according to the dean of writers on the subject of organizational culture, Dr. Edgar Schein, organizational culture is the realm of leadership.

> *These dynamic processes of (organizational) culture creation and management are the essence of leadership and make you realize that leadership and culture are two sides of the same coin* (Schein, 2010, p. 3).

The 2019 survey was the instrument we used to assess the impact of leadership on personnel retention in a quantitative manner. The survey featured an array of questions that were distributed as follows:

---

[1] If you're a current or aspiring leader, you need to understand organizational culture and Schein's <u>Organizational Culture and Leadership</u> is perhaps the best work on the subject. See the references section for details.

- Demographics – 4 questions;
- Elements of retention – 1 question (7 responses required);
- Leadership impact on retention – 7 questions; and
- Leadership attributes – 18 questions.

The survey was administered from June through August of 2019 and sent to 22,771 recipients. We received 1,364 total responses, of which 1,010 contained complete data. Now it might seem that 1,010 out of 22,771 responses, a response rate of 4.4%, is not sufficient. But thanks to two guys named Krejcie and Morgan, who wrote one of the definitive works on sample size for research activities, 1,000 valid responses are more than sufficient as a sample size to produce generalizable results to a much larger population (1970)[2].

DEMOGRAPHIC RESULTS

Figure 2 below classifies the respondents according to the type of operator who employs them. Figure 3 classifies the respondents by whether they do or not work for Fortune 500 companies.

---

[2] If you've ever wondered why political polls typically use a sample size of 1000 potential voters, you can thank Krejcie and Morgan.

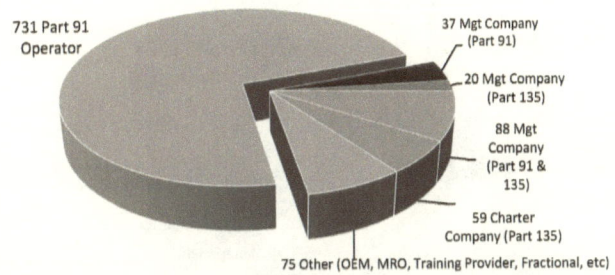

Figure 2. Respondents by operator type.

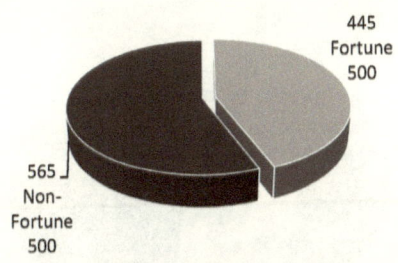

Figure 3. Respondents by company classification.

Figure 4 depicts the respondent's professional skill area. Interestingly, *Management* was not one of the responses provided to the question. The group identified as *Management* in the Figure is composed of those who selected *Other* as their response and wrote in *Management* or a leadership title in the area provided for identifying *Other* skills. It would seem that those respondents felt *Management,* or a leadership title, classified them more accurately than their skill of origin.

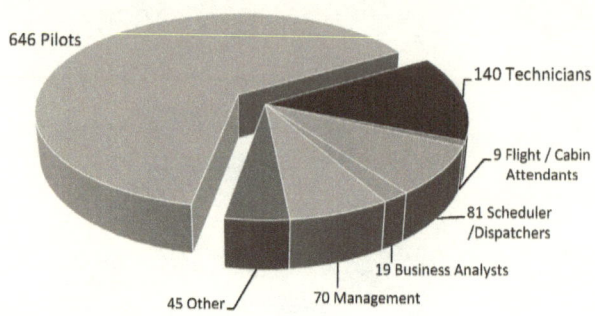

Figure 4. Respondents by professional skill.

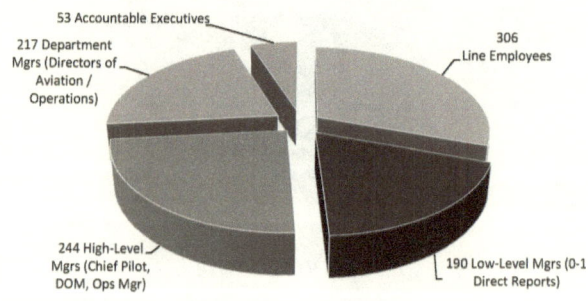

Figure 5. Respondents by organizational level.

Figures 5 and 6 illustrate the level of the respondent within his or her organizational structure. Figure 5 depicts the actual level, and Figure 6 shows the respondents divided into *Leaders* and *Followers*. For purposes of this study, low-level managers, those with *Manager* in their job title but with a maximum of one direct report, were included in the *Followers* category.

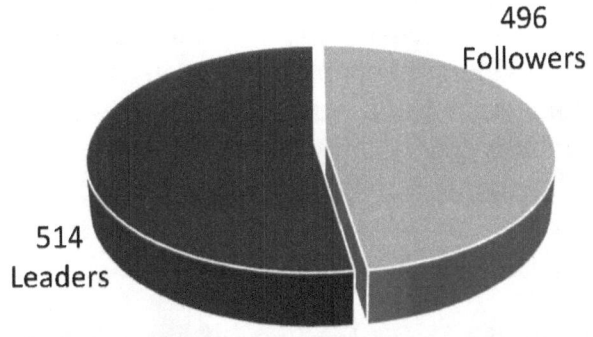

496
Followers

514
Leaders

Figure 6. Leader / Follower classification.

ELEMENTS OF RETENTION

The first non-demographic question asked respondents to rank order seven elements of retention. The respondents ranked those elements as follows:

1. Quality of Life
2. Compensation
3. Benefits
4. Leadership Actions / Attributes
5. Organizational Culture
6. Individual Value / Morale
7. Opportunities for Advancement

While items 4, 5, and 6 might seem to be confounding variables/classifications to a certain extent, from an observational perspective, it is interesting that after quality of life, compensation and benefits, leadership actions/attributes was the first area identified by the respondents. Note that while the leadership of an aviation department might have some impact on quality of life, compensation and benefits, leadership has a direct effect on the remaining areas.

SATISFACTION WITH CURRENT ORGANIZATION

The second non-demographic question was a crucial one for the study and one that lingers in the background of any organization where retention issues are present. We provided the respondents with a simple statement:

I am considering leaving my current organization.

We asked them to respond using a five-point Likert scale where the choices were:

1. Strongly Disagree
2. Slightly Disagree
3. Neutral / Undecided
4. Slightly Agree
5. Strongly Agree

The results appear below in Figure 7, and the accompanying statistics appear in Table 1.

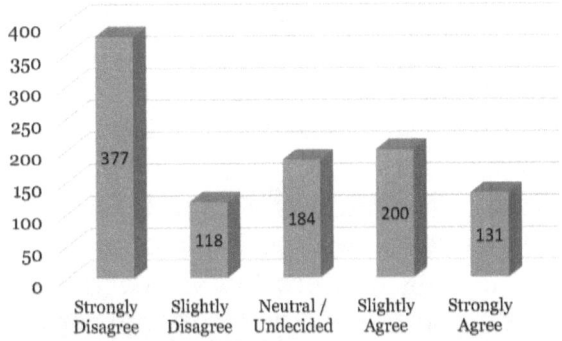

Figure 7. I am considering leaving my current organization.

Overall Mean	2.59
Leaders Mean	2.20
Followers Mean	3.00
Levene's Test for Variance	F = 2.483, p = .115
Means Statistically Different?	No

Table 1. Statistics from I am considering leaving my current organization.

The overall mean for all respondents was 2.59, or under Neutral / Undecided, so most respondents were not considering a departure from their current employers. It would seem that upon observation, the means for *Leaders* and *Followers* are different from one another. But Levene's test for variance[3], which assumes that the means are the same for both *Leaders* and *Followers*, produced a nonsignificant result, so from a statistical perspective, the means are not different.

The next question was a natural follow-up. We asked respondents to choose a destination if they were considering or were to consider a departure from their organization. The results appear in Figure 8.

Part 91 Corporate Operators were the number one selection of the group with the airlines as the number two choice. The low number of those choosing the airlines is probably a reflection of the fact that those who were not considering a departure were not included in the respondents analyzed for this question.

---

3 Levene's Test analyzes the hypothesis that the variances in different groups are equal (i.e., the difference between the variances is zero). It performs a one-way analysis of variance (ANOVA) on the deviations (i.e., the absolute value of the difference between each score and the mean of its group). A significant result indicates that the variances are significantly different – therefore, the assumption of homogeneity of variances has been violated. When samples sizes are large, small differences in group variances can produce a significant Levene's test (Field, 2013). Levene's test is best suited to data that is non-normally distributed as our data is here (Statistics How To, 2014).

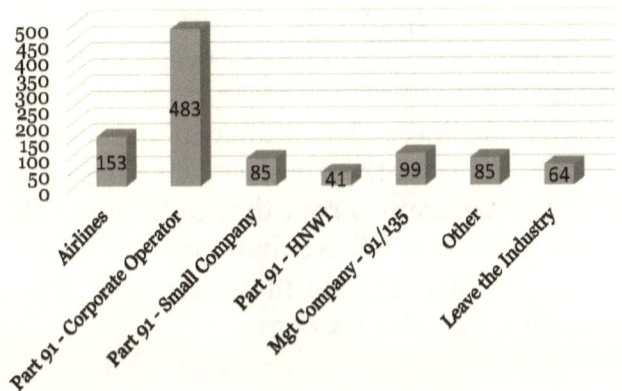

Figure 8. Destinations for departing employees.[4]

THE IMPACT OF LEADERSHIP ON RETENTION

The remaining questions on the survey dealt directly with the subject of leadership, specifically leadership traits and the impact of leadership on retention. The first two questions set the stage for the discussion of leaders and their traits in Part II. The final two will be discussed in the conclusion of this book.

The first question asked *Leaders* and *Followers* to respond to this statement using the same five-point Likert scale described above:

If I am considering or were to consider leaving my organization, the quality of department leadership would be a factor in that decision.

---

4 HNWI = High Net Worth Individual

The results appear in Figure 9 below. The accompanying statistics in Table 2 reveal an interesting disparity. While the overall mean rests solidly on the *Agree* answer, Levene's test for variance shows that the means between the *Leaders* and *Followers* are statistically different. From that difference, we can infer that *Followers* believe that quality of leadership is a more significant factor in a decision to leave the organization than the *Leaders*.

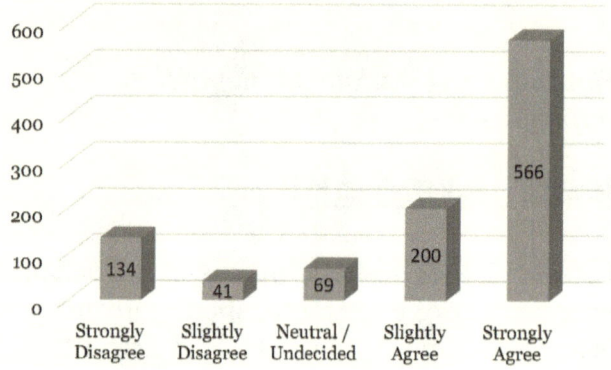

Figure 9. Quality of leadership as a factor in departure from the organization.

Overall Mean	4.01
Leaders Mean	3.88
Followers Mean	4.16
Levene's Test for Variance	$F = 24.311, p = .000$
Means Statistically Different?	Yes

Table 2. Statistics from Quality of leadership as a factor in departure from organization.

The next question is the last one we will cover in this section. We asked *Leaders* and *Followers* to respond to the following statement with the five-point Likert scale:

The attitudes and actions of leadership have an effect on personnel retention.

The results for this statement appear in Figure 10 and the statistics in Table 3. *Leaders* and *Followers* are in alignment here.

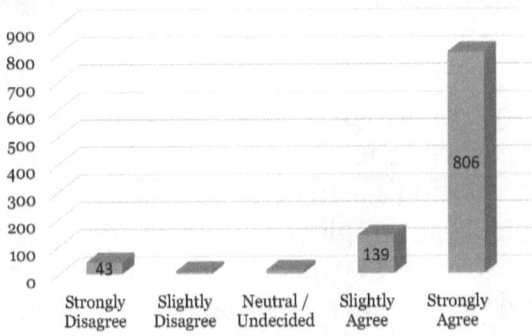

Figure 10. Attitudes and actions of leadership have an effect on personnel retention.

Overall Mean	4.64
Leaders Mean	4.61
Followers Mean	4.67
Levene's Test for Variance	F = 2.482, p = .115
Means Statistically Different?	No

Table 3. Attitudes and actions of leadership. have an effect on personnel retention.

CONCLUSION FOR PART I

We've examined the personnel retention model and looked at the research that led to the 2019 study. We've described the study itself, discussed the demographics, and divided the respondents into *Leaders* and *Followers* depending on their level in the organization. We noted that when questioned about the elements of retention, respondents ranked quality of life first, echoing the findings of the 2017 research, compensation second, benefits third and the remaining elements, the leadership elements, fourth through seventh. We saw that while *Leaders* and *Followers* were in alignment about not leaving their current organizations, we saw a statistical disparity, a misalignment, between *Leaders* and *Followers* when it came to the question of whether an organization's leadership would be a factor in the decision of an employee to leave the organization. Finally, we saw that *Leaders* and *Followers* equally believed that action and attributes of leadership have an effect on retention. In Part II, we'll get into the trenches with actual leaders and see those actions and attributes first hand.

BUSINESS AVIATION LEADERS

ATTRIBUTES AND ACTIONS

INTRODUCTION TO PART II

Attribute (Noun): a quality, character, or characteristic ascribed to someone or something // leadership attributes

Synonyms: affection, attribution, character, characteristic, criterion, diagnostic, differentia, feature, fingerprint, hallmark, mark, marker, note, particularity, peculiarity, point, property, quality, specific, stamp, touch, trait (Merriam-Webster, 2019).

Bolman and Deal, in their book <u>Reframing Organizations</u>, aren't particularly complimentary on the use of leadership attributes or traits to describe leadership in action. As they review the scholarly literature on what they describe as *trait research*, they conclude that area of research:

> *...tells us that leaders, compared to non-leaders, tend to be smarter, more creative, more extraverted and agreeable, and better at thinking outside of the box. They have more social skills and stronger needs for power and achievement. This research tells us something about what leaders are like, but not much about what they do (Bolman, L.G., Deal, T.E., 2013, p. 347).*

I have to disagree with that conclusion. Leadership traits or attributes reflect who a leader is and what he or she believes. Look at the definitions above. An attribute, a trait, is part of a leader's character, and we all act through our character, whether we realize it or not. We act through who we are, to do what we do. So, in essence, leadership attributes or traits are *exactly* how leaders do what they do.

It seems that the vast majority of popular literature agrees with me. Most leadership books you pull off the shelves will discuss the attributes or traits of good leaders. One of my favorite books about leadership is Taking Charge, by Maj. Gen. Perry Smith. Written in 1986, the precepts in the book are timeless. In the opening chapter, Smith details 20 key fundamentals for leaders, most of which are leadership traits (1986). Those fundamentals set the reference for the entire book. But Smith isn't alone in his use of traits to establish the baseline for leadership. John Maxwell's bestselling classic entitled 21 Indispensable Qualities of a Leader, lists and describes 21 attributes of leaders and how leaders can assume those attributes and become the person others will want to follow (1999). Max De Pree, in his book Leadership is an Art, which has become something of a bible for the business world, presents several vital ideas for effective leadership, all of which revolve around the attributes and actions of the leader (2004). But these three authors are not alone. If you do an online search using the keywords *leadership traits*, you'll receive well over 200,000,000 hits. The top articles from publications like Forbes, Corporate Finance Institute, and Inc.com will feature "key traits" of leaders and will often have several "top traits" featured. Using attributes or traits as a lens through which to examine leadership appears to be a common practice.

For this book, I approached the use of leadership attributes or traits in two ways. First, when I interviewed each of the leaders you will read about in the following pages, I asked them to describe the attributes or traits that had worked the best for them over their careers and to relate some stories or anecdotes as examples. I asked them to provide illustrations of their leadership style, illustrations of their character in action, through the use of the traits that had worked for them.

Second, as part of the 2019 study, I asked respondents to rate the importance of the following fifteen leadership attributes and to rank their top three. I can't provide scholarly references to support my choice of these fifteen attributes. I'll merely say that after 35 years in my own leadership journey, these were the attributes that leaped out at me. These attributes appear in Table 4 along with overall, *Leaders* and *Followers* rankings, respectively. It is interesting to note that several of the attributes are ranked differently, depending on the level and perspective of the respondent.

Trait	Overall Rank	Leader Rank	Follower Rank
Integrity	1	1	1
Lead by Example	2	2	2
Communication	3	4	3
Empowerment	4	3	4
Credibility	5	5	6
Advocacy	6	4	5
Transparency	7	7	7
Vision	8	6	10
Humility	9	9	8
Selflessness	10	11	9
Passion	11	10	12
Courage	12	12	11
Engagement	13	13	13
Decisiveness	14	14	14
Determination	15	15	15

Table 4. Leadership attribute ranking.

In the pages that follow, we'll examine each

attribute, in detail, through the eyes and actions of the men and women who lived it and led with it.

PART II

CHAPTER ONE

INTEGRITY

THE DEFINITION

Before we discuss this trait or any of the ones that follow, we must first agree on terms. In each case, we'll start with a dictionary definition and then drill down on that definition in the context of leadership.

The dictionary for a definition(s) of integrity are direct and concise.

1. *Firm adherence to a code of especially moral or artistic values: incorruptibility*
2. *An unimpaired condition: soundness*
3. *The quality or state of being complete or undivided: completeness* (Merriam-Webster, 2019).

Some who have tried to capture the concept of

integrity have often resorted to a saying that has been used so frequently it has become trite.

> *Integrity is doing the right thing even when no one is watching.*[5]

According to Palanski and Yammarino (2007), integrity is discussed most often in the context of leadership, perhaps because of the high level of influence that a leader can exert of his or her subordinates. Through a review of scholarly literature, they contend that integrity can be defined as wholeness, authenticity, word/action consistency, consistency in adversity, or in terms of mortality and ethics that can include honesty, trustworthiness, justness, openness, or compassion (Palanski, M.E. & Yammarino, F.J., 2007).

THE RESEARCH

Now that we have a sense of what integrity means, let's see what the research reveals about it. In the 2019 study, I gave the respondents a one-liner definition that I felt captured the concept of integrity in a leadership role and even perhaps integrity on a personal level:

> *I can trust what my leader says.*

---

5   This quote is often misattributed to C.S. Lewis, but it's actually a paraphrase of a Charles Marshall quote in Shattering the Glass Slipper (C.S. Lewis Foundation, 2019).

I asked the respondents to rate integrity's importance as a leadership attribute, from 1 – 7, and I used the results of the 1 - 3 rankings of all the attributes to determine where respondents placed it on the list of values.

Overall Mean	6.56
Leaders Mean	6.56
Followers Mean	6.57
Levene's Test for Variance	$F = .217, p = .641$
Means Statistically Different?	No

Table 5. Respondent ratings on the importance of integrity.

As shown in Table 5, *Leaders* and *Followers* were aligned in their opinions about the importance of integrity. Integrity was also ranked as the number one attribute, by both *Leaders* and *Followers* alike.

THE LEADERS

DON HITCH

Don Hitch is the former Vice-President, Flight Operations, for a company on the west coast. He wanted to be a pilot for as long as he can remember and gained his private, commercial, and instrument ratings while working at a fixed base operator (FBO) in Sacramento, California. Since his first full-time job in aviation in 1984, he has held multiple leadership positions and has had over 16 years of experience in senior management.

In 2006, Don was hired as the General Manager of Aviation Methods (AMI), a company that acted as the 14 C.F.R. Part 135 certificate holder for TAG Aviation. In 2007, he was promoted to President of AMI. Unfortunately, the FAA relieved AMI of its 135 certificate in the fall of 2007 for reasons which still seem somewhat arbitrary. But, during his tenure at AMI, Don took a company that was considered the most challenging TAG entity and turned it into a thriving organization by creating a culture of trust in the organization. Before the FAA arrived in 2007, Don was regularly petitioned by employees from TAG who asked him for positions inside of AMI because they had heard about the culture that had been created.

Don and I worked together at the now-defunct JetDirect, an ambitious business venture which attempted to combine the 14 C.F.R. Part 135 certificates of ten separate companies, including TAG Aviation[6]. In 2007, after the FAA revoked AMI's certificate, TAG was purchased by JetDirect, and TAG's managed fleet was absorbed under the JetDirect umbrella. Don was hired by the CEO of JetDirect, initially as a Client Responsible Officer and a key figure on the TAG/JetDirect Integration

---

[6] Those who are familiar with the rise and fall of JetDirect know that there were several other corporate names used during its short but tumultuous existence. For the sake of simplicity and to avoid possible legal issues, JetDirect has been used here.

Team. When JetDirect decided to split its fleet into Part 91 and Part 135 segments, Don was appointed as Vice-President of Part 91 Operations, which gave him responsibility for over 75 aircraft based all over the United States.

Two times during his tenure at JetDirect, Don had to make tough decisions that were guided by his sense of integrity, and both decisions came with consequences. The first occasion had to do with a high-profile client with bases on both the east and west coast.

"This particular client had continually pushed me on safety issues," Don says. "But I stood my ground. After a few minor but telling safety-related events, the client purchased a new aircraft, staffed it with a new crew, and then demanded that we issue them a waiver to operate in 'lower than standard minimums.' The waiver was denied with explanations, but the client subsequently terminated the contract. Losing a client of this size was difficult, but we wanted to ensure that safety and standards were the primary focus."

The second occasion came during JetDirect's financial decline[7]. Don had been instrumental in bringing the flight department of a high-visibility

---

7 Looking back over the history of the JetDirect debacle, the financial descent is somewhat easy to see, but at the time, those of us who were trying to keep clients happy and keep aircraft operating safety were blissfully unaware of the dire state of the company's financial affairs. I was National Chief Pilot of the company from November of 2007 until June of 2009.

entertainment company to JetDirect as a new management client. Almost immediately, there were financial issues. Payments the client made to the company were not being used to address invoices for the client's aircraft and operations. Eventually, payroll checks for the client's staff began to bounce.

"I aggressively petitioned the senior leadership of JetDirect to fix this problem," Don says, "and I was repeatedly reassured about the company's financial soundness. But the payroll checks for this client continued to bounce. In early 2009, I couldn't tolerate the situation any longer. I refused to continue to be a part of the ongoing failure to perform and I resigned in protest."

Don's resignation surprised senior leadership and was the beginning of many others to follow. It was the first major symptom of the company's final descent into bankruptcy (Hitch, 2019).

Integrity can come with a price. Don Hitch was willing to pay that price. So was Milton Hobbs.

MILTON HOBBS

Milt Hobbs is the former Director of Aviation for a Fortune 10 company located in the Northeast. He has since retired. His father was a small-town electrical contractor in northeastern Pennsylvania. When Milt was 17 years old, his dad had a time-critical job that had to be accomplished and required some parts from Pittsburgh. He walked into the local airport and chartered a Piper Cherokee to retrieve them. The pilot asked Milt if he would like to ride along, and Milt jumped at the opportunity. He has had the "aviation disease" ever since.

After graduating college with a degree in political science, Milt went to Tulsa to acquire his aviation ratings. Later, while working in Greenville, North Carolina as a flight instructor, he saw a Lear Jet freighter land and went out to meet the pilots. Soon after, he interviewed with the freight company and landed his first jet job. Since then, Milt has compiled over 44 years in the industry. Milt has 25 years of leadership positions and was in his former job for 13 years (Hobbs, 2019).

Prior to that position, Milt was the Director of Aviation for a cable/entertainment company that had dual headquarters on Manhattan and Long Island. The company operated S-76 helicopters that flew between the two offices and logged up to 5,000 legs per year, often as many as 30 in a day. The company had a difficult CEO who often challenged the pilots on weather decisions. On any day he was flying, the CEO required that the pilot-in-command of the helicopter for that day's flight call him at 5:00 AM to make the weather call for a flight four hours later, at 9:00 AM. Given the dynamic nature of the weather environment on both Long Island and Manhattan and the fiery nature of the CEO, the pilots were understandably concerned about their jobs when they had to make a hard call on the weather at 9:00 AM that was different from their prediction at 5:00 AM. Rather than sit back and let the CEO have his way, Milt put himself in the line of fire and told his pilots, "I'll be fired before you will."

It wasn't long before Milt had to take the stand for his pilots that he had promised.

A few months later, one of Milt's helicopter pilots called the CEO at 5:00 AM and told him the weather would be adequate for the trip into Manhattan that day. Unfortunately, the weather worsened during the ensuing hours, and the pilot had to call the CEO back and tell him the weather had deteriorated and the flight that day would not be possible. The CEO was furious. He hung up the call with the pilot, called Milt, and demanded that the pilot be fired. Milt refused and told the CEO he wouldn't do that, and if the CEO wanted to fire anyone, it would have to be Milt. After several minutes of intense conversation, the CEO backed off and told Milt: "You win this time. The next time, you're fired."

Milt replied: "The answer will still be the same; my job is to keep both you and the company safe" (Hobbs, 2019).

Integrity, and the trust that is generated by it, often means accountability, sometimes for the leader, and other times for those she or he supervises.

DEB PROSINSKI, CAM

Deb Prosinski is the Head of Aviation for a Fortune 100 company located in the Northeast U.S. She went to the University of Massachusetts to study hotel and restaurant management. Always looking for unique internship programs while she was in college, she saw one that offered a flight attendant position with the IBM flight department. She applied to the program, was selected, and spent the next six months flying IBM executives all over the country.

When she graduated from college, she was offered a position with Marriott and a position as a flight attendant on a new Gulfstream G-III, recently purchased by Bausch and Lomb. She chose the latter. As the only flight attendant on the aircraft, Deb spent the next years seeing the world on the G-III, but due to unfortunate circumstances, the aircraft was sold. Deb took the opportunity to learn how to be a scheduler and eventually wound up in a flight department in New England. She worked her way up through the ranks and was ultimately chosen to be the Director of Aviation for the department. Deb has an FAA Dispatcher's certificate and an NBAA Certified Aviation Manager (CAM) credential. She has been in leadership positions for over 15 years (Prosinski, 2019).

Before she became a Head of Aviation, Deb was the scheduler for a one-aircraft operation but would also book seats on the corporate shuttle. On one particular day, she received a call from the pilots of the shuttle asking when the passengers would show for the day's flight.

"That's when I realized that the passengers had already canceled, and I had not passed that information on," Deb says. "Since there were no passengers on the outbound flight, I had basically dispatched a roundtrip flight with no passengers at a cost of roughly $4,000. I apologized profusely to the pilots, but then I had a decision to make. No one knew what had happened except the pilots and me.

I could leave things as they were or call my boss and admit my mistake."

Deb's integrity compelled her to be accountable. She told her boss (Prosinski, 2019).

ROBERT RANCK

Bob Ranck is the former President and CEO of Orbis International, a global NGO that transforms lives through the prevention and treatment of avoidable blindness. He has since retired. Bob's father was a jack-of-all-trades operations worker for several airlines while Bob was growing up. Bob saw what airline captains could earn and set himself on a course to an aviation career, to include the United States Air Force Academy[8] . But once he graduated from the Academy, Bob's goals changed, and he spent a thirty-year career in service to his country as an Air Force Officer, including a tour as Commander of the prestigious 89th Operations Group, which provides transportation to the White House, Cabinet, and Congress. Bob has over 30 years of leadership experience (Ranck, 2019).

When Bob was a squadron commander at Andrews Air Force Base, his squadron had classified communications materials and gear, overseen

---

[8] Full disclosure, Bob and I were classmates at USAFA and spent our last two years there in the same cadet squadron, CS-27.

by a Technical Sergeant Jones[9]. The classified communications section was inspected, failed the inspection, and TSgt Jones lost his job. He was transferred to the squadron orderly room,[10] and placed under the supervision of the non-commissioned officer in charge (NCOIC) of the orderly room, a senior NCO whom Bob greatly respected. After a few weeks with TSgt Jones assigned to the orderly room, Bob walked into the room one morning to find that TSgt Jones was not at his desk. When he asked the NCOIC about Jones' absence, the NCOIC see told him, "Jones doesn't do Mondays."

Shortly after that, Jones arrived smelling of beer. When that sequence of events was repeated the next Monday, Bob had Jones driven to the base hospital for a urinalysis. Jones' blood-alcohol level was dangerously high, .16. Jones had told Bob that he hadn't had a beer since the previous Friday evening. Bob gave him non-judicial punishment under Article 15 of the Uniform Code of Military Justice and sent him to rehabilitation. When Bob was told that in-house rehab wasn't available, he found a way to get Jones into an in-house program and learned that Jones' liver function was only 10% of normal, hence the reason for the beer smell. Since Jones' body couldn't process the beer, the only place for it to go was out of his pores. Jones finished rehab, apologized

---

9 Not his real name.

10 A squadron orderly room is the administrative hub of the squadron.

to Bob and returned to his duties. Eventually though, he returned to drinking, and Bob wound up going to a circle of chairs for Jones at the base counseling center. Each of the participants in the circle was trying to build Jones up using empathetic and supportive phraseology. Bob was more direct.

"I'm invested in you," Bob said. "Now stay sober, or I'll kick your ass out of the Air Force."

While other members of the counseling circle were aghast at Bob's remarks, what he said made the difference for Jones. Jones returned to his duties. Ultimately, he finished his career and retired from the Air Force. Shortly after Jones' retirement, Bob received an emotional communication from Jones' daughter. In it, she thanked Bob for "giving me my dad back" (Ranck, 2019).

A leader's insistence on integrity for themselves and their personnel can have a beneficial and persistent effect on an organization's culture as Joe Segarra and Bill Korner will attest.

JOSEPH SEGARRA

Joe Segarra is the COO of the Rich Entertainment Group and the Senior Vice President of Finance. He is also the accountable executive for the flight department at Rich's. Unlike other corporate executives in charge of flight departments, Joe's assignment to the job wasn't random. Joe's exposure to aviation came through his financial expertise. As Director of Tax for Rich's, Joe had to assist in an audit from the Internal Revenue Service that dealt with the use of the company aircraft, a Falcon 50. The audit was successful for the company, and no deductions were disallowed. The Chairman/Founder of the company liked Joe's work and commended him.

Soon after, Joe built a business case to trade in the Falcon 50 for a Falcon 900B via a like-kind exchange. After that transaction, Joe was involved every time an aircraft was bought or sold, and he became progressively more involved with the flight department until he was eventually appointed to oversee it. Today Rich's operates a small fleet that includes three aircraft, all in the Falcon family.

Joe's take on integrity and organizational culture is simple. "I try to live and act it every day," he says. "It's the way we must conduct ourselves. It starts at the top and works its way down. It has to be embedded in the culture. And when it's there, it makes things work" (Segarra, 2019).

WILLIAM KORNER

Bill Korner is the Chairman and CEO of Flight Research, Incorporated, a training and flight test provider in Mojave, California. Bill grew up wanting to fly aircraft. He built model aircraft in his basement and went to nearby McGuire Air Force Base with his dad to fly them. As the USAF aircraft flew overhead, Bill and his dad would watch them, and his dad would remark, "it must take a very special person to fly those."

But the funds were not available for Bill to pursue his aviation dreams until he was a sophomore in college and he found out that the Army would pay for helicopter training. Bill was commissioned a Second Lieutenant, completed the Field Artillery Basic Course and Rotary Wing Flight Training, and left for Vietnam 30 days later. Highly decorated, he flew over 200 combat missions with the iconic First Air Cavalry Division in Vietnam, flying CH-47 Chinooks, OH-6 Cayuse and UH-1 Huey's.

Following Vietnam, Bill transferred his commission to the USAF, and was the outstanding graduate of his class in all of USAF pilot training, amassing the highest grades ever attained in the history of the program, and winning the prestigious Daedalian trophy. Bill also flew 25 combat missions in Desert Storm.

Following active duty in the USAF, Bill has had a distinguished career in business. He was the former CEO of Rand McNally and was a founder and CEO of Comp USA. Having always wanted to invest in aviation, Bill bought Flight Research in 2013 and put a new team in place. The company has become the premier provider of in-aircraft Upset Recognition and Recovery Training in the world. Bill also founded the International Flight Test Institute (IFTI) in 2011. IFTI performs flight test support and flight test training and education for pilots, engineers, and organizations from all over the world.

Bill is a believer in the impact of integrity on the culture of an organization and the subsequent impact that culture can have on business.

"You need to build the culture of the business," he says, "integrity and the right team are central to that culture. Culture is your 'ethos,' it's what you stand for. You need to preach the culture, work on the culture, at least 50% of the time. If you build the culture right, and the leadership team and strategy are right, the business will be successful."

Bill's thoughts on integrity, culture, and business seem to be paying off. Since 2013, Flight Research and International Flight Test Institute have experienced rapid growth and expansion (Korner, 2019).

Sometimes, when you work for a leader who believes in integrity, the integrity you demonstrate in return can result in recognition and promotion. Keren Mclendon believes she owes her success to just that.

KEREN MCLENDON

Keren Mclendon is the President and CEO of Robinson Aviation, an Oklahoma-based company that provides multiple services to both the civilian and military sectors of aviation. Her story of success is one that is almost stranger than truth.

After moving to Oklahoma in 1994 with her husband at the time, she found herself getting stir crazy at home. Keren examined a few classified ads in the local paper, and found a position for a part-time accountant, a good fit for her bachelor's degree. Sid Robinson, the founder of Robinson Aviation, interviewed her. He told her that he had put bids in for two contracts in the FAA Contract Control Tower program and if the company won the contracts, they'd stay in business, but if they didn't, the company would shut its doors. Robinson beat the competition and was responsible for getting 15 towers up and running in a period of weeks. Keren's job went from part-time to full-time immediately. She was promoted from accountant to Controller, then from Controller to CFO, then to CFO/Vice President for Contracts and Administration.

In 2002, Sid told Keren to get a law degree, and Keren graduated, third in her class, in 2007. Sadly, Sid passed away later in 2002, and the company went under a new president, but he and Keren worked well together. In 2016, he wanted to sell the business, and Keren was elevated to President and CEO.

Keren credits her success to Sid Robinson. "I learned the value of integrity from Sid," she says. "Honesty and integrity are the reason I am the CEO today. People know they can trust me."

When the new owners asked her about the state of the company after they purchased it, Keren didn't gloss over the flaws or issues. She was brutally honest in her assessment and laid out the entire company situation. As a result, the new owners insisted she run the company (Mclendon, 2019).

Integrity can be difficult, as Don Hitch and Milt Hobbs have shown us. It forces accountability, as Deb Prosinski and Bob Ranck have demonstrated. It has a direct impact on the culture of an organization, as Joe Segara and Bill Korner explained. Sometimes, as Keren Mclendon's story reveals, it can generate favorable recognition and even promotion, when similarly minded people are in charge.

THOUGHTS FOR LEADERS ON INTEGRITY

Integrity, trustworthiness, honesty, accountability are easy virtues to demonstrate when there is no pressure to act otherwise. It's when we're placed in the crucible, when we're under pressure, that difficulty may come. According to Avery Blank, a senior contributor to Forbes Magazine, there are three ways to maintain your integrity in difficult workplace situations.

1. **Remember your values and what initially motivated you.** When we reconnect with our ethical center, it can often make the decision track clearer;
2. **Rethink what it means to be comfortable with your decision.** Being comfortable doesn't necessarily mean you're doing the right thing. Leadership can be lonely when you have to stand up for your convictions. Be prepared to be uncomfortable; and
3. **Think about how you want to be remembered.** Placing yourself in the future and looking back on your decision can often provide clarity that thoughts in the moment do not. Do you want to be remembered for doing the right thing or the easy thing? (Blank, 2018)

A PERSONAL REFLECTION ON INTEGRITY

Tests of integrity can come in many forms in our

industry. Some can be large and obvious; others can be smaller and more insidious.

I remember a situation when I was a newly hired captain for a charter company based in Long Island. I was flying a Hawker 800 to Baton Rouge, Louisiana and back. This flight occurred a week or two after Hurricane Katrina ravaged New Orleans and the surrounding area.

We landed at Baton Rouge, and our passengers went about their business, which was only going to take them a few hours. Our FBO was being used as a resupply center, and there were stacks of pre-prepared meals lining the walls in every public room of the building. Since we couldn't leave the FBO to eat dinner, we asked if we could have a couple of meals to eat. The FBO management encouraged us to have as many as we could consume, so my co-captain and I took one each and ate them in the break room area of the building. Soon after, our passengers returned, and we took off for Long Island.

As we were letting down into the terminal airspace for our destination, my co-captain, a very senior employee in the company, turned to me and produced what looked like a stub from a restaurant-style cash-receipt and offered it to me.

"You're entitled to at least $20 for a meal," he said. "The fact that meals were free doesn't mean you shouldn't get reimbursed. I carry a stack of these things for occasions just like this. Fill it out and file it with your expense report."

I was going through some extreme financial difficulty at the time, and $20 - $30 would have helped my situation. No one would have been the wiser. But I remember thinking to myself, "I'm not sure what my integrity is worth, but I think it's worth more than $20."

I didn't submit a receipt.

A little over a year later, I was returning home from a contract trip to Morocco. I had flown the trip for a large management company based in Teterboro. Since the captain I had flown with lived just off the New Jersey Turnpike and on my way home to Delaware, he had asked for a ride. Along the way, he asked me to stop at an Applebee's restaurant.

It wasn't for a meal. He went into the restaurant and came out with a $25 Applebee's gift card a few moments later. When he got back into the car, he opened his wallet and proudly displayed his collection of the cards.

"See what this card says?" he asked. "It says 'eatin' good in the neighborhood.' I'm entitled to a $25 meal after a flight like this. I just get a gift card instead, file the expense as a meal and take my family out to dinner. The company owes that to me. You should go in and get one too."

I politely refused, and we completed the drive in silence. I wasn't called back for another trip on that aircraft.

The fact is that we all face the small tests of integrity before we get to a stage where we're approving aircraft transactions, selecting vendors, and dealing with contracts, all of which could have an element of potential financial gain. But it is often in those small tests that the muscles of integrity are built and maintained, when we make those small, conscious decisions, by ourselves, when no one is looking.

Some additional words on Integrity for the Second Edition:

In the time period between writing the two editions of this book, I came across something that shed a different light on the concept of integrity.

I try to start every day with some "quiet time" during which I read scripture, books about scripture, and spend some time in prayer. One of the books I've been reading is called <u>Handbook to Leadership</u> which presents a biblical view of leadership using scripture to illustrate its teaching points. While nearly everything I've encountered in the book has applicability whether the leader is Christian or not, one of the readings was particularly poignant.

The writers begin by saying that the definitions of the terms ethics, morality, and integrity often get confounded and people use them interchangeably. But, the writers say, the three terms are separate and distinct. They go on to argue that a clear understanding of integrity requires leaders to understand those separate definitions and how they interrelate.

Usually, I'm leaning back on my sofa and drinking coffee while I read during the morning, but those words caused me to sit up and take notice, largely because of the research and interviews I presented in this chapter. I too always thought that ethics, morality, and integrity were approximately the same thing. Turns out, I was wrong.

The writers of <u>Handbook to Leadership</u>, Kenneth Boa, Sid Buzzell, and Bill Perkins, provide these definitions for the terms:

- **Ethics** is a defined standard of right and wrong; good and evil – what we ascribe to;
- **Morality** is a lived standard of right and wrong, good and evil – what we actually do;
- **Integrity** is good, sound, integrated – how ethics and morality coincide (2007).

So, what does this mean? Well, it's a little like an audit. Auditors might not like the processes an organization has in place, but typically, they're more focused on how well an organization follows its own guidance. The strict definition of integrity is like that – it's indifferent to a particular set of ethical standards. It's more about compliance than right or wrong. I can have disgusting ethics, but if I abide by them, I'm integrated. I have "integrity." I can have terrible ethics but choose to do the right thing, and while that might be good, it's not integrated. I don't have integrity.

The point here is that for leaders, for any of us, strictly having integrity isn't enough. The value of integrity is found in the code of ethics we follow and the moral steps we take to abide by those ethics. We've all seen terrible leaders who had great integrity. Their ethics were self-centered and/or power-focused and they lived in accordance with those ethics. Hence, to lead well, indeed to live well, our integrity must demonstrate adherence to an ethical standard that rises above – an ethical standard that is in itself admirable – an ethical standard that will make others want to follow us.

CHAPTER TWO

LEAD BY EXAMPLE

THE DEFINITION

A definition for lead by example would seem to be self-explanatory:

> *To act in a way that shows others how to act* (Merriam-Webster, 2019).

Easy to say, but what does that look like in practice? Brearley (2019) defines it as "setting the standard and expected behavior for one's subordinates in the workplace." He stresses the effect of leadership by example, and subordinates' response to that practice on the culture of the workplace. He also issues a warning that the heads of organizations are always leading by example, because subordinates are always watching (Brearley, 2019).

Victor Lipman, a writer for Forbes magazine, has some interesting comments on the concept:

I was never a big fan of former U.S. Secretary of Defense Robert McNamara (one of the architects of the Vietnam War), but on one matter I thought he was dead right: He always felt a primary responsibility of management was, as he put it, to be "more Catholic than the Pope."

This had nothing to do with religion, of course, but everything to do with setting the right kind of example, the absolute best "tone at the top."

As a manager, or leader at any level, you can choose not to lead by example... and not play by the same rules you expect others to. But why would you want to? That is, if you want to have the best chances of succeeding.

There are two highly practical reasons why leading by example makes excellent career and business sense.

1. *It's effective.*
2. *It makes people want to follow you* (Lipman, 2016).

THE RESEARCH

In the 2019 retention study, I described lead

by example with the following sentence and asked respondents to rate the importance of it. The results appear in Table 6 below.

Sets the example through his or her actions.

I also used the respondents' 1-3 ranking to determine where lead by example fell in the overall list of attributes.

Overall Mean	6.40
Leaders Mean	6.43
Followers Mean	6.37
Levene's Test for Variance	$F = .575, p = .448$
Means Statistically Different?	No

Table 6. Respondent ratings on the importance of lead by example.

As shown in Table 6, *Leaders* and *Followers* were aligned in their opinions about the importance of leadership by example. That trait was also ranked as the number two attribute, by both *Leaders* and *Followers* alike.

THE LEADERS

CRAIG OLSON

Craig Olson, whom I quoted in the introduction

to this book, is the Vice President of Aviation for a Fortune 500 company based in the Pacific Northwest. He has been in aviation his entire adult life. After graduating with an aviation degree from Central Washington University, Craig took a line service job at Kenmore Air in Seattle, Washington. He started work as a pilot in 1988, and after performing flight instructor, charter pilot, and floatplane pilot duties with Kenmore, he joined the United States Navy.

Craig spent a career in the Navy flying the F/A-18 Hornet and served with the Blue Angels Air Demonstration Team twice. He still holds the record as the longest-serving pilot on the team.

When he retired from the Navy in 2014, Craig flew for a high-net-worth family for a few years before he was recruited into the Chief Pilot position for a well-known company in the Northwest. He was promoted to Vice President of Aviation in early 2018. Craig has over 12 years of leadership experience.

Leadership by example is the central tenet of Craig's leadership style. He believes that by setting the example, by always trying to do the right thing, he motivates his people to achieve a higher standard and inspires them to a continuous pursuit of excellence. This approach has yielded highly beneficial results many times in his aviation and leadership career, but it has proven especially effective in two particular instances.

Craig has the record as the longest-serving Blue Angel pilot because he returned to the team after a year away when the Blues suffered an accident and lost a pilot. Craig was called back to fill the lead solo position, one of the most demanding roles on the team. The team's morale was low, and the emotional strain of losing a fellow teammate was palpable throughout the organization. The morale had to be restored, and the mission had to be resumed. Craig came aboard and threw himself back into the role.

"I had to set an example of confidence," Craig says. "I had to generate trust in my skill set. I wanted the team to know they could rely on me. They needed to feel that we could still function as a team."

Shortly after Craig's return to the team, they were flying air shows again. The Blues finished their schedule that year, only losing two shows in the transition.

The second notable instance where Craig's leadership by example paid dividends is in his current position. In the last year, a significant change has been occurring in Craig's organization as part of that organization has been split off into a separate operation. The transformation has generated tension, uncertainty, and anxiety in his organization.

"I've had to manage through that tension," Craig says. "I've had to be open about events as I become aware of them, share information with the group, and try to be a positive role model, even a cheerleader. I've had to lead my people to a place where they are a tighter, stronger team and inspire them to maintain an upward trajectory. I spend a lot of time walking the deck plate, so my people can see me and talk to me, and I can learn of issues and deal with them in the moment instead of letting them fester.

"It's been quite a journey," Craig concludes.

There's still a lot to be resolved. But we're on a good course as a team, and that's what matters" (Olson, 2019).

Craig Olson led by example through significant changes in two organizations. Jeff Lee had to lead by example to change the culture of one of the most established flight departments in the country.

JEFF LEE

Jeff Lee is a former Director of Aviation for two Fortune 500 flight departments. He currently serves at the Executive Director, Business Aviation Development, at FlightSafety International.

Jeff grew up in Alaska, where seaplanes and boats were common forms of transportation. When it came time to choose a college, Jeff won an appointment to the United States Air Force Academy. He graduated with the class of 1974, while the legendary Brigadier General Robin Olds[11] was the Commandant of Cadets. After he finished Undergraduate Pilot Training at Williams Air Force base near Phoenix, Arizona, Jeff drew an assignment as a T-38 Instructor Pilot at Sheppard Air Force Base in Wichita Falls, Texas.

Upon completion of his tour of duty there, Jeff

---

[11] Robin Olds was one of the most inspiring and colorful combat leaders in USAF history. His autobiography, Fighter Pilot, showcases his leadership style and his accomplishments in a stirring first-person account. (Olds, et al. (2010) Fighter Pilot. New York, St. Martin's Press.)

opted to leave the USAF, pursue an engineer position at IBM, and fly with the Air National Guard at Burlington, Vermont. When the Air National Guard unit converted to a new aircraft type and put him on hold, Jeff walked across the street to fly helicopters with the Army National Guard.

After three years of engineer duties and flying for the Army, Jeff decided he needed a change, and he applied to an internal job advertisement for the IBM flight department. He joined the department in 1983 and was selected for promotion to Chief Pilot in 1991 and Director of Aviation in 1993. In an effort to retain personnel, Jeff developed the IBM Compensation Survey[12], a data-driven tool to capture and analyze compensation for business aviation personnel. Jeff retired from IBM in 2010 after 30 years with the company and was hired as the Director of Aviation for American Express three days later. He retired from Amex in 2016. Jeff has spent over 25 years in business aviation leadership positions.

Jeff's take on leadership by example is blunt and direct. "I'll do the dirty jobs no else wants to do," he says. "I'll work harder than anyone else, lead from the front, and tell my people 'here's what we have to do, and here's how we get there'".

Jeff credits his success at IBM at being able to see

------

[12] The IBM Compensation Survey is considered the "gold standard" in business aviation compensation surveys. While its applicability is somewhat limited, by design, its data collection and analysis methods are among the best in the industry.

the needs of the company, determine how the flight department could add value, and lead his people, through his example, to provide that value.

"It was about walking the talk," Jeff Says. "I had to make my people understand that our mission was never about flying airplanes. Our mission was about making the company successful through the service we provided."

It is useful to note that while there are still a few corporate flight departments that operate in silos[13] today, most tend to be fully integrated with the company they support. In the 1990s, silo-style operations were rampant. Getting a flight department to a place where they accepted Jeff's perspective, at that time, would have required a significant culture change.

Through Jeff's leadership and direction, the department realigned itself to provide better value and support to the company, even as it went through downsizing in the early 1990s and had to adapt to the company's net losses in the years beyond. Jeff also led his team to provide more visibility between the flight department and the company's senior leadership, leading one of the company's senior vice president (now the current CEO) to remark that the flight department was the most responsive service

---

[13] Silo-style operations are used here as shorthand to connote flight departments that operate in a corporate vacuum and isolate themselves, either intentionally or unintentionally, from their parent corporations.

organization in the company.

"We pursued several operational enhancements to increase that responsiveness," Jeff says. "We were certified for category 3A approach minimums in the Falcon 2000, which gave us more capability in flight operations. It was also a source of pride for the department. In addition, we were an early adopter of airborne high-speed data communications, to allow company executives to be more productive inflight (Lee, 2019).

Jeff Lee set the example as a spokesperson for the value his department added to the company. Dan Wolfe's example is related, but slightly different. Rather than speak about the value of the flight department to his company, Dan actively sells that value, on a daily basis.

DANIEL WOLFE

Dan Wolfe is the Vice President of the Nationwide Aviation Business Center. Dan's father was retired Air Force, so Dan grew up around military bases. He had a knack for fixing things and gave some thought to running his own motorcycle repair shop, but as Dan puts it, "I realized that was more work than what I wanted to do. I decided to go into aviation instead."

Dan took a job in an aviation repair center at Kent State University and paid for his education there as well as his pilot ratings. While he had the opportunity to join the Air Force and the Navy, neither service could guarantee him a pilot slot, so he stayed where he was and performed Assistant Chief

Flight Instructor duties at Kent State. Since his job also involved turning wrenches on business aviation aircraft, he became acquainted with the industry while performing those tasks.

It was an acquaintance that made an impression. After working his way through a few flying jobs, including a brief stint at a regional airline, Dan started work at Nationwide 29 years ago. He has over 24 years of leadership experience.

In 2016, Dan was named a Living Legend of Aviation, due to his record in the industry and his extensive work with the Kiddie Hawk Air Academy.[14]

For Dan Wolfe, leadership by example is about modeling the behavior and the attitude you want your subordinates to have.

"I'm about the value we bring to the table," he says. "I'm constantly selling our capability to everyone who comes through our doors as well as to the folks downtown. It feels like I'm a politician running 24/7, but never getting elected. My people see me setting that example, and it's important that they do."

In the spirit of sharing that value, Dan turned the flight department's building at the CMH airport into a business center, featuring conference rooms and team-building facilities that provide off-site meeting

---

[14] The Kiddie Hawk Air Academy is a non-profit, 501 (c) (3) organization dedicated to introducing, educating, and sparking children's interest in aviation Learn more at: https://kiddie-hawk-air-academy.myshopify.com.

locations for headquarters personnel.

"Our value is showcased to the entire company now," Dan says, "almost every day."

Dan hasn't been afraid to argue that value when challenges have occurred. On two occasions, his department has been subject to NetJets evaluations. Rather than push back on the reviews, Dan welcomed them and brought in an unbiased analyst from his company's finance department to manage the assessment and provide a report to the CFO. Neither occasion resulted in a change to the department or its operations.

Similarly, when the company made a corporate acquisition and a shuttle service was required, rather than try to source the operation inhouse and make the department larger, he contracted Chautauqua airlines to run the shuttle program and saved the company $27 million over four years[15]. The example set by his actions built credibility for himself and the department (Wolfe, 2019).

Dan Wolfe's positive actions modeled the behavior he wanted his people to see. Mark Chaney learned, the hard way, that his people were watching his example and drawing conclusions from it. Sometimes, those conclusions were not outcomes he intended or desired.

---

[15] Calculated in reference to Arthur Andersen's Lost Productivity Numbers.

MARK CHANEY, CAM

Mark Chaney is the Senior Director of Aviation for a Fortune 1000 beverage company. He is the youngest son of a World War II aviator who flew in the Ferry Command during the war. While his three older siblings went to college after high school, Mark wanted something different. Since a job at the airlines required a college education or an inside recommendation, Mark was advised to become a technician co-pilot to make his way into aviation. He attended Airframe and Powerplant school and got his rating as a private pilot.

When he finished school, Mark began his maintenance career working on light aircraft in Chattanooga, Tennessee. That started a two-decade journey that eventually landed him in his current position. Along the way, he obtained a bachelor's degree in accounting and served in multiple Director of Maintenance positions. He also had to decide between being a pilot or a maintenance technician. He chose the latter and hasn't looked back. Mark has over 22 years of aviation leadership experience.

"Your people are always watching you," Mark says. "What you do, what you say, is important. And I've sent the wrong message on at least one occasion without intending it."

One instance came during a period when Mark was leading his department through a change in location from an airport in Tennessee to one in North Carolina. While the facility in North Carolina was under construction, and Mark had people and aircraft at both locations, he would frequently travel between the two, often due to very short notice tasking by the executives above him. Since company aircraft flew between the two locations regularly, Mark would jump aboard a company aircraft whenever he could to make the journey.

"Here I was, going to meetings with my people and telling them to do the right thing," Mark says. "And then one day, my Chief Pilot, who was a good friend of mine, came into my office and closed the door.

"'You're setting a bad example,' he said. 'You're flying between our two locations, but you're asking your people to drive. How do you think that looks?'

"I was stunned," Mark says. "That had never occurred to me. From that point forward, I drove between our locations whenever it was possible. And when we worked a company-sponsored event at a NASCAR race at our North Carolina location, I put all the Tennessee members of our team on the company jet, and I drove."

Mark learned a lesson from this episode that caused him to change another element of his behavior.

"At our facility in Tennessee, I used to always park directly in front of their hangar," Mark says. "When we completed the move to North Carolina, I made a practice of parking furthest away from the hangar, so my team members could have the closest parking spots available. I was going to shut that down from the beginning of our time there. My people weren't going to see the boss take advantage of his position."

Mark's example resonated in several positive ways with his subordinates as well. On one occasion, during the first year after the move to the new hangar, there was an issue with the department's fuel farm, which was not co-located with the refueling pit on the ramp for the aircraft.

"One of my maintenance techs had sumped the fuel filter located in the pit and noticed some debris in the filter. The tech wanted to overlook the debris, but the pilot of the aircraft to be fueled confronted him. There was an altercation. I had to intervene."

It would have been easy for Mark to take the technician's side of the issue, especially given his maintenance background. But he knew he had to rise above. Mark listened to both sides of the issue, agreed with the pilot, and disciplined the technician. The example he set in a moment of potential favoritism set an example for his entire organization.

GLENN GONZALES

Sometimes, leadership by example means spending time in the trenches with your people. Glenn Gonzales exemplifies that behavior. He's not only a flying leader, he's also a flying CEO. Glenn is the CEO and Co-Founder of Jet-It; an innovative fractional operator and he grew up in Houston with a passion to fly. That passion was stoked by frequent visits to the Johnson Space Center while he was a student and it culminated in an appointment to the U.S. Air Force Academy. Glenn graduated in 1999, went to Undergraduate Pilot Training and then became a first assignment instructor pilot in the supersonic T-38 Talon trainer. Glenn went on to fly the mighty F-15C

Eagle air-to-air fighter at Langley Air Force Base and moved up to the role of Senior Flight Commander. He left the Air Force for the private sector in 2009 to join Gulfstream and was almost immediately furloughed in the economic downturn that occurred the same year. But Glenn didn't let that deter him. He had a project management background and went to work for Spectrum Communications as a new business development and program manager. When he re-joined Gulfstream in 2012, Glenn became a new aircraft demonstration pilot and discovered that he had a knack for sales. He left Gulfstream in 2014 to join the Honda Aircraft Company and became the Regional Sales Manager for the northeast United States. While he was still at Honda, he saw a gap in the business aviation fractional market and built a business model to address that gap. Jet It was formed in 2017, funded in mid-2018, and received its first aircraft later that year. Glenn now leads an executive team of four experienced business leaders and oversees a company of 134 employees – and he also flies.

"I've always loved flying," Glenn says, "but that's not main reason I do it as CEO. I like to lead from the front. And you can't do that in an office. You've got to get into the cockpit and your people need to see you there.

"Besides," he continues, "it's great quality control. I want to do the best I can to ensure the ownership experience is consistent for our customers. By being on the line and interacting both with them and my team members, I can do that.

"The other thing is that I don't want to ask my team members to do things that I'm not willing to do," Glenn says. "I worked the day after Thanksgiving, and I'll be working over Christmas. I want them to see me making the same sacrifices that I'm asking them to make" (Gonzales, 2021).

To lead by example, leaders have to be very deliberate in their actions and their words. The circumstances can involve tragedy and change, like Craig Olson's, cultural change, like Jeff Lee's, demonstrating value, like Dan Wolfe's, the movement of an organization, like Mark Chaney's, or getting into the trenches with your team, like Glenn Gonzales'. But in each case, the choices these leaders made in their words and their actions provided a tangible example that their people could see and follow.

THOUGHTS FOR LEADERS ON LEADING BY EXAMPLE

The U.S. Navy's Sea, Air, and Land Forces (SEALs) have a creed, an ethos, that is highly worthwhile reading. One of the lines is particularly relevant to this discussion:

> *We expect to lead and be led. In the absence of orders, I will take charge, lead my teammates and accomplish the mission. I will lead by example in all situations* (Greenberg, 2015).

So exactly how does a leader lead by example? Inc. magazine's Brent Gleeson offers seven mechanisms to do that.

1. **Get your hands dirty**. Do the work and know your trade. Work alongside your people and maintain an in-depth understanding of your industry and business;
2. **Watch what you say.** Actions speak louder than words, but words themselves can have a direct impact on morale. Be mindful of what you say, to whom, and who is listening;
3. **Respect the chain of command.** One of the fastest ways to confuse your personnel and damage their morale is by going around them. All team members need to respect the leadership at every level;
4. **Listen to the team.** Don't be so consumed with providing direction that you forget to stop and listen. One good sign of leadership is awareness and admission of the fact that you don't know everything. Listen and get feedback from the team regularly;
5. **Take Responsibility.** As the leader, it's always on you. If one of your team members makes a mistake, you need to take responsibility. Blame rolls uphill, not downhill;
6. **Let the team do their thing.** Stop micromanaging. Communicate the mission, vision, values and goals, then step back and let the team innovate. And if you insist on micro-information, you are, by

definition micromanaging; and

7. **Take care of yourself.** Wellness and fitness are essential for good leadership. Get in shape and lead from the front (Gleeson, 2013).

A PERSONAL REFLECTION ON LEAD BY EXAMPLE (OR HOW NOT TO)

Everything a leader says matters. Even if it might seem inconsequential at the time.

When I was in the Air Force, I spent one year as an executive officer for a two-star general, the Director of Plans and Programs, at Headquarters Air Combat Command, at Langley Air Force Base, Virginia. The general's questions were so important that every question he asked turned into an official task for the division he queried. The tasks had to be answered via email or paper package (if it was classified) and required a staff summary sheet and signoff by the division head. The tasks were numbered and tracked and sometimes required follow-up, which was the substance of my job as an executive officer. As a captain/major, it was my job to track down the colonels and get them to answer the general's questions. One of the things I admired about the general I served is that he never asked questions idly. If he asked a question, there was a reason behind it, and he needed the answer.

So, with that experience behind me, you'd think I'd learn to watch what I said when I was in a leadership position of my own. Sadly, not so much.

A few years ago, when I was Director of Aviation

for a large flight department, I received a promotional gift from a vendor. As I recall, it was a Christmas basket with candy and associated vendor swag. As was my custom, I put it on a table in our breakroom and let the folks in the department take whatever they wanted out it. The next day, another similar gift arrived from another vendor, and I repeated the process. During one of the two occasions, while several of us were in the break room, one of my junior personnel asked me, "Why do you get this kind of stuff?"

I responded with, "It's good to be the king," in my best Mel Brooks, Louis the XIV impersonation, thinking that everyone would know I was quoting a line from "History of the World, Part I."

I used the same line on a few other occasions, always with humor and thought I was quite witty. Several months later, when I had a 360-degree leadership review, I learned that several of my junior personnel had resented that line. "He thinks he's a king," was the gist of their comments.

I was shocked.

It never occurred to me that my people would take something like that seriously. Like Mark Chaney, I had to learn a lesson the hard way. When it comes to leadership by example, it's often as much about what you say as what you do. And every word matters.

PART II

CHAPTER THREE

COMMUNICATION

THE DEFINITION

The term communication can invoke a wide variety of denotations and connotations, but in its most basic terms, communication is simply:

A process by which information is exchanged between individuals through a common system of symbols, signs, or behavior (Merriam-Webster, 2019).

While the act of communication can be defined somewhat easily, it's importance cannot be overstated. In his classic work, <u>The 21 Indispensable Qualities of a Leader</u>, John C. Maxwell entitles his chapter on the subject as Communication: Without It You Travel Alone (Maxwell, 1999). To illustrate the importance of communication, Maxwell quotes

Gilbert F. Amelio[16], a former CEO of the National Semiconductor and Apple Corporations:

> *Developing excellent communication skills is absolutely essential to effective leadership. The leader must be able to share knowledge and ideas to transmit a sense of urgency and enthusiasm to others. If a leader can't get a message across clearly and motivate others to act on it, then having a message doesn't even matter (Maxwell, 1999, p. 23).*

THE RESEARCH

In the 2019 retention study, I described communication with the following phrase and asked respondents to rate the importance of it. The results appear in Table 7 below.

Keeps me informed.

---

[16]   Gilbert F. Amelio, Ph.D. was a technology researcher who rose through the ranks to become President of Fairchild Semiconductor. He became President and CEO of National Semiconductor in 1991 and turned the company around in his five-year term there from 1991 to 1996. He was subsequently recruited to be CEO of Apple during its downturn in the mid 1990's and was ousted after only 500 days in the position. It is widely speculated that Steve Jobs, who had recently returned to the company, was responsible for Amelio's departure.

I also used the respondents' 1-3 ranking to determine where communication fell in the overall list of attributes.

Overall Mean	5.98
Leaders Mean	5.93
Followers Mean	6.03
Levene's Test for Variance	$F = 1.230, p = .268$
Means Statistically Different?	No

Table 7. Respondent ratings on the importance of communication.

As shown in Table 7, *Leaders* and *Followers* were aligned in their opinions about the importance of communication. But *Leaders* and *Followers* differed in their rankings of it. *Leaders* ranked it fourth, after empowerment. *Followers* ranked it third.

THE LEADERS

GUIDO VISCONTI

Guido Visconti is the Director of Aviation for a Fortune 500 company based in the Chicago area. He's the son of Italian immigrants who came to the U.S. in the early 1950s with nothing but the clothes they were wearing. They rode bicycles until Guido was in high school because they couldn't afford a car. Guido did well in high school, and after graduation, he was accepted into a college chemical engineering program. At the same time, he noticed that Concordia University had an aviation program where he could major in business and minor in aviation. His schedule would alternate time between the classroom and the airport.

"That was the first day of the rest of my life," Guido says. "I became a flight instructor early in my sophomore year, was recruited to be the Chief Pilot of another flight school soon after, and I managed all aspects of that school's operation."

Over the next several years, Guido built and ran a small charter company, worked for a large Milwaukee charter company, and later became a Standards Captain on an account for a large Fortune 500 bank managed under TAG aviation. He joined his current organization in 2001 and assumed Director of Aviation duties in 2015. He has 26 years of leadership experience.

Guido ranks the ability to communicate as his number one, go-to, leadership trait.

"You have to listen actively," he says. "You have to not only hear what people are saying; you have to understand why they're saying it. That kind of communication builds rapport and trust."

While communication with peers was important, Guido found that active listening was most important with his superiors and subordinates.

"I've been pursued and promoted throughout my career because of the people I've worked for," he says. "I listen to them carefully, I'm enthusiastic about learning from them, and they respect that I think."

Guido was promoted to his current position while his department was in a period of significant flux. His predecessor had retired abruptly after occupying the Director position for many years. While the department and its operations may have appeared satisfactory, the lack of transparency due to the authoritarian leadership style of the previous director had demoralized the department.

"When I took over, I had no transition material," Guido says. "No data, no history, only empty file cabinets. I also discovered we had pending lease turn-ins on two older aircraft, but no information on how our processes worked. It was a mess."

Guido knew he had to understand exactly where they were, map out where they were going, and rebuild trust inside and outside the department.

"Listening was key to this process, to this rebuilding," he says. "I had to be direct with my people. I told them we could dwell on the pain and drama of the past, or we could learn the lessons and move on. It turned out to be a long and tedious process. I had to revamp and rebuild the department's identity and regain the trust. I had to show my people I was working on their behalf and the organization's, by listening to them and communicating what I was doing and why."

Part of that communication process was a conversation with senior leadership about the role and goals of the department within the company. This conversation took place in increments over the course of two years.

"I had to convince leadership that we needed to

change the culture of our organization to provide them with better, safer service," Guido says. "I told them we could do things the way we always had, or we could strive for industry best practices where people and process were concerned. The latter approach would be more costly than our legacy practices, but the result would more directly align with our values and requirements" (Visconti, 2019).

Guido Visconti achieved a better state for his department and the morale of his people through open communication. Kellie Rittenhouse built an entire management business using the same skill.

KELLIE RITTENHOUSE, CAM

Kellie Rittenhouse is the Director of Aviation for Hangar Aviation Management, LLC. She started college as a journalism major, transitioned to an English education major, but after graduation, she chose a job that used neither of those skills. She became a receptionist at what was then Clark Aviation in Bloomington, Illinois, but her responsibilities there went beyond meeting the people who came through the doors. She also sold charters, coordinated the trips, and dispatched them. Through her job, Kellie became enamored with aviation and wanted to increase her knowledge of it. She attended schedulers and dispatcher's conferences to build her expertise and gain additional training.

When Kellie's husband, a professional pilot, was moved to Pontiac, Michigan, she moved with him and found a job at the same airport with Pentastar

Aviation. She worked as a receptionist there for about 18 months, hoping to gain increased responsibility as she had in her previous job. When that didn't happen, she moved down the field to the Volkswagen flight department.

In 1998, when the Daimler-Chrysler merger occurred, Pentastar called her back, and she returned to become the Scheduler for the company's Part 91 and Part 135 operations, utilizing 20-23 aircraft and flying worldwide. Kellie's responsibilities included scheduling 75 pilots and 15 flight attendants, as well as dealing with the spouses of the employees they transported. During the time she performed these duties, she earned her FAA Dispatcher's certificate to increase credibility with those with whom she worked.

When Daimler sold all core businesses, including aviation, a few years later, Edsel Ford purchased the aviation division and put it under the Pentastar brand. Kellie transitioned to flight operations and ran the Pentastar dispatch center, a 24/7/365 function. While running the center, she also handled Ford's travel, which tended to be very challenging. Kellie's thoroughness in that function impressed Ford, and he decided that he wanted the customer experience that he was receiving replicated across the organization. Kellie built an owner services division and served as the liaison between owners and the company and reported directly to the president of Pentastar and Ford himself. When problems began to emerge in the FBO part of the business, Ford assigned her to fix it. "Teach them the Pentastar way," he said. Kellie was promoted to Director of Customer Relations, and in that position, she built training programs for over 200 employees.

In 2011, a consultant recruited her to be a Scheduler for a new aircraft operation that was starting on the field. In this position, she would not only schedule aircraft and crew but also have accounting and tax responsibilities as well. As the operation grew from one plane to several over the next three years, she worked as part of a three-person team with the Chief Pilot and Director of Maintenance. Eventually, the need for an overall leader in the organization became apparent, and she was promoted to Director of Aviation. Kellie has over 20 years of leadership experience.

Kellie attributes much of her success to a style of communication that goes far beyond the words involved. "Listening is the most important part of the communication process," she says. "You have to understand not just what people are saying, but why people are saying it and how they are saying it. You have to adapt yourself to their style of communication and use that style to communicate back. You have to do your best to read people."

Kellie's first communication challenge came when she was performing crew scheduling duties for Pentastar. She had to work with Chrysler Aviation's Vice President of Flight Operations.

"That operation had a lot of moving parts," Kellie says. "I ended up building a chart of who flew what so that I could get the right people into the right airplanes. But it was more than that. I had to have regular discussions with the VP of Flight Ops and his Chief Pilot and about scheduling parameters. Those two guys provided mentorship and guidance, but I learned the importance of listening for what people are really saying, and often that goes beyond the words. Those skills were especially important when I'd have to handle calls from crew members who were angry about their flight assignments. I found that if I listened beyond the words and applied some empathy, I could usually find a way to make things work and deal with their issues. It was about putting myself in their shoes."

But Kellie is quick to admit that she hasn't always seen the right cues in a communications exchange.

"We had a CEO traveling on one of our jets, which was scheduled to fly to Mexico to meet a head of state. His aircraft had a mechanical issue at departure time, so I was sent out to his jet to bring him into the building and get him a private room for a conference call. It was a big room and had a grand table that had quite a bit of history to it. I told him a story about the table, and it soon became apparent he didn't want to hear it. I got him on the phone and got out of there.

"My timing was terrible," Kellie recalls. "The story was not a good use of his time. Although I ended up building a good rapport with him eventually, I learned that I had to have better awareness in situations like that. I needed to learn how to read the room, how to read people."

For Kellie, reading people is a lot about asking the right questions and listening to the answers.

"Many times, we solve the wrong problem," she

says. We can get more concerned with our rules and processes than what the customer wants. We need to ask the right questions. Except where safety issues are concerned, 'no' is never the right answer. We have to present options. We need to turn plane talk into plain talk whenever possible" (Rittenhouse, 2019).

Communication can be general and organizational, as Guido Visconti showed us. It can be organizational and personal, as Kellie demonstrated. But sometimes, it has to be strictly personal, and it has to convey bad news. Colin Powell has been quoted as saying, "Bad news isn't like wine. It doesn't improve with age.[17] " Both Jad Donaldson and Tony Kern were placed in situations where they had to use their communications skills to convey bad news in a timely manner.

JAD DONALDSON

Jad Donaldson is the Director of Aviation for Harley Davidson. He wanted to fly since he was three years old, although as he was growing up, he was told he should get a "real job" first. He started flying gliders at the age of 12 and soloed at 14. When the time came for college, Jad chose a school with an electrical engineering program, Tri-State University in Angola, Indiana. But when he wasn't in class, he spent every waking hour at the Angola Airport, and

---

[17] I have not found the original source document for this quote although it has been widely attributed to Powell.

by his third year in college, he had obtained all of his ratings.

Jad finished school with a variety of degrees and went to work for a local manufacturing company that had locations in nine different states. Since he was able to rent a Cessna 310R from the local airport for $175 per hour, Jad convinced the CEO that flying his personnel to the various locations in the C-310R was more cost-effective than driving and the CEO agreed.

After flying there for a few years, Jad moved to Michigan and took a position with the University of Michigan Survival Flight, a medivac operator that supported the University's hospital. Jad obtained his airline transport pilot rating shortly after he was hired and remained there for seven years. During his tenure, he used his flight and electrical engineering expertise to contribute to the development of a portable heart-lung machine that could fit inside an aircraft cabin.

Jad applied to join Avfuel's flight department on the advice of a co-worker, became the department's Chief Pilot after two years and Director of Aviation shortly after that. In 2015, Jad was recruited to be the Director of Aviation for Harley Davidson when the previous Director left to take another position. Jad has over 20 years of leadership experience.

Jad is about building trust with the people in his organization, telling people what they need to hear, not necessarily what they want to hear. This attitude was tested a few years after he took the Director position at Harley when it became apparent that the department would have to be downsized.

"The financial cues were obvious," Jad says. "The market was shrinking, and it wasn't long before I was given about four months' notice by the executives above that the department would lose one of its two aircraft. For safety reasons, I couldn't tell my team about the department's fate, but I still had to make preparations for it. In the meantime, the company's human resources department was not managing information related to the downsizing well, and my people were losing their focus. I had to preserve safety. I put one aircraft into an out-of-service status, and the Chief Pilot and I flew all the department's missions on the remaining aircraft."

Before the formal announcement of the downsizing was released, one of Jad's pilots came into his office and shut the door. "I just saw a great opportunity in Chicago," the pilot said.

Jad had a choice to make in that moment. He could remain silent, or he could communicate the bad news without violating the guidelines of the company. He didn't hesitate. "You should be looking at that opportunity," he said.

The pilot smiled at him, thanked him for his candor, and left the office. When the department was summoned for the final announcement of the downsizing sometime later, the same pilot came to Jad a few minutes before the meeting and told him, "I think this is going to be a lot harder on you than on me. Thanks to you, I'm good."

As it turned out, all three of the employees who were laid off in the downsizing landed well, and the pilots were given a recurrent training event before they departed. Jad's willingness to communicate the bad news with tact made a substantial difference in that process.

TONY KERN, ED.D.

Dr. Tony Kern is a well-known figure in our industry. His work in the fields of both human performance and human attitudes in the cockpit has significantly added to knowledge in the aviation safety field. He continues to challenge aviation personnel to perform at their highest level[18]. Interestingly, Tony didn't start his life intent on a career in aviation.

After graduating from college in 1978, Tony initially decided he was going to teach school. But then, on January 2, 1979, he walked into the Marine recruiting office in Ann Arbor, Michigan, and told the recruiter he wanted to see what they have to offer and vice versa.

The marine talked to him for a few minutes and said, "You know Tony, with a college degree, you might be able to get into Officer Training School. Unfortunately, we're full for officers right now. But go next door to the Air Force. They usually come in late, but they might be able to do something for you."

The Air Force recruiter's tardiness resulted in the

---

[18] Tony's books, Redefining Airmanship and Flight Discipline are outstanding works and highly recommended. In a previous leadership role, I bought copies of both books and made them required reading for my pilots.

Air Force's gain. Tony signed on with the Air Force, and after taking the mandatory entry exams, he was selected for Undergraduate Navigator Training after he completed the Air Force's Officer Training School (OTS) at Lackland Air Force Base in San Antonio, Texas. While he was at OTS however, he began to see the lay of the land, and he realized that he wanted to be a pilot instead of a navigator.

After being told multiple times that the transition from the navigator track to the pilot track was impossible, Tony persisted in asking the question to OTS Commander. His persistence paid off. The night before his graduation from OTS, he was called into the Commander's office. He recalls a sinking feeling.

"Being called in the night before graduation probably meant they had discovered something in my performance that would prevent me from graduating," Tony says.

As he stood at attention in front of the Wing Commander's desk, the Colonel looked at him and said. "Kern, you've been a pain in the ass. When you throw your hat in the air tomorrow morning, you'd better catch it. You are to report to pilot training next Monday at Vance Air Force Base."

Following completion of pilot training, Tony was initially assigned as a first-assignment instructor pilot, but his father had suffered a heart attack, so Tony was given an assignment as a tanker copilot in Michigan to be near his ailing father, who lived alone. From there, Tony went to McConnell Air Force Base to fly tankers, upgraded to aircraft commander, and worked in the wing scheduling shop where he was asked to rewrite the wing's operating procedures for a new aircraft that would soon arrive.

Tony's operational and staff work was recognized, and he was selected as initial cadre for the B-1B bomber. He soon upgraded to instructor pilot and examiner in the aircraft. After a subsequent tour as an Associate Professor at the Air Force Academy, Tony retired from the Air Force and took a civilian position as the National Aviation Director of Aviation for the United States Forest Service, the largest non-military government aviation program in the world. In 2003, he left government service to form what is now Convergent Performance, a multi-million-dollar company that provides Human Reliability and Performance Training for a worldwide clientele.

Tony believes in directness when talking to his employees. Newcomers to his company are given the same, no-nonsense rules.

"We trust you fully from the beginning. We only have a few rules. Don't F-up my team...Do not lie to anyone about anything. Violate either and you're gone. We work hard around here and have fun doing it, but if you need a lot of pats on the back, or someone to tell you what do every day, you don't belong here."

When there is misconduct in his organization, Tony believes in forceful, constructive intervention. In one case, he needed to counsel a new business development employee who had an aggressive attitude toward her fellow employees, especially when she was under stress. She had a habit of shifting blame for failing to meet targets. That violated the two rules. Tony confronted her on her behavior, and she agreed to change it. Soon after, though, it was apparent that she had resumed that behavior, and she was quickly terminated from the company. The word has spread to each new employee since that time. Convergent is serious about the basics. In a word – it's their culture.

Tony also strongly believes that his employees are strong enough to take constructive criticism

"Every self-regulated organization needs negative feedback," Tony says. "It's like the Blue Angel's debrief. For the first 20 minutes, no one is allowed to say anything positive. They have to focus on what they did wrong. That requires direct conversation. Direct communication. It requires that you deliver the bad news and not be afraid to do that[19]" (Kern, 2019).

Together, Guido Visconti, Kellie Rittenhouse, Jad Donaldson, and Tony Kern have shown us the importance of open and direct communication from leaders to their people. Whether it is managing change, like Guido and Jad experienced, building the organization as Kellie has shown us, or just being direct with new hires about expectations for

---

[19] While I was in the Air Force, I tried out for the Thunderbirds twice. During the process, I witnessed multiple briefings, shows and debriefings. The debriefs were detailed and direct. Even the slightest errors were thoroughly examined and discussed. It's been said that the Thunderbirds have never flown and will never fly a "perfect' show. But they certainly work at it. I've never witnessed a Blue Angel debrief, but Tony's remarks show the same orientation.

performance as Tony has related, communication acts as the oil in the gears of the organization, for without it, the organization can come to a grinding halt.

THOUGHTS FOR LEADERS ON COMMUNICATION

John C. Maxwell has four simple guidelines or truths for effective communication.

1. **Simplify your Message**. The key to effective communication is simplicity. Forget about impressing people with big words or long, complex sentences. As Napoleon Bonaparte used to say: "Be clear, be clear, be clear;"

2. **See the Person**. Focus on the people with whom you're communicating. Know your audience. Build the message to connect with that audience. Keep the message to accomplish the task and to fit into the designated time. People believe in great communicators when those communicators believe in people;

3. **Show the Truth**. Credibility precedes great communication. Believe what you say. Ordinary people become extraordinary communicators when they are fired up with conviction. It's also important to live what you say, after you say it; and

4. **Seek a Response**. The goal of all communication is action. When you speak,

give people something to feel, something
to remember, something to do (Maxwell,
1999).

When paging through leadership books in
preparation for writing this book, I came across a
book called <u>The Powell Principles</u>, by Oren Harari.
In that book, the only principle or chapter devoted to
communication is about listening. Harari says that in
a conversation with Powell, one would be struck by
how intently Powell listens. "In fact," Harari says, "he
seems to be more inclined to listen than be listened
to" (Harari, 2003, p. 11). Harari goes on to say
something about listening that I found very apropos:

*When managers ascend the corporate
hierarchy, they sometimes become afflicted
with a curious problem: their ears get smaller
and their mouths get bigger. Perversely, the
more they say without hearing, the less likely
they are to be heard. Leaders who shut up
and listen not only learn a lot, but carve out
an environment where others are willing to
listen to them. Encouraging communication
at all levels of the organization—and listening
to the dialogue that results—raises the bar on
individual and group performance* (Harari,
2003, pp. 11-12).

A PERSONAL REFLECTION ON COMMUNICATION

Perhaps the best lessons in communication I ever

experienced came while I was flying fighters in the Air Force. As a flight leader, you brief the mission to one to three other pilots, maybe more if it was a training mission with two-seat aircraft in the flight. You led the mission, and when you came back through the doors, you went into the room to debrief. When the briefing room door was shut, the rank came off, and you listened to all the things you messed up, often voiced by pilots who were junior. I've been on the giving and receiving end of these debriefs more times than I can remember.

When I was on the giving end, as a wingman or instructor, I tried to be direct, but respectful in my remarks. When I was on the receiving end, I couldn't control either the tone or breadth of the comments that came from my flight members, and those remarks came in all modes and flavors. There was no quarter expected or given.

In Fighter Weapons School, there were many sorties where it was three instructors and me. The instructors took pages of notes on my performance in the air– an impressive feat in a pre-LASTE[20] A-10 with no autopilot. When we landed, the debrief was detailed and lengthy. When I was checked out as a

---

[20] LASTE – Low Altitude Safety and Targeting Enhancements, was the system that brought the A-10 into the modern era with a computing gunsight, enhanced stability and an autopilot. Before it was installed in the early 90's, we shot the gun and dropped bombs manually, using the same techniques as World War II aviators used in the 1940s.

Mission Commander, both in the A-10 and in the F-16, it was me and up to 100 other aircraft, all with pilots who had their opinions about what had been done well or not. The debriefs could be hours long.

In all of those cases, I had to sit (or stand) there and face the music, regardless of how it was delivered. There was no room for my ego, hurt feelings, or thin skin. The goal was to listen, to learn, to improve my performance, and to execute the mission better.

In the world of business aviation, we can all lead better if we approach communicating with our people with the same mentality. If we remove our ego from the communication process, we listen more acutely and we speak more empathetically, we develop our leadership, improve our organization, and, most importantly, we execute our mission better.

PART II

———— CHAPTER FOUR ————

EMPOWERMENT

THE DEFINITION

Empowerment can mean different things to different people. The dictionary definitions, however, seem to be straightforward.

1. *The act or action of <u>empowering</u> someone or something: the granting of the power, right, or authority to perform various acts or duties*
2. *The state of being empowered to do something: the power, right, or authority to do something* (Merriam-Webster, 2019).

Page and Czuba (1999) performed a comprehensive literature review on the concept of empowerment. After initially concluding that the term was not well defined in the sources they consulted, they constructed a general definition of it that is process-oriented:

> *...empowerment is a multi-dimensional social process that helps people gain control over their own lives. It is a process that fosters power (that is, the capacity to implement) in people, for use in their own lives, their communities, and in their society, by acting on issues that they define as important* (Page, N. & Czuba, C.E, 1999).

Page and Czuba emphasize the social aspect of empowerment since it occurs in relationship to others. They also insist that empowerment is a path, a journey, a process, that develops over time as work occurs within it (Page, N. & Czuba, C.E, 1999).

In contrast, Steven R. Covey viewed empowerment as a natural function of trust on the part of leadership.

> *By extending trust, you empower people. You leverage your leadership. You create a high-trust culture that brings out the best in people, creates high-level synergy, and maximizes the ability of any organization—whether it be a business, a school, an NPO, or a family— to accomplish what it sets out to do.* (Covey, S.M.R. & Merrill, R.R., 2006, p. 228)

THE RESEARCH

Empowerment is a difficult concept to capture in a brief sentence. In the 2019 retention study, I described it with the following phrase and asked respondents to rate the importance of it. The results appear in Table 8 below.

Gives me the resources to do my job and trusts me to do it.

I also used the respondents' 1-3 ranking to determine where *Empowerment* fell in the overall list of attributes.

Overall Mean	6.16
Leaders Mean	6.19
Followers Mean	6.13
Levene's Test for Variance	$F = 2.187, p = .139$
Means Statistically Different?	No

Table 8. Respondent ratings on the importance of empowerment.

As shown in Table 8, *Leaders* and *Followers* were aligned in their opinions about the importance of empowerment. *Leaders* and *Followers* differed in their rankings. *Leaders* ranked it third, and *Followers* ranked it fourth.

THE LEADERS

Tony Kern[21] and Jad Donaldson have similar approaches to empowerment. Tony believes in some instances; the best decision can be not to lead.

"I refuse to lead talented people conventionally," he says. "Sometimes, the best approach is not to lead at all but to make people make their own decisions. You need to challenge them, make them figure it out, and let them figure out how to generate the work required in the time available. There are certain people who thrive in that environment because they understand they won't be put in a false box of time and requirements to meet a self-imposed deadline that reduces innovation and the quality of work."

"But really," Tony continues, "it's about the team you select. Ninety percent of leadership is the setup. Project work is like a playbook. The trick is to get the team to design the playbook and hold themselves accountable to it. That's the way you empower people. That's the way you get things done" (Kern, 2019).

Jad Donaldson's approach to empowerment is similar to Tony's.

"I don't ever want to be the smartest guy in the room," he says. "I want the right thing for my people and my company, so it's not about me being right, it's about everyone being right. Empowered people can change the department. They can change the

---

[21] Tony's and Jad's bios and introductions appear in Part II, Chapter Three.

company. That's why when they come into my office and ask me what I think about some question or some issue, I immediately turn it around, and I say, 'No, what do you think?'" (Donaldson, 2019).

Candace Covington and Chris Raskob have built their entire leadership styles around empowerment. Each related a specific instance where empowerment made a significant difference to their team and to their operation.

CANDACE COVINGTON

Candace Covington is the Senior Director of Aviation for a software company based in the Bay Area of California. Candace's working life started in Colorado, where she worked in the field of graphic design. But one day, when she was home recovering from an illness, she read Richard Bach's Bridge Across Forever[22]. The book prompted her to take up flying as a hobby, but once she had obtained her private and instrument ratings, she decided to pursue a career as a professional pilot.

Candace researched flight schools and found one she liked in San Diego, California. She moved to San Diego, expecting to stay there only three to five years, but destiny had a different plan for her, and she would end up remaining there for 26 years.

Candace obtained her commercial and instructor

---

22 Bach, R. (1984) Bridge Across Forever. New York, William Morrow and Co., Ltd.

ratings and soon found herself performing charter duties, flying Navy personnel between North Island and San Clemente Island. The flying job turned into a base manager position in San Diego. When the Navy contract expired, Candace partnered with an established repair station to start her own charter company to service another government contract. She ran the company as the Director of Operations for several years. Eventually, that contract also expired. By that time, Candace had found her way into Part 91 operations, where she was hired to acquire aircraft and run a two-aircraft department. She ran that operation out of two locations and performed Chief Pilot duties at the Carlsbad base. As much as she enjoyed the job, the lure of international flying beckoned, and Candace applied to a major telecommunications company in the Southern California area. She rose to Senior Director of Aviation in that company and remained there for almost 11 years. She transitioned to her current position in March of 2019. Candace has 25 years of leadership experience.

Candace's theory of empowerment is similar to what we've seen previously. "It starts with open communication," she says. "Being able to debate at the table with no hard feelings. Conversations can't get personal. It's about high-performing individuals pushing for the same goal. Different personalities, engaging passionately, as a team, in the best interest of the organization. The goal is the good of the organization. My goal in that process is to support the people and remove any obstacles for their success."

While Candace's theory might be conventional,

she chose a method of implementation that is unique and showcases the way she empowers the people on her team.

"Every new employee affects the culture of the organization, for better or for worse," she says. "So, we are relentless in our hiring practices. Since teams do better work than individuals, we built a hiring team to handle recruiting and screening for new employees. I wanted the people on my team to have ownership in the hiring process to ensure diversity and buy-in for new team members. My 'ask' of each member of the hiring team was to read a book called The Ideal Team Player[23] and to use that as a philosophy and guide to hiring. There was competition in the department for seats on the hiring team. Everyone wanted to be a part of the process."

But the real test of the concept and Candace's empowerment of the team came when the team worked through a list of candidates for an open position and found none that were a good fit for the culture of the organization.

"The hiring team was deeply concerned," Candace said. "'They came to me and told me there was no one who worked, no one who fit into our culture. 'What are we going to do?' they asked.

"I told them not to worry. We'd find a plan B, even if that meant starting over. That gave them relief. It

---

[23] Outstanding book for hiring and assessing personnel in any organization. Lencioni, P. (2016) The Ideal Team Player. Hoboken, N.J., Jossey-Bass.

told them I trusted their decision. They felt we hadn't compromised" (Covington, 2019).

Empowerment is about trusting your people. Candace Covington demonstrated that in a tangible way. So did Chris Raskob.

CHRISTOPHER RASKOB

Chris Raskob is the Director of Aviation for Cummins, Inc., based in the Midwest U.S. He always had a passion for things that flew. He grew up in Albuquerque, around hot air balloons, and after a flight in one, he was hooked on aviation. He started fixed-wing training in high school and took the exam ride for his private pilot certificate the day after his 17th birthday.

Chris chose to attend Purdue University, a college known for its aviation program. He performed flight instructor duties there after attaining his other ratings.

Before he graduated, Chris was offered an interview with Piedmont airlines, and he took a position there as a first officer after he completed college. He quickly upgraded to captain, but after the attack on 9/11, he decided the airlines weren't going to offer a bright future, at least in the near term.

A friend recommended that he apply for a first officer position with Cummins, Inc., and that set him on an unexpected course. Chris climbed the ranks in the department to captain, safety officer, and Chief Pilot. He assumed the Director of Aviation position in 2013. In addition to his corporate duties, Chris works in a family charity foundation where he has served in leadership roles for his entire life.

"I try to create an environment for people where they can grow, excel and achieve their full potential," Chris says. "I try to empower them. A big part of that is communication. I work on my communication skills every single day. Whether it's a one-on-one conversation, communications inside the group, outside the group, or even outside the company."

One example of the empowerment Chris offers his people is the safety committee in his department.

"Our safety committee is a cross-section of the team, and everyone wants to be involved," he says. "I stay clear and let the members of the committee do their thing. These days, they're working on process improvement. They've had process improvement training, so they know how to find issues and fix processes. Now they're identifying issues with our processes and recommending solutions. It's good stuff and will make our team better."

Perhaps the best example of empowerment Chris shared was in the set-up and execution of his department's corporate shuttle operation.

"Our company sends many people to locations that are expensive and difficult to get to," he says. "Lee Blake, our Shuttle Manager, latched on the idea of a shuttle soon after we hired him as a pilot. After becoming Shuttle Manager, he identified the need for a larger jet that could transport more people to those locations cheaper than the airlines. I gave the project to Lee and my Maintenance Manager and let them run with it. All I did was facilitate. They built the business plan, selected the aircraft, and worked the transaction to acquire and outfit it. The first time I saw the jet, it was on our ramp, painted, equipped, and ready to go. Now that aircraft flies 11,000 people every year" (Raskob, 2019).

Empowerment comes with challenges, and those issues often involve communication and oversight. Deb Prosinski[24] experienced this when one of her aircraft had a mechanical problem.

"As a rule, I don't micromanage," Deb says. "I treat people like grown-ups and let them perform their jobs in a way that works best for them. But sometimes, requests for information can be misinterpreted.

"We had a flight coming back from somewhere in Europe, and it had to make a stop in Maine. While it was on the ground, it had a mechanical problem that was going to delay its departure. We realized we were going to have to send a helicopter to Maine to retrieve the passengers because the jet crew wasn't going to be able to complete the mission within the limits of their duty day. When I called the captain of the jet to find out what was happening with her aircraft, I could tell she thought I was calling because I didn't trust her. I had to reassure her that I wasn't questioning her judgment; I just needed the background and information to provide explanations to those above. I had to reassure her that I trusted her decisions on the situation" (Prosinski, 2019).

---

24 Deb's introduction and bio appear in Part II, Chapter One.

MARCELA WHITE

Marcela White has had to work similar communication issues in the balance between empowerment and oversight. Marcela is the General Manager/Owner of Tavero Aviation Jet Charter Corporation, a Charter/Management Business based in Houston, Texas, that she co-owns with her husband.

When Marcella graduated from college, she decided to begin a career in real estate, but it wasn't long before she decided real estate wasn't for her. Her sister was working for a small charter company and invited Marcela to join her, brokering charters. That started Marcela on a remarkable 30-year journey that ended up with her current position. Currently, Tavero has 13 aircraft in its fleet. Marcela has 34 years of leadership experience, with the last 20 years of it in her current position.

Tavero's organizational culture is team-oriented and empowers its employees to make decisions.

"Our culture is less about the job description," Marcela says, "And more about the success of each flight."

To keep that culture of empowerment in place, however, requires her to take great care in her style of communication. She learned that through experience.

"It is in my nature to understand, and in order to do that I have to ask a lot of questions," Marcela says, "but I have to do that in a way that doesn't come across as a threat. I have to be careful to question in a way that doesn't sound like I'm challenging. Because it's not what you say to your people, it's what they hear.

"I remember this one time when we had a jet on the ramp and the passengers were going to show soon, but the jet wasn't fueled. Our fuel provider wanted to fuel the aircraft, but they couldn't because the jet's fuel valves weren't opened. I called the co-pilot and communicated verbatim what the fuelers had communicated to me. that the jet fuel valves were not open. Because this communication came from me, his boss and not the fueler, he felt compelled to open them without first discussing this action with his captain. Due to a series of mishaps, the fueler erroneously put more fuel than necessary as the fueler inadvertently completed a fuel request from a different aircraft on the ramp. I learned a lesson that day, that I will not forget. I need to be careful about how I communicate. I never intended for him to open those valves without discussing this with his other crewmember, but he interpreted that as a directive from his boss. I watch what I say, and I watch how I say it."

Marcela's use of empowerment and focus on communication has built trust from her employees. She has been direct with people inside and outside her organization to build that trust.

"I do not sugarcoat my communication," she says. "I am honest and fair. If you've done a great job, then I'm going to acknowledge that. However, if you've done an inferior job, I'm also going to point that out."

Marcela related another story that provided a lesson on the importance of communication and empowerment.

"We had a charter going into Montana with a former president on board," she says. "The captain lowered the landing gear but had conflicting indications in the cockpit. He could tell the gear was down but couldn't verify it was locked. We spoke on the radio and I told him to do what he needed to do, and we'd support him. His actions taught me a lot about communication in a tense situation. His confidence and composure kept everyone in the cabin calm and collected. Everything turned out well, but it was his demeanor and ability to effectively communicate the issue at hand and a provide a resolution that kept that customer coming back for many years. I would like to believe that the culture we created helped him to do that.

"Empowerment isn't just about communication with your employees," Marcela concludes. "It's also about standing up for them; showing them you support their decisions. Empowering your employees to do their best with the best interest of the company in mind is paramount. Everyone in our company, including me, will make a mistake. How you handle that mistake will keep employees loyal. There is no price for loyal employees. They will represent you well even when you are not around. You cannot have a loyal employee if they are not happy in their environment, and without an empowering culture in the workplace" (White, 2019).

Tony Kern and Jad Donaldson have offered perspective on how to lead people with empowerment. Candice Covington and Chris Raskob provided specific examples of empowerment in action. Deb Prosinski and Marcela White illustrated clear communication in the process of empowerment. Together, these leaders have shown us how empowerment builds trust in organizations and motivates employees to higher levels of performance.

THOUGHTS FOR LEADERS ON EMPOWERMENT

Inc. magazine's Kevin Daum, an entrepreneur and best-selling author, writes: "If it were easy to empower your employees, then everyone would do it" (Daum, 2013). The leaders in this chapter have made it look easy, but the concept of empowerment in action might be difficult for many of us to envision. To assist in understanding what empowerment looks like in practice, Daum provides some systematic guidelines that capture much of what our leaders have said.

1. **Foster Open Communication.** Top-down communication isn't open communication. Provide channels for safe communication from your subordinates and let them know their input is valued, even if you choose to go a different way;

2. **Reward Self-Improvement.** Budget dollars and time toward professional development training for your people. Help them set a plan for growth and reward them as they advance;

3. **Encourage Safe Failure.** Give employees mechanisms and projects that won't compromise the operation or department.

Allow them to learn the lessons that come when they don't succeed;

4. **Provide Plenty of Context.** Context is about vision. Vision for the department or vision about a project. It's on you as the leader to impart your vision;

5. **Clearly Define Roles**. Roles provide boundaries, and boundaries provide structure. Establish specific roles so that employees can work more cooperatively and efficiently together;

6. **Require Accountability**. People need to know when they're meeting expectations and when they're not. It's hard for employees to maintain accountability if they don't understand the consequences of failure;

7. **Support Their Independence**. Leaders who constantly look over the shoulders of their employees are babysitters, not leaders. And, as mentioned above, by requiring micro-information or constant updates, you're inserting yourself into your employees' processes. Give your people the room to stretch out. They might stumble, but they'll learn a lot in the process and become empowering leaders themselves one day; and

8. **Appreciate Their Efforts**. Praise your people for their work and successes. Your subordinates feel that their participation is valued and appreciated. If you have to

ask how your people are doing, if you don't know how they're doing, you're probably not performing well as their leader (Daum, 2013).

A PERSONAL REFLECTION ON EMPOWERMENT (OR HOW NOT TO)

One of my favorite quotes about empowerment comes from an unexpected source, General George S. Patton, Jr.

Never tell people how to do things. Tell them what to do and they will surprise you with their ingenuity (Business Insider, 2015).

I've built my leadership style around that quote, but there was a time when I allowed it to lure me into complacency. A few years ago, I was recruited to build a flight department for a corporation in the Midwest. Initially billed as a one-aircraft operation, it quickly expanded to two aircraft, and the required staff doubled in size. We needed a flight operations manual (FOM) that was compliant with the International Standard, Business Aircraft Operations (IS-BAO)[25]. With Patton's quote in mind, I assigned the task of building the FOM to the senior pilots in our organization. I gave them a template, instructions that

---

[25] IS-BAO is an internationally accepted code of best practices for business aircraft operators. See www.ibac.org for more information.

I thought were reasonably precise, and empowered them to go forth and conquer, eager to be impressed by their ingenuity. I also gave them a time constraint, the targeted date for our initial IS-BAO audit, one year from the day we began operations. Then I busied myself with the multitude of other tasks the director of a new department has to deal with and put the FOM on the back burner of my mental stove.

Months passed. From time to time, I would ask the pilots how the FOM was progressing and receive expressions of confidence. I satisfied myself that the job was getting done.

Then we had the audit, and we nearly flunked it. The FOM we had produced was a barely useful product and still carried elements of the template in it that weren't replaced with our department's name or logo. In the weeks that followed, we engaged a vendor, furiously reworked the FOM, and resubmitted it. We were awarded our IS-BAO registration shortly thereafter.

After the dust settled, we debriefed this incident together. I told my team that I had not provided sufficient oversight and accepted responsibility for the outcome. My team members were quick to point out their own deficiencies in the process and together, we put a stronger FOM process in place for future revisions and updates.

There's a saying from many of the superhero movies: "With great power, comes great responsibility." Where empowerment is concerned, I'd say the same applies. With great empowerment of your people comes great responsibility as a leader.

As leaders, we can say that we empower our folks to succeed, but if we don't do it systematically and responsibly, we must be prepared for the consequences. Whatever they may be.

PART II

— CHAPTER FIVE —

CREDIBILITY

THE DEFINITION

When we think of credibility in a leadership role, the dictionary definition of the word might seem surprising.

1. *The quality or power of inspiring belief;*
2. *The power for belief* (Merriam-Webster, 2019).

Yet, Sandy Allgeier, in her book <u>The Personal Credibility Factor</u>, defines the word in almost identical terms.

When others believe, trust and have confidence in you, you naturally receive their respect – you are someone with personal credibility (Allgeier, 2009, location 261).

She goes on to state that credibility is a function of our behaviors and the observations of those around us and is either enhanced or damaged by the ongoing decisions we make and the behaviors we demonstrate (Allgeier, 2009).

Steven R. Covey's definition of credibility goes beyond the personal factor and ties into the professional. He believed there are four "cores" of credibility in a professional environment.

1. **Integrity.** Are you congruent? Do you act in accordance with your values and beliefs?
2. **Intent.** What is your agenda? What is your motive? What is your purpose? What is your agenda?
3. **Capabilities.** Are you relevant? Do you have the talent, skill, knowledge, and capacity to perform?
4. **Results.** What's your track record? What have you accomplished? (Covey, S.M.R. & Merrill, R.R., 2006)

THE RESEARCH

So how do we capture and measure the concept of credibility in a professional context? For the 2019 retention study, I attempted to describe it with the following phrase and asked respondents to rate the importance of it. The results appear in Table 9 below.

Knows what he/she is doing in their role.

I also used the respondents' 1-3 ranking to determine where credibility fell in the overall list of attributes.

Overall Mean	6.13
Leaders Mean	6.15
Followers Mean	6.11
Levene's Test for Variance	$F = 1.564, p = .211$
Means Statistically Different?	No

Table 9. Respondent ratings on the importance of credibility.

As shown in Table 9, *Leaders* and *Followers* were aligned in their opinions about the importance of credibility. There was some misalignment in the rankings, however. *Leaders* ranked credibility as the number five attribute, but *Followers* ranked it as number six, after advocacy.

THE LEADERS

STEPHANIE CHUNG

Stephanie Chung is the Chief Growth Officer of Wheels Up, an innovative private jet provider. As I have related the experiences of other leaders thus far in this book, I have condensed their biographical information, so I could get to their thoughts about the leadership attributes they personified. Stephanie's story is different. As a study in leadership credibility, her demonstration of that attribute is intertwined with her story. To understand her credibility, we need to understand her life.

Stephanie's father was a Master Sergeant in the USAF, and she was surrounded by aircraft taking off and landing all around her during her childhood. She fell in love with aviation, knew she wanted to be in aviation, but couldn't determine what she wanted to do. She would see pilots and flight attendants but decided she didn't want to be either.

Stephanie started her aviation career on the tarmac, loading bags for Piedmont Airlines in Boston. She loved working on the ramp and being with "the guys." Her first promotion took her from the ramp to the ticket counter, and it was there one of the airline's vice presidents told her, "I always see you serving the customer with a smile on your face - you should get into sales." Stephanie saw an internal opening for a sales automation position. She didn't know what it was, but it was sales, so she applied. She was selected to interview, but the interviewer told her that the position was a promotion for someone who was already in sales. He advised her to go back to her area and immerse herself in sales, then apply, if she saw an open sales position.

"I'm the child of a soldier," Stephanie says. "I follow instructions."

Stephanie returned to her home base with a purpose. She made a routine of completing her usual shift and making her way down to where the salespeople worked. She focused on getting to know the sales staff and understanding what they did. When U.S. Airways bought Piedmont soon after, sales positions began to open up. Stephanie applied and got the job because she had built a relationship with the salespeople. At 25 years old, she became a sales representative for U.S. Airways in Connecticut.

Her first few months in the new position were difficult, but the training she received was comprehensive and thorough. U.S. Airways' sales training program lasted a year and consisted of four, three-month cycles. Every quarter, Stephanie spent one week at the Xerox Sales University. Each day, she was taught sales skills for eight to ten hours, received homework for the evening, and repeated that itinerary the next day. After her week in training, she'd go back to her territory and ride to sales calls with her boss, who would evaluate everything she did. Then, she'd work her territory for the remaining two weeks of the quarter. The company invested substantial time and money into her during the year-long training program, and Stephanie was grateful for it. It gave her a foundation in sales and provided a competitive advantage. She had to strive to meet the aggressive quota set by her boss, but she learned from her and grew to love the job. She hit her quota that year and performed so well she was recruited by one of her customers into a new job with a new company.

Stephanie's next position was Corporate Sales Manager for Delta Dream Vacations. Her former customer had become President of the company and told her to "find business in unlikely places." Stephanie took that advice to heart. She looked at different affinity groups to include minorities, LGBT clientele, and females. That process taught her to think out of the proverbial box.

"A normal salesperson looks in pathway A," she says. "But I looked in pathway B. Consistently."

Stephanie performed well and she would have stayed with the company, but life intervened. When the time came for her child to be born, she left Delta Dream Vacations to be a stay-at-home mother.

"I lasted about three weeks," Stephanie said. "That's the hardest job on the planet! I realized that I wasn't cut out for it. I had to get out and do something. A friend of mine invited me to sell Mary Kay cosmetics with her. Five weeks later, I won one of those Mary Kay cars."

Soon, Stephanie was one of the top ten Mary Kay salespeople in the nation, winning five cars in the five years she was with the company.

"I learned a lot about leadership in that job," she says. "People need praise, and they need recognition. People respond better when they get it. Many times, it's not nearly as much about the reward itself as it is about the praise and recognition. Another thing I learned is that to be successful as a leader, you need to develop your people. You need to challenge them. You need to make them successful."

But Stephanie yearned to return to her aviation roots. When Bombardier recruited her for a position in charter sales, she eagerly accepted a job at Skyjet, Bombardier's charter company.

After her sales territory was assigned, Stephanie looked for leads in a place where no one else was looking, in the backwoods of Mississippi. She found one there – a company called Sanderson Farms, a single plane operator that was located, quite literally, in the middle of nowhere. When she called them to set up her first visit, the representative from Sanderson was incredulous.

"You're coming out here?" he asked. "No one has ever done that before."

Stephanie got on a plane, rented a car, and drove two hours. Sanderson gave her a gift merely for showing up. It turned out that the company needed supplemental lift for certain events, and Stephanie sold it to them. That sale was the beginning of her rise to become the number one sales producer at Skyjet.

Before long, she was promoted to National Sales Director for the company. Her boss gave her only one directive: "Have your team do what you do," he said.

Now she was in a leadership position and had to put the lessons she had learned to work.

"But I was lucky," Stephanie says. "Sales and leadership share a common element, the need to connect with people. I spent my childhood on a series of Air Force bases. I was a professional 'new kid.' When you're always the new kid, you have to learn to read people and make friends. I learned how to connect with anybody.

"I learned some other things growing up around solders. I learned the importance of saying what you mean and meaning what you say. Military people don't do fluff. They communicate directly. I saw soldiers in pressed uniforms with shined boots. I saw them running in formation. They exemplified excellence. That sunk in for me. The other thing I saw was how cause and effect worked. If a soldier screwed up, he stood at attention for hours on end. Our family lived on base, and if I screwed up, my father heard about it. Actions have consequences, and if you don't do what you should do, bad things can happen."

Stephanie's leadership style was molded by her experiences as a military brat and by her own ability to perform. She demanded excellence of herself and required it from her subordinates.

"Do what you say," she tells her people. "And meet your deadlines."

Under Stephanie's leadership, Skyjet went from obscurity to stardom. At that time in Bombardier Aerospace's history, it was the only division in the corporation that turned a profit.

Later, while Stephanie was attending an NBAA BACE[26] event, she had the opportunity to interact with the President of the Skyjet and Flexjet. She was at Bombardier's chalet at the static display, and she was watching how a small team of executive assistants was being overwhelmed with the constant flow of people into the chalet. Rather than stand on the sidelines, Stephanie jumped in to help them. When her peers stood in the way of the personnel flow, Stephanie told

---

26 National Business Aviation Association (NBAA) Business Aviation Convention and Exhibit, a yearly event that takes place in either Las Vegas or Orlando. One of the largest yearly conventions in the nation, the number of attendees regularly exceeds 20,000 people. See www.nbaa.org for more information.

them to move.

"We could never do that," one of the EAs told her. "You never know who is watching and what they'll say about you."

The President of Skyjet and Flexjet was impressed. "You worked," he said. "You pitched in, and you helped. Others were standing around, but you rolled your sleeves up and got to work." He hired her to be the Vice-President of Sales for Flexjet's Western Region soon after.

"His decision was based on my brand," Stephanie says. "And you always have to ask yourself, how will your brand be discussed when you're not in the room. How do you want it to be portrayed? For me, it was about being real and being credible. What people saw with me was what they got. And they knew that."

Stephanie remained in the vice-president position for seven years and spent a total of 15 years at Bombardier. But when the merger with Flight Options occurred, she and many of her colleagues in senior leadership were forced out. She had multiple job offers within the industry, but she decided to go in a different direction and start her own business. She opened a coaching and consulting practice that focused on leadership communication as a tool to drive sales. She also offered intense sales training to help those in sales positions make their quotas. Stephanie's specialties included coaching executives on the importance of sales and how to speak to salespeople. In the same vein, she coached sales teams on how to understand the rest of their organizations. One of her best clients in the coaching practice was JetSuite.

Thanks to Stephanie's coaching efforts, JetSuite's sales team realized significantly higher levels. As part of the coaching process, Stephanie became friends with JetSuite's CEO. When JetSuite's headquarters moved from California to the Dallas-Fort Worth area and JetSuite X was created, the company needed a new president for JetSuite. Stephanie was offered the position. She was president of JetSuite for about two years and then transitioned to her current position (Chung, 2019).

When viewed through the lenses of credibility as discussed by Allgeier and Covey above, Stephanie Chung's example aligns precisely with the points outlined by both authors. Her performance satisfies Allgeier's criteria because it inspires belief from both her superiors and subordinates alike. The reason that inspiration occurs is due to her satisfaction of Covey's measures of credibility.

- She's congruent in words and actions;
- Her intent is ethical and beneficial;
- Her capabilities are highly visible; and
- Her results are a matter of record.

Stephanie Chung's credibility is function of who she is and her journey in life. Bob Agostino's journey is different, but his credibility has been built in the same manner.

ROBERT AGOSTINO

Bob Agostino is the President of a private aviation

company in North Texas and the former Aviation Director for Bombardier. He grew up in Western Pennsylvania and soloed in his first airplane while he was still in high school. He attended college in Rochester, N.Y. and attained his commercial, instrument, multi-engine, and instructor ratings during and immediately after his senior year.

"I only fell in love twice in my life," Bob says. "The second time was with my wife 39 years ago, but the first time came before that when I was going out to the airport to do a flight for my commercial license. I heard this loud, screaming whine. It came from a Lear 23. I crawled over the fence between me and the jet so fast that I tore my pants in the process. The crew let me have full access to that jet, and it was the most beautiful thing I had ever seen."

After college, Bob instructed aerobatics for foreign nationals who were going into Navy flight training. His first business jet job came as the pilot for a man who was an icon in sports and business aviation, Arnold Palmer. Bob flew for Palmer and others and continued to build his aviation expertise over the years.

In 1993, he was recruited to be the Aviation Director for Learjet, then based in Wichita, Kansas. In 2002, when Bombardier consolidated flight demonstration operations for the company in Wichita, Bob was promoted to Aviation Director for both the narrow and wide-body flight operations, where he served until his first resignation/retirement in 2008.

"I had enough when I left Bombardier," Bob says.

"I'd been in one management job or another since 1978. I needed to depressurize."

But it was not to be. Bob had barely moved to Pennsylvania to begin his retirement when he was recruited to be the Vice President of Operations for L.J. Aviation at the Arnold Palmer Regional Airport in Latrobe. Bob re-wrote the operations manual for the company and settled into the job. He wasn't there for long. A high net worth individual in the Dallas-Fort Worth area called Bob to run a flight department, an FBO, and serve on the executive team at an OEM specializing in a future supersonic business jet. Bob has been in his current job(s) for 11 years and has been in leadership positions for over 40 years.

Throughout his career, Bob has dedicated himself to the pursuit of the highest levels of aviation competence, for himself, for his people and for the industry.

"At Bombardier, we worked with flight test for the Lear Jet 45 and the Challenger 300," he says. "We also performed some post-certification testing on the Global Express. My pilots were going to be up for the task. I put them through a mini test pilot course at the National Test Pilot School and made them undergo upset recognition and recovery training. I wanted them to be competent and credible. Credibility and safety are based on competence, and competence is based on capability. Training makes you capable."

While he was at Bombardier, thanks to his strong belief in training, credibility, and capability, Bob founded the now world-famous Bombardier Safety Standdown, a yearly event in which safety experts from the industry speak to an enthusiastic audience of hundreds of aviation personnel.

"The first time we did it, we had like five or six pilots," Bob says. "I wanted the unvarnished truth about safety from someone who had credibility, so I got Gene Cernan[27] involved as a hook for people to attend. His credibility spoke for itself. I wanted people to hear about safety from someone who had lived it.

"And speaking of credibility, Gene showed me that in action. He was truly an inspirational person. I checked him out in the Lear 45 to show him was what business aviation and business jets were like. We did stalls and falls over the Hutchinson Airport. Here's a guy who has flown all sorts of jets and gone into space, but he didn't take anything for granted. He respected the jet and what we were doing, and he threw himself into the program. And let me tell you, I worked his ass off. He ended up with a type rating in the Lear 45, and he was proud of it."

Even today, the pilots in Bob's operation are trained at a level that leaves many other departments far behind. They do water survival training in live conditions in the Gulf of Mexico, and they attend upset recognition and recovery training on a regular, recurring basis. They've even done supersonic upset

---

27 Eugene Cernan was an Apollo 17 astronaut and the last of the Apollo astronauts to set foot on the moon. He passed away in 2017. See https://www.nasa.gov/astronautprofiles/cernan for more information.

training so they could be conversant with abnormal flight conditions in the transonic and supersonic flight regimes[28].

"The greatest job is getting passengers safely from point A to point B," Bob says. "That's our calling and it takes knowledge and focused planning. My people perform at the highest levels of safety because they're highly competent. I don't want our passengers to have the slightest doubt about their credibility or their capability."

As we noted above, a leader's credibility is about inspiring belief in their followers. Bob's dedication to his people and their competence has generated high morale in the organizations he has led. Perhaps one of the best indications of his ability to inspire came from the mouth of Gene Cernan himself.

"At Bombardier, every member of the flight test team got a black jacket," Bob says, "but they only got them when the rest of the team decided they were ready. That group was so highly trained, so tight and so professional that when Gene came to visit us about a year after he'd been typed in the Lear 45, he was amazed at how well the department worked. He told us that we reminded him of a fighter squadron on a ship, which from a Navy guy, is about the highest compliment you can get.

---

28 Flight Research (See Bill Korner's introduction and bio in Part Two - Chapter One) is the only URRT vendor that provides training in this envelope. It consists of one ride in the T-38 Talon aircraft.

"But," Bob says, with a smile of pride, "as good as that team was, my current team is better" (Agostino, 2019).

Through the examples that Stephanie and Bob have provided, we can see that credibility is more than a mere leadership trait. Like some of the other attributes we've discussed in this book, credibility is a product of a leader's character – a manifestation of not only what a leader is but who that leader is as well.

THOUGHTS FOR LEADERS ON CREDIBILITY

Credibility is a comprehensive trait that encompasses many of the others we'll discuss. While I defined it narrowly in the research, a leader knowing what he or she is doing can be interpreted in a defined skill sense or a broader psychological sense. Alice Scarlet, in an article in All Business Magazine, provides nine steps to leadership credibility that encompasses both interpretations.

1. **Give respect, earn respect.** Respect is a two-way street between leaders and subordinates. If you don't respect your subordinates as people and professionals, don't expect respect in return;
2. **Trust is an essential asset.** This speaks to the importance of integrity in a leader, as Covey discusses above. Leaders are credible when they do what they say they'll do;

3. **Your loyalty goes a long way.** You demonstrate your loyalty to your people when you take the blame for the organization's issues instead of blaming subordinates and when you stand up for them when the organization isn't treating them fairly;

4. **Be accountable for your actions.** If you make a mistake, own it, fix it and move on;

5. **Focus on your goals and beyond.** A leader should keep sight of her goals and continually create strategies to move the organization to achieve them;

6. **Don't speak, Act!** Actions speak louder than words. Be decisive. Don't be afraid to get your hands dirty;

7. **Be an expert at what you do.** Technical competency, per Bob Agostino's example, is essential. Regardless of your area of expertise, pilot, technician, dispatcher, perform your tasks well;

8. **Keep learning.** Stay abreast of new trends, new information, and new regulations. Credibility is often about knowledge. A leader should know his stuff; and

9. **Honesty is the best policy.** This speaks once again to a leader's integrity. Without it, there can be no inspiration and no credibility (Scarlet, 2019).

A PERSONAL REFLECTION ON CREDIBILITY

The Air Force, like any other large bureaucracy, has leaders that run the gamut in credibility and capability. During my twenty years in the service, I found that the most credible leaders were the ones who could fly the jet well. The basic unit of the Air Force is the squadron, and two best squadron commanders I worked for were god-like in their respective aircraft.

Mud Moore, whom I mentioned in the introduction, was one of the pioneers of tactics in the A-10 and was with the aircraft from the time it was fielded until he retired in the late 1990s. When he was the Commander of the 78th Tactical Fighter Squadron at RAF Bentwaters/Woodbridge, we would fly sorties to the four air-to-ground gunnery ranges that lined the east coast of the country. Mud would regularly have the best scores in the bombing and strafing events we performed. His history and his proficiency in the jet inspired a degree of respect that his successor, a pilot who had never flown the Hawg before and needed a squadron commander slot for promotion, could never match.

When I transitioned to the F-16, I had a squadron commander in the 62nd Fighter Squadron at Luke AFB named Rob Kesterson. Rob or "Roo" as we called him, had spent his entire career in the Viper and could make it do some incredible things that most of us couldn't match. Like Mud, he regularly beat his flight mates on the bombing range, but he could also kick your butt in an air-to-air engagement. He made both missions of the F-16 look effortless, and his briefings, flight leadership, and debriefings were executed with the highest degree of professionalism. His expertise, his credibility in the aircraft, demanded respect.

But what made both of these men worthy of respect is that in spite of their history in their aircraft, they made the effort to stay current and to stay proficient. In spite of their many other responsibilities and duties, they worked hard at staying good in the aircraft. Their proficiency was not just a function of their training or their history; it was a function of their discipline and their respect for the jet and the mission. It was a function of their character.

Today, decades later, the examples that Mud and Roo set still resound for me. They led from the front because they had the technical credibility, the discipline, to be there.

As aviation leaders, we should strive for the same.

PART II

CHAPTER SIX

ADVOCACY

THE DEFINITION

The dictionary definition of advocacy might seem a bit redundant.

The act or process of supporting a cause or proposal: the act or process of advocating something (Merriam-Webster, 2019).

In the realm of leadership, we can find ourselves focusing on different causes depending on the mission or the environment. Still, the cause that should command our most intense focus is that of our people, either as individuals or collectively as a team. In the context of our discussion in this chapter, we will define advocacy as the willingness of a leader to stand up for his or her people, particularly to those above.

Laura Stack, a hall-of-fame speaker who goes by the moniker "The Productivity Pro," believes that the real test of a manager is successfully fighting for the team (2014).

> *Your team members may not expect you to fight for them in any sense. Most of us have seen too many self-serving CYA maneuvers over the years to really be surprised when a leader slinks off into "every-man-for-himself" territory. So why not surprise them by facing your in-house rivals like a team player?* (Stack, 2014)

She urges leaders to present their needs forthrightly and clearly to the echelons above, make it clear that while the leader is still a team player, he or she is prepared to move around the bureaucracy and stand up for his or her people. To have the courage to take one for the team if necessary (Stack, 2014).

THE RESEARCH

Given the context above, I defined the trait of advocacy with the following simple sentence for the 2019 study, and I asked respondents to rate the importance of it. The results appear in Table 10 below.

Isn't afraid to stand up to those above.

I also used the respondents' 1-3 ranking to

determine where advocacy fell in the overall list of attributes.

Overall Mean	6.04
Leaders Mean	5.96
Followers Mean	6.12
Levene's Test for Variance	$F = .006, p = .939$
Means Statistically Different?	No

Table 10. Respondent ratings on the importance of advocacy.

It would be tempting to conclude that *Leaders* thought that advocacy was less important than *Followers* did, but the data doesn't allow that. The results from Levene's test, as shown in Table 10, indicated the two means are not statistically different, so *Leaders* and *Followers* were aligned in their opinions about the importance of advocacy. But there was substantial misalignment in the rankings. *Followers* ranked the attribute as number six, but *Leaders* ranked it as number eight, after both vision and transparency.

THE LEADERS

JAY ORWIN

Jay Orwin is the former Director of Aviation for a company located in Michigan, where this story takes place. He is currently the Director of Aviation for a California Corporation. Jay got his start in aviation when he was ten years old. He had two uncles, one who flew for a small freight operation and would let Jay ride along, and another uncle who had a remote cabin and would let Jay ride with him as well. When Jay was 15, one of his aunts bought him ground school lessons and his first flight. After that, Jay was hooked. He worked summer jobs, cutting grass and washing trucks to pay for flight lessons. His hard work paid off, and Jay received his private pilot certificate just after his 17th birthday.

When the time came to choose a college, Jay opted for a school with a flight program, Western Michigan University. He entered college in the fall of 1996 and participated in the precision flight team during his time at the university. After he graduated, Jay and one of his fellow flight team members were looking for internship programs, and Jay wound up at his current employer's operation. He spent six months there, flying in the right seat of a King Air 350. He liked the company, and he liked his boss, but while he was flying in and out of the home airport, he'd see airliners landing and taking off and felt like he wanted to try commercial aviation. He was hired at Mesaba Airlines and went to work as a first officer.

"It was great at the beginning," Jay said. "But I began to feel out of place. I was conscientious, and I could hold my own as a pilot, but some of the pilots I flew with had bad skills or bad attitudes or both. The union mentality began to wear on me as well. Then 9/11 happened, and I left the airlines behind."

Jay remembered the pleasant experience he had at his current employer as an intern and applied for a full-time position there. He was hired in 2003 and was fortunate to have a boss who developed him and groomed him to run the department. In early 2014, Jay became the Director of Aviation for the department.

Shortly after stepping up to the Director job, Jay was placed in a position to stand up for his people. In fact, he had to stand up for the whole department.

"I spent four months shadowing my boss before I took the reins in January of 2014," Jay says. "I spent the first nine months just getting my feet on the ground. Then, in the winter of that year, the company began a series of planned executive leadership changes. In conjunction with those changes the new team embarked on a transformation that culminated in business spin-offs and a home office restructuring which included the flight department. During that time, I was tasked with completing a comprehensive review of the operation, staff, and the fleet. I presented my findings knowing that it would be a challenge to exit unscathed. I was told 50% of the staff and half of the jets had to go. I did not believe that our analysis supported that type of reduction, but the decision was made, and it was my responsibility to implement.

"Then September rolls around, and I get called into a meeting on a Friday. I'm told that there had been a last-minute decision made to disband the entire department. The announcement is to be made the following Monday. I had the wonderful task of going back to the department and telling everyone."

Jay was forced to lay off everyone in the department, with the temporary exception of a small team who would help with the disposal of the department's assets. He also hired a personnel agency to help with the transition of the team to other positions.

A short time after the decision was made to disband, Jay was asked to arrange a few charter flights. Upon completion of these flights, Jay's boss relayed the message from company senior leaders that they would like to re-analyze the merits of an in-house department and would like numbers comparing in-house to fractional and chartered options.

Now Jay had the opportunity to fight for his people and his department again. He built a thorough analysis that showed, based on historical and forecast utilization, an in-house department was less expensive and provided a more consistent experience than either fractional or charter providers. After that data was presented to the CEO, the CEO responded. "Bring it back to what we originally planned," he said.

"I started making phone calls," Jay says. "I couldn't call everyone, but the people I did call came back."

But then Jay had a new task to accomplish. "We needed to replace one of our aging aircraft," he says. "It was nearly 20 years old and lacked many of the technological enhancements that improved safety margins. Additionally, dispatch reliability began to creep lower and our maintenance budget began to creep higher.

Jay went to his boss and the senior leadership team and made a case for aircraft replacement. Jay's plan was accepted, and the team began to execute.

Today, Jay's company operates a Phenom 300E and a Falcon 2000LXS, and he is more relaxed in his job. But he looks back upon his baptism by fire as a valuable experience.

"There were a lot of sleepless nights," he says. "But at the end of the day, what matters is your people and standing up for them. While I wouldn't recommend it, losing your job can be somewhat liberating!" (Orwin, 2019)

Jay Orwin's story of support for his people ended well for him and his team. John Rambo's did not.

JOHN RAMBO

John Rambo is the former Head of Aviation for a major financial institution located in the Philadelphia area. Like many of the other leaders in this book, John started his career in aviation at an early age. When John was 15, his father took him on a sightseeing ride for fun in a Cessna 172. John immediately fell in love with flight and would ask for pilot books for Christmas and birthdays. Once he learned that his friend's father was a certified flight instructor, John began taking lessons for $25 per hour and received his private pilot's certificate the day after his 17th birthday.

John pursued his education in Professional Pilot Technology at Indiana State University. After his junior year, he landed a job in his home state of Pennsylvania. He decided not to return to school for his senior year and to work at the Pottstown Limerick Airport, where he performed line service duties, flight instruction, sightseeing flights, and even worked in a small maintenance facility on the field. At the time, John had fulfilled all his core classes, except for his general electives. He felt that he felt hands-on experience outweighed traditional education.

One summer, John flew sightseeing flights at the Ocean City, Maryland airport, where he met some skydivers and became curious about parachuting. After a few jumps, he was offered a job flying in exchange for skydiving lessons. Soon after, he took a full-time position with a company called FreeFall Express, which operated DeHaviland Twin Otters and Pilatus Porters as a jump aircraft. John met other jumpers that were also established pilots as well. These relationships opened the door to jet time. John took a position flying Lear Jets with a charter company where he quickly accumulated hours as pilot-in-command.

After 1,000 hours in a Lear 35, John was promoted to captain and attained his Airline Transport Pilot certificate. Soon after, he transitioned to another charter company where he rose through the ranks to the Chief Pilot position. He worked closely with the FAA on the company's manual suite and learned how to coordinate documents quickly through the agency's processes.

But the lack of work/life balance and low compensation led John to look for a position with more growth potential and stability. Eventually, he found a job with the flight department of a major financial organization in the Philadelphia area. John had to work his way through the ranks once again, starting as a first officer, then working his way up to captain, then Chief Pilot, Director of Aviation and eventually Assistant Vice President and Head of Aviation. John worked with this organization for 18 years and led the department for three years.

As a new department head, John faced many of the same challenges as other managers. Perhaps the most complicated one was balancing the conflicting expectations of senior leadership, his team, and their internal customers during a period of change management. Before John assumed his new role, the department had been deteriorating for several years. The fleet was becoming obsolete, and compensation had not kept up with industry standards, which resulted in both mechanical issues and staffing dilemmas.

"One of the first hurdles I had to deal with was the implementation of IS-BAO," John says. "My team and I wanted to implement it, but senior leadership did not understand the benefits. They thought it was too expensive and didn't really bring any return on investment. I had to take the time to put it into terms they could understand. Once I did that, they were on board.

"My folks also wanted to implement an ASAP program with the FAA, and current management didn't want to do that either, but I pushed the issue with my superiors. I brought a continuous improvement team in house to train my people. I made one of my guys a safety manager and gave the other young leaders in the group the tools they needed to implement the programs the department wanted. We implemented IS-BAO and the ASAP program in record time. It was a fantastic experience, and I was really proud of my team. I learned that if you stand up for your people and give them the room to accomplish great things, they'll do just that."

But the next time John had to stand up for his people, things didn't work out so well. When their current aircraft began to manifest several mechanical problems, the company acquired an additional aircraft that came with its own issues. This particular aircraft was not the one John had recommended because it did not offer a favorable long-term solution. Senior leadership had forced the purchase of a less expensive aircraft and did not consider the cost of maintenance and near obsolescence of this particular model.

As he struggled to get the aircraft situation under control, John lost a pilot due to inadequate compensation during an industry-wide pilot shortage. He told his leadership that they needed to adjust pilot compensation, provided them with documentation and white papers, and forecasted the departure of good employees. Leadership ignored him a second time. Two additional pilots resigned, both citing low compensation and better opportunities as the reason for their departure. John went to his management to make a stand for better pilot compensation to stabilize the department. Instead of being receptive to his presentation, the management terminated him.

"I'm not sorry I did it," John says. "I did the right thing. I stood up for my people. As a leader, my top priorities going in were to develop and initiate a plan to repair the existing damage and move the department forward. I wanted to make sure my team was compensated fairly, the planes we were flying were safe, and my successors were set up appropriately to execute our plan. That said, I accomplished what I set out to do."

But John is reflective about that experience.

"The initial shock of my termination made it hard to remember and accept the end result," he says. "I guess I always knew termination might be a possibility when you're dealing with reorganizations and change management, but it was still disheartening at first. In retrospect, I realize I could have approached certain situations differently, but I've grown and learned from that experience, and it may have been the most valuable lesson I've learned as a leader" (Rambo, 2019).

Jay Orwin's approach to advocacy was data driven. John Rambo's approach was about what was right for his team and his people. Another Director of Aviation's approach combined both of those elements.

DIRECTOR X

Director X is the Director of Aviation for a major corporation located in the Northeast U.S who wishes to remain anonymous. His aviation career didn't begin until after he graduated from college and was attending graduate classes.

Director X worked for several small businesses

immediately after college, but none of them piqued his interest, and he applied to law school. It was while he was there that he decided to learn how to fly. He took flying lessons in the summer at a Part 141 school and gave himself a four-year timetable to get all of his ratings. Eventually, he attained his CFI and multi-engine ratings and was hired for a position flying a Mitsubishi MU-2 in the Northeast U.S.

Director X transitioned to a charter job and then to the regional airlines, flying Beechcraft 1900s all over New England. But it didn't take long before he determined that the airline life was not for him.

Director X made the rounds of the largest business aviation airports in the New York City area, Morristown, White Plains, and Teterboro, giving resumes to anyone who would let him through the front door. He was hired by a company that eventually became one of the largest financial groups in the United States, and he has been at the same hangar, working for the same company since that day. He has worked his way through the ranks from line pilot to Director of Aviation and has over 19 years of leadership experience.

Director X's approach to standing up for his people revolves around his credentials and credibility.

"When I have to make my case to my leadership," he says. "I have to argue for the right thing and use data to back it up. I have to be able to sell my solutions to the people who control the money."

Using this approach with his superiors, Director X was able to resolve two critical situations that occurred at the same time in his department.

"Many years back, when I was Chief Pilot," he says, "I recognized two currents, which I believed, had they converged without intervention, could have posed a significant risk to our ability to meet scheduling demands.

"One, we were slated to take delivery of new aircraft, which were a technological leap into the next generation, both in systems and avionics. Two, we had a significant demographic bubble of pilots who were quickly approaching retirement age. My concern was that these pilots, about 30% of our staff, would either not want to, or would not be able to, take on the challenge of learning to fly and operate these aircraft, which were about to become the mainstay of our fleet. The risk I perceived was that they would retire *en masse*, decimating our pilot ranks, and effectively crippling our operation. Were this to come to pass, our business and our people would have been profoundly negatively impacted."

Director X developed a compelling business case, in which he proposed solutions. He presented the case to his senior management. It was reviewed, discussed, and the solution was implemented. As a result, he instituted a rational and pragmatic, planned reorganization of the pilot staff in a fashion that was fair, equitable, and appealing to all. It also allowed the department to maintain business stability and continuity.

"A good leader needs to detect impending risk and develop and implement strategies to foreclose on that risk and avoid undue disruption to the business function," Director X says. "And that includes making a case for your organization and your people to your superiors when the situation demands it" (DirectorX, 2019).

Sometimes, leaders face either a less than optimum status quo or the tides of impending change, where their people are part of the equation. When these events occur, leaders have a choice to make. They can stand back and allow events to unfold, or they can stand up for their people. Jay Orwin, John Rambo, and Director X have shown us that when leaders advocate for their personnel, they generate a powerful impact in the lives of those people and the future of their organizations. They have shown us that effective leadership demands action, regardless of the personal cost.

THOUGHTS FOR LEADERS ON ADVOCACY

According to the management experts at Mindtools.com (2018), when a leader advocates for his or her people, it shows subordinates that the leader is on their side and builds long-term loyalty, trust, credibility, and morale in the team. It also gives subordinates a confidence boost. If leaders are placed in a situation where standing up for their people is necessary, the following guidelines can help:

1. **Know Your Values**. As leaders, we need to know what we'll stand up for and what we won't and that means we need to know our own values;
2. **Analyze the Situation and Assess**

Risks. Gather the facts about the situation. Do you have both sides of the story? Have you spoken to everyone involved? Explore the behavior of the person or people you're defending, if applicable. Does that behavior undermine the team's mission or support it?

3. **Decide on Action**. If you believe your person or persons are justified in their actions, support them fully. If they weren't, take responsibility for their actions and take steps to make sure the situation in question doesn't reoccur; and

4. **Defend Appropriately**. Plan what you're going to say to your superiors in advance if you can. Explain why you're standing by your people, if they were in the right, and what you're going to do to resolve the situation if they weren't. Be diplomatic but assertive and do your best to use empathy to see things from your superior's perspective (Mindtools, 2018).

A PERSONAL REFLECTION ON ADVOCACY

Advocacy can involve a host of issues and take place at different levels. Most recently, I've had a chance to see several flight department leaders standing up for their people regarding the same issue that cost John Rambo his job –compensation.

Full disclosure here. The research I've done into pilot retention over the last few years has led me to a consulting practice in that area. I've performed retention studies for more than 60 flight departments, either through other companies or independently, and I've become an accidental aviation compensation geek in the process. I know the major surveys intimately, I've gotten well acquainted with the U.S. Bureau of Labor Statistics data. Between the surveys and BLS data, I've developed a method to analyze and predict compensation that is quite precise. As I have analyzed compensation trends over the past few years, one trend has been indisputable – aviation compensation levels are rising at more than twice the rate of increase in the private industry marketplace.[29]

There are aviation departments and company leaders who have chosen to ignore this trend and have lost personnel as a result. As I noted in Part I, 63% of the operators in the 2018 survey had lost at least one pilot to a position elsewhere, and nearly a third of the pilot force, 29%, had changed jobs since 2015. During that same period, 33% of the operators had lost at least one technician to a position elsewhere, and 22% of the technician force had changed jobs. The number one reason cited for departure among both the pilot and technician populations was compensation.

---

[29] From a comparison of the base salary and total cash compensation numbers from 2020 and 2021 NBAA and Gallagher Compensation Surveys. The average increase in compensation across all positions was about 7.5%, compared to 3.1%, the average compensation increase for all private industry according to the U.S. Bureau of Labor Statistics.

The data is compelling.

But some aviation directors and managers are fighting to keep their people. I've had the privilege of helping them by providing them precise data to use in their discussions with those above them. These leaders know what they need to do, and they aren't afraid to state the facts or stand up to their superiors. I've spent hours on the phone and exchanged multiple emails with them as we discussed honing the data to provide the emphasis they wanted.

The courage these leaders have shown, the grit, and the determination to do what was right for their people have been impressive, but one aspect of their approach was more inspiring than anything else. These leaders put their people first, put themselves second, and were willing to do battle with their superiors for the sake of the men and women working for them. They stuck their necks out on the politically difficult subject of compensation because they knew it was the right thing to do for their people and their organizations.

These leaders, like the ones cited earlier in this chapter, show us what real advocacy is about.

PART II

——————— **CHAPTER SEVEN** ———————

TRANSPARENCY

THE DEFINITION

Since transparency is the state of being transparent, the dictionary definition of this trait requires us to use the noun form of the word. I've included the definitions regarding the physical aspects of the term because they provide clarity into the literary ones.

1. *Having the property of transmitting light without appreciable scattering so that bodies lying beyond are seen clearly, allowing the passage of a specified form of radiation (such as X-rays or ultraviolet light), fine or sheer enough to be seen through*
2. *Free from pretense or deceit, easily detected or seen through, readily understood, characterized by visibility or accessibility of information especially*

concerning business practices (Merriam-Webster, 2019).

Note that the last part of definition two is tailored specifically to the discussion in this chapter, an indication of the pervasive use of it in the context of leadership and business.

Stephen Covey combines some of the definitions in his explanation of the term:

Transparency—is about being open. It's about being real and genuine and telling the truth in a way people can verify. It's based on the principles of honesty, openness, integrity, and authenticity. I also like to include the principle of light, because when something is transparent, light will flow through it. In the words of former U.S. Supreme Court Justice Louis Brandeis, "Sunshine is the best disinfectant." It cleanses. It dissipates the shadows. It casts out the darkness. It enables people to see. It gives them a sense of comfort and confidence because they know there's nothing being hidden (Covey, S.M.R. & Merrill, R.R., 2006, pp. 153 - 154).

THE RESEARCH

For the 2019 study, I used a phrase to capture an element of transparency, particularly as viewed from the subordinate perspective.

Doesn't keep secrets.

I also used the respondents' 1-3 ranking to determine where transparency fell in the overall list of attributes.

Overall Mean	5.69
Leaders Mean	5.62
Followers Mean	5.75
Levene's Test for Variance	$F = 1.442, p = .230$
Means Statistically Different?	No

Table 11. Respondent ratings on the importance of transparency.

The results from Levene's test, as shown in Table 11, indicated the two means are not statistically different. Hence, the *Leaders* and *Followers* were aligned in their opinions about the importance of Transparency. Both groups also ranked it as the number seven attribute.

THE LEADERS

TODD DUNCAN

Todd Duncan is the Chairman of the Board for Duncan Aviation, the largest privately held business jet support facility in the world. Todd grew up in a business aviation family. Duncan Aviation was started in 1959 and initially focused on aircraft sales and brokerage. Todd's grandfather, Donald, and father, Robert, were working in the company when Todd was born, and he got his start in the business in the late 1980s after he graduated from college. At the time, he had his private pilot's license, but apart from actual flying, he knew very little else about the industry. Todd initially worked in aircraft sales a few years after the company started, concentrating more on its aircraft service and support offerings than pure aircraft sales. After five years, Todd left the company to try his hand at a family restaurant endeavor. He learned a lot about customer service and leadership and enjoyed working in food service, but his heart was in aviation. So he returned to Duncan Aviation after three years and hasn't looked back.

"I just loved the flying side of it," he said. "And business aviation is about people. I wanted to get back to that."

Todd took a position on the component repair and overhaul side of the company and worked his way up to President of that division. In 2007, he became Chairman of the Board for Duncan. He has over 20 years of leadership experience.

"I'm about supporting our people," Todd says. "I work with and develop teams inside the company, and transparency is an important key to do that. When I was growing up, we were a company of 300 people. Now we're nearly 2,300 strong. You can't have successful growth on that scale without being open with your team members."

During the business aviation depression after the

financial crash of 2008, Todd knew it was essential to keep his team members informed. He worked with Duncan Aviation President Aaron Hilkemann and the rest of the senior management team to develop a companywide email newsletter that was sent every Friday at 3:00 pm. In the newsletter, the entire company was informed about the status of the industry, the condition of the company, the schedule for incoming business, and what the leadership team was doing about all of it.

"2008 was a good year, and based off that year's performance, we paid team members a healthy profit-sharing bonus in January 2009," Todd says. "And 90 days later we lost a third of our business, about $150M of potential revenue. We reacted with across-the-board with pay cuts where senior leaders took a larger cut than middle managers and other team members. We suspended the 401(k) company match and halted tuition reimbursement and non-critical training programs. We shared the details. Yet shortly after that, we still had to conduct the company's only layoff. We knew we had to do it properly and openly. We tried to treat people fairly by evaluating every person and every job and making the best possible decisions. It was a very dark time and there were a lot of sleepless nights, but we kept our entire team informed, every step of the way. There were no surprises.

"The industry was slow to recover and the pay cuts lasted a long time," Todd continues, "but then, near the end of that period, we could see that a lot of new business would be coming our way soon. We had to invest in a new paint facility while we were still operating in a lean mode, so the company was positioned to accept the new business. Building then would be a smart decision for the longevity of the business and best long-term for our people. In many companies, spending money on a construction project in the middle of a downturn could have a serious impact on employee morale. We avoided those issues by being completely transparent about the project. We made sure everyone knew that we were building the new facility, and more importantly, we made sure everyone knew why we were building it and what we believed it would mean to them in the future. Open communication was the key to that entire project."

Sometimes, transparency can be shocking to people who haven't seen it in a corporate environment. Duncan Aviation has owned its facility in Battle Creek, Michigan for 22 years. But when the facility was acquired in 1998, it wasn't an easy transition for the employees in that facility.

"It's not the culture in a union state like Michigan for a company to be open and transparent," Todd says. "We created an awakening for our team members there. They were stunned about how open and transparent we were. It was a huge difference for them because their culture and beliefs didn't encourage such openness. Our leadership team had to convince them that the transparency was essential not only to morale but also to success. For example, we showed them how at Duncan Aviation, pay scales weren't arbitrary. They came with career development. If you come into our company at Tech

I, you can be a Tech III in a given time interval with appropriate development. There were no secrets to advancement and promotion. Everyone knew what to expect. That was a game-changer for them" (Duncan, 2019).

Todd Duncan used transparency as a tool to facilitate change inside his company. Elizabeth Dornak found it equally essential for change she had to manage in her own organization.

ELIZABETH DORNAK

Elizabeth Dornak is the Director of Aviation for a Fortune 500 corporation based in the Philadelphia area. Elizabeth was born in Australia and was fascinated with airplanes from an early age. She began taking flying lessons at age 14, soloed at 16, and had her private pilot certificate at 17. She didn't know how to make a career in aviation, so when she enrolled at Purdue University, she planned on a pre-med track for her major.

That lasted exactly one semester. Elizabeth transferred into the university's aviation program for the second semester and stayed the course, graduating with a Bachelor of Science in Aviation Technology. After performing flight instructor duties for about 18 months, she was hired by Pan Am Express Airlines. They were flying ATR-42s at the time and needed simulator instructors.

But the handwriting was on the wall that Pan Am wasn't going to be around much longer. Elizabeth had a friend who worked for a Fortune

500 flight department based in the mid-Atlantic. She interviewed and was hired as a First Officer. She's been there ever since. Over a career spanning more than 30 years, she flew multiple aircraft types and worked her way up through several managerial positions. She was recently promoted to Director of Aviation.

Elizabeth's leadership style emphasizes open communication and transparency, both of which were critical for her to deal with a significant change that recently occurred inside her organization.

"We had to split an old, established flight department into two independent departments," she says. "That's more difficult than starting from scratch. It's a journey, and you have to take everyone with you. I'm completely transparent with my team members. One of my responsibilities is to translate the goals and expectations from downtown and communicate a vision to keep my people focused on what they can control and to disregard things they can't control. Transparency allows the team to understand what's happening behind the scenes and helps them to keep their focus. It keeps them engaged" (Dornak, 2019).

Craig Olson's[30] organization went through a structural change very similar to Elizabeth's company. Craig credits transparency as a critical factor in managing that change.

"When the department separated into two organizations, it was extremely challenging," he

---

[30] Craig's introduction and bio appear in Part II, Chapter Two.

says. "We were all still living under the same roof with some of the same employees but two different payrolls and two different companies - even different missions and mindsets. You can't imagine the issues a situation like that can generate. It seemed like every stone I picked up, 15 crabs ran out from under it. The thing that helped us to get through the change was me being transparent with my people. As long as I had the green light from leadership, my team knew what I knew when I knew it. That's one of the reasons I'd spend so much time walking the deck plates, so that I could share information with them, and they could ask questions. I made it clear to them that I wanted their input, and when I could accommodate it, I did" (Olson, 2019).

Transparency helped Elizabeth Dornak and Craig Olson manage the change of a departmental reorganization. It also helped Kevin Nichols manage the change as his department transitioned to new aircraft.

KEVIN NICHOLS

Kevin Nichols is the former Senior Director of Conagra Brands' flight department, based in Omaha, Nebraska. He has since retired. Kevin didn't start his professional life as a pilot.

After graduating from college, Kevin became a schoolteacher and taught music and band in Chicago and St. Louis.

But he had an embedded love of aviation. As he was growing up, he had an uncle who was a longtime corporate pilot in St Louis, and Kevin and his sister would get to ride along with him in small airplanes when they were little.

When Kevin lived in Chicago, he began to spend time at DuPage Airport, watching airplanes. He decided to take flying lessons and saved money from his teacher's salary to take one lesson a month. Later, when he moved back to St. Louis, he took a second job to pay for flight training.

Kevin's professional aviation career began with Decatur Aviation Airlines in 1980. But he soon transitioned to a corporate flight operation, working for the Brown Shoe Company that was headquartered in St. Louis. Kevin spent 15 years there and worked his way up through the ranks to Assistant Chief Pilot. Eventually though, he was recruited by the flight department for the Union Pacific Railroad, headquartered in Omaha, Nebraska. After five years there in a captain role, he left Union Pacific to lead a start-up flight department in Omaha as Aviation Manager. About two and a half years later, that flight department was dissolved, and Kevin went to Conagra Brands as a captain. Over the next few years, he worked his way to Chief Pilot and then eventually to Senior Director of Aviation for the department. Kevin has over thirty years of leadership experience.

"You have to be transparent with your people," Kevin says. "You have to be vulnerable, and you have to let people know what's going on. I encourage my people to talk to me, and I want everyone to participate in the way we run the department. You can say you have an open-door policy, but the way you get your people to talk to you is through being transparent with them."

Transparency was essential for Kevin and his department as they navigated 2018, or the "Year of Change," as he calls it.

"We had previously downsized our fleet, and the decision was made to modernize our fleet with new, larger, longer-range aircraft," Kevin says. "Those aircraft needed to be outfitted with newer technology, technology that didn't make sense for our legacy aircraft. Prior to delivery of the aircraft, we experienced some pilot attrition due to retirement or transition to the airlines. We had to go into the hiring mode. During the middle of this process, my mother died, which made it all even more difficult. But I was open with my team about the changes and kept them informed every step of the way. The team pulled together, and got the necessary training completed, and we managed the transitions together.

"The cool thing here is that we didn't miss a beat with safety, service, and efficiency," Kevin continues. "And that's where transparency and open communication were particularly important. We discussed the warning, cautions, and risks as we transitioned, even as our flight utilization increased. I let the team run with the responsibilities of safety and standardization and whatever new procedures that were required. We worked together as leaders and partners. The whole process was facilitated by transparency (Nichols, 2019).

Jad Donaldson[31] also relied on transparency to deal with change when he became the Director of Aviation at Harley Davidson.

"When I took over, the department was operating autonomously and needed to be brought back into the company," Jad says. "Several people in the department who were still loyal to the previous director had political agendas of their own. I had to separate one of them immediately. He was toxic to the group, and he was definitely on his own page. I realized I had to let the group know exactly what was on my mind and be transparent with them. I held a department meeting with HR present to discuss the separation, and I was blunt with them.

"'The train is leaving the station,' I told them. 'And if you're not on board, then you need to get off.'

"One of the technicians asked, 'Whose train is it?'

"'It's the CEO's train,' I answered. 'We are no longer making our own rules.'

"The transition wasn't easy, but we became a better, more integrated department because of it," Jad concludes. "And when the dust cleared, of the ten original members of the department who were there when I took over, seven of them were gone" (Donaldson, 2019).

Todd Duncan, Elizabeth Dornak, Craig Olson, Kevin Nichols, and Jad Donaldson have showcased the need for leaders to be transparent to their subordinates, particularly during times of change.

---

[31] Jad's introduction and bio appear in Part II, Chapter Three.

While their situations and solutions were unique, each used transparency as an essential tool to keep their organizations moving forward and keeping their people on board in the process.

THOUGHTS FOR LEADERS ON TRANSPARENCY

So how does a leader create transparency in his or her organization? Covey (2006) provided some simple advice:

Tell the truth in a way people can verify. Get real and genuine. Be open and authentic. Err on the side of disclosure. Operate on the premise of 'What you see is what you get.' Don't have hidden agendas. Don't hide information (Covey, 2006, p. 157).

Writing in the <u>Harvard Business Review</u>, two distinguished professors of business offer advice that is a bit more detailed. They discuss the importance of creating a culture of candor and the role of the leader in creating that culture. They argue that leaders need to be the role models for the behavior they want the culture to exemplify (O'Toole, J. & Bennis, W., 2009).

Leaders must share more information, look for counterarguments, admit their own errors, and behave as they want others to behave (O'Toole, J. & Bennis, W., 2009).

On a more granular level, O'Toole and Bennis

(2009) recommend the following:

1. **Tell the Truth.** Leaders who are candid and predictable show that the rules of the game aren't changing and that decisions won't be made arbitrarily;
2. **Encourage People to Speak the Truth to Power.** Leaders must first trust others before others will trust them. Clearheaded leaders and managers appreciate openness and encourage that behavior in their subordinates, or as one leader said: "The only messenger I would shoot is one who arrived too late;"
3. **Reward Contrarians.** Organizations with healthy cultures continually challenge their assumptions. That work can't be done by a leader who is alone in a room; it requires leaders who listen to others;
4. **Practice Having Unpleasant Conversations.** As beneficial as candor can be, it can cause unintentional harm if done awkwardly or inappropriately. Leaders should practice the delivery of feedback to employees whose performance is not up to par to encourage growth for the employee and not resentment;
5. **Diversify Your Sources of Information.** To understand the culture of their organization, leaders need to meet and speak with different people with different perspectives and even different

biases. By limiting their sources of information, leaders can get a very skewed view of their organization's culture;

6. **Admit Your Mistakes.** When a leader owns up to his or her mistakes, it disarms their critics and makes employees more apt to own up to their own mistakes;

7. **Build an Organizational Architecture that Supports Candor.** This begins with the creation of norms and practices that sanction truth-telling, but it can extend to ethics and even to hiring; and

8. **Set Information Free.** Some leaders tend to keep a great deal of information private that could easily and usefully be shared wisely. Sharing information in the right culture allows for additional analysis on the part of employees. It also demonstrates trust (O'Toole, J. & Bennis, W., 2009).

A PERSONAL REFLECTION ON TRANSPARENCY (OR HOW NOT TO)

The leaders in this chapter have provided some superb examples of transparency. They have implemented it well and gleaned commendable results. Here's an example of the opposite condition.

In a past life, I attempted to create a culture of true transparency in an organization I was leading. While my initial efforts were successful, as the organization grew and time passed, I neglected the maintenance piece, and the culture of transparency deteriorated.

Sometimes, as organizations grow, cliques can form, and personnel can perceive they are outsiders. As my team grew, acquaintances and friendships between some team members caused cliques to develop, and as it turned out, one of the cliques consisted of three members of my leadership team.

I would regularly gather information from my leadership team about the state of the organization and the morale of their personnel and receive rosy reports. It never occurred to me that the information I was receiving might be skewed, biased, or not in tune with the rank and file.

Eventually, it became clear that I did not see the "big picture" in my organization because I had limited my sources of information. When I took the time to talk with every single person in my group, I realized the extent of my error. Not only was the culture of transparency in disarray, but also trust in leadership, and trust in me had been affected as well. I learned that factions and fissures had developed inside my team and that I was clueless about those conditions. It was a sobering lesson.

What's the moral of the story? Just because you have an outstanding culture of transparency in your organization today, doesn't mean you'll have one tomorrow. One of the things O'Toole and Bennis (2009) emphasize is that real transparency requires ongoing effort, sustained attention, and constant vigilance. Leaders would do well to keep that in mind.

CHAPTER EIGHT

VISION

THE DEFINITION

The strict definitions of vision, in the noun form, don't seem to render a meaning we would find relative from a leadership perspective, although some of the definitions are close.

1. *The act or power of imagination, mode of seeing or conceiving*
2. *Unusual discernment or foresight, direct mystical awareness of the supernatural usually in visible form*

Nearly every leadership book or article you might encounter will tell you how vital leadership vision is, but very few, if any, will attempt to define it. Smith (1986) equates leadership to planning.

The great leaders of our time have been not only effective operators and decisionmakers, but also people of vision who have had a marvelous sense of what was possible, how to set and articulate goals, and how to motivate their people to strive successfully for these goals. Great leaders tend to be great planners (Smith, 1986, p. 119).

But if we take the definitions above into account, vision is more than planning. In its essence, vision is about an act of imagination that sees or conceives the future. Leadership writer Mitch McCrimmon agrees.

Visionary leadership paints an inspiring picture of what an organization can become. It points towards a new future, a change in direction, and hence provides leadership (McCrimmon, 2019).

John Kotter, the author of the classic work, Leading Change, describes vision this way:

Vision refers to a picture of the future with some implicit or explicit commentary on why people should strive to create that future (Kotter, 1996, p. k 644).

THE RESEARCH

I borrowed from Kotter's definition when I created the summary phrase to measure respondents' views on the importance of vision in the 2019 study.

Has a clear view of where the organization must go.

I also used the respondents' 1-3 ranking to determine where vision fell in the overall list of attributes.

Overall Mean	5.44
Leaders Mean	5.47
Followers Mean	5.39
Levene's Test for Variance	$F = 3.855, p = .050$
Means Statistically Different?	<u>Yes</u>

Table 12. Respondent ratings on the importance of vision.

The results from Levene's test, as shown in Table 12, indicated the two means are, in fact, statistically different. Hence, *Leaders* and *Followers* disagreed in their opinions about the importance of vision. This lack of alignment was highlighted in the rankings of vision between the two groups. *Leaders* ranked the attribute 6th while *Followers* ranked it in 10th place.

THE LEADERS

ED BOLEN

Ed Bolen is the President and CEO of the National Business Aviation Association (NBAA). When asked about how he found a career in aviation, his answer comes in one word – serendipity.

Ed grew up in Salina, Kansas. Thanks to the presence of the nearby Schilling Air Force Base, home of the 310th Strategic Bombardment Wing, Salina was an Air Force town. When the base closed in 1965, the community was forced to turn the airport into a community asset. Ed's father and grandfather both served on the airport board, and Ed grew up listening to them discuss the airport's fate.

Ed attended the University of Kansas and then went to law school at Tulane University in New Orleans. After law school, Ed found his way to Washington, D.C., where he served as General Counsel to the Senate Committee on Labor and Human Resources, and as Legislative Director to U.S. Senator Nancy Kassebaum (R-KS). One of the topics the Senator was passionate about was general aviation. She thought that OEMs[32], particularly OEMs located in Wichita, needed protection from frivolous lawsuits.

At the time, general aviation pilots were crashing light aircraft, and OEMs such as Cessna, Piper, and Beechcraft were being sued by the pilots or their families. While the OEMs were winning the lawsuits,

---

32 An acronym for Original Equipment Manufacturer – common shorthand in the aviation industry for aircraft manufacturers.

it cost them about $500,000 per occurrence to prove it wasn't the aircraft's fault. Cessna had stopped building airplanes, and Piper had gone into bankruptcy.

Senator Kassebaum wanted to place limitations on legal action against OEMs. Ed was instrumental in the passage of the resulting legislation, the General Aviation Revitalization Act of 1994, which implemented those limitations and allowed the general aviation industry to rebound.

In the process of passing the act, Ed interacted with nearly all of the aircraft manufacturers, and that led to the General Aviation Manufacturers Association (GAMA) recruiting him as senior vice president and general counsel in 1995. In 1996, GAMA's board of directors promoted him to president and CEO. In 2004, Ed was selected to be the President and CEO of the NBAA. He has over 24 years of leadership experience.

Ed believes that vision plays a crucial role in a leader's success at the helm of an organization, a belief that was instilled in him by other leaders who have influenced him in his career.

"I've been fortunate to have met and been mentored by some outstanding leaders like Senator Kassebaum, Ed Stimpson,[33] the former President of GAMA, Russ Meyer, the Chairman and CEO of Cessna, and Alan Mulally, former President and CEO

---

33 Ed Stimpson was also a founding member of GAMA. He passed away in 2009.

of Boeing's Commercial Airplanes Group and Ford Motor Company. These were all big-picture people, and they could articulate a clear vision and clear goals and find ways to bring people together around those goals. Alan would have weekly meetings where he'd go through a list of items related to his goals so everyone would be aware of the progress on the goals, and he could ensure open communication about them."

Ed's vision has resulted in successful action in both crisis management and long-term scenarios. The crisis management scenario came about in 2005.

"We had planned to host our annual convention in New Orleans in October of 2005," Ed says. "But in August of that year, Katrina hit the Gulf Coast area and devastated the city. Facilities and infrastructure to support the event were nonexistent. The NBAA didn't have much time to adapt. We needed to move the event. The vision for the event, the goal for it, was to make it a great show, in spite of the challenges. Our people rose to the occasion, and through a great deal of hard work by the team, we secured Orlando as a site, and the event was successful. We even raised a lot of money for the Katrina relief fund. That was a clear and well-defined goal, and we executed it superbly."

One longer-term goal involved NBAA's lobbying efforts with Congress and interaction with business aviation personnel to improve the industry. That goal paid off when the time came for a critical Congressional vote on air traffic control privatization.

"The business aviation community has dedicated, talented, and engaged members," Ed says. "We have wanted to mobilize our membership on a grassroots level to effectively communicate with Congress. NBAA has been developing software to make it easier to contact Congress and our state, regional and local groups have helped out. A year ago, when the House was preparing to vote on H.R. 2997, which would have authorized ATC privatization, we were able to use that software to inform and engage the NBAA membership base. We generated 10,000 responses in 24 hours. That mobilization resulted in 10,000 communications with Congress, and we were able to dissuade the House from passing the bill" (Bolen, 2019).

Ed Bolen's vision provided the means to support and protect the business aviation industry. Brian Proctor's vision provided the means to change an important segment of it.

BRIAN PROCTOR

Brian Proctor is the President and CEO of Mente Group, LLC, a retained agency that offers consulting in all aspects of private aviation. He grew up with a father who loved aviation. But Brian followed a different path.

After he graduated from the University of Richmond, Virginia, Brian accepted a commission in the U.S. Army. He worked as an infantry officer and later as an intelligence officer. Brian is a graduate of the Army's prestigious Ranger school, a leadership course designed to develop the ability to accomplish multiple, high-quality projects under heavy mental and physical stress. It was while Brian was in the Army that a life event changed his attitude about aviation – he married a pilot. He and his wife Karen wound up in Savannah, Georgia, and after he served a tour in Kuwait, Brian decided to leave the Army for a more stable job.

Brian moved to the Dallas Fort-Worth Area of Texas, working for Transamerica Corporation. After about 17 months, Brian made the transition to aviation consulting and acquisition. He rose to Chief Operating Officer in one firm, founder board member and president of another, and decided to start his own company, Mente Group, LLC, in 2009. Mente is a retained firm that offers consulting in all aspects of private aviation. Brian has over 24 years of leadership experience.

In 2017, Brian was elected as the President and Chairman of the Board for the National Aircraft Resale Association (NARA), which was later rebranded as the International Aircraft Dealers Association (IADA). His vision in that position has been about cleaning up the aircraft broker space.

"There are a lot of 'bedroom brokers' in our industry," Brian says. "These are people who have a cell phone and a computer and are buying and selling multi-million-dollar aircraft for clients. In real estate, you have to go to school and get a license to buy and sell houses that are a fraction of the price of a business jet. We have none of those requirements in our industry. So, for the last three years, we have been working on accreditation for brokers and a certification program to certify individual standards, ethics, and client delivery. We're trying to create an environment to move IADA, our members, and the industry to the next level. My goal, my vision, is to explain the future to our members, show them where they are, show them where we're going, and help them to get there."

As a result of Brian's work, more brokerage companies are applying to membership in IADA, over sixteen in 2019. The most in any previous year were seven. Brian's vision also led to the development of a website called Aircraft Exchange (www.aircraftexchange.com), where all aircraft listed for sale by IADA brokers are listed. Standardized templates for Letters of Intent (LOIs) and Aircraft Purchase Agreements (APAs) are also available.

"What is being put in place today will shape the future," Brian says. "For too many years, there used to be an opinion out there that NARA was a 'good old boy' network of people who did deals together. That perception got our organization to a crisis point. But now, we're moving in the right direction" (Proctor, 2019).

Brian Proctor's vision was about the improvement of our industry. Kirsten Bartok's vision is about the innovation of it.

KIRSTEN BARTOK TOUW

Kirsten Bartok Touw is the Co-Founder and Co-Managing Partner of AirFinance, a company that specializes in the structured finance, leasing, and financing of aircraft with a focus on emerging markets. She took a circuitous route to an aviation career. The story of that career is an expression of the vision she has shown both in aviation operations and aircraft finance.

Kirsten started her professional life in private equity investments and venture capital. After working for the investment banking division of Goldman, Sachs, and Company, she was hired by J.P. Morgan Partners, the global private equity arm of J.P. Morgan Chase. Kirsten later became a partner in Alpine Investors, a San Francisco-based middle-market private equity firm, where she led investments in the services, transportation and aerospace markets, among others. It was at Alpine that she was initially exposed to business aviation.

"We were looking at investing in FBOs," Kirsten says. "And I knew nothing about aviation. I knew financial analysis and how to buy companies, but I needed to understand the basics and eventually the nuances of business aviation. To do this, I partnered with experienced aviation professionals. I brought the business acumen and they brought the aviation knowledge."

Soon after, Kirsten, and another individual who brought the aviation expertise, ended up personally investing in an FBO located in the Sacramento Area of California that also provided aircraft sales, charter, and maintenance services.

"We did this deal personally, because the business wasn't profitable enough to be of interest to the private equity firm I worked for," Kirsten says, "but my aviation partner and I still found the business model compelling."

Unfortunately, the FBO quickly burned through the investment, and Kirsten and her partner were forced to replace the management team. Together, she and her partner set about revamping and reorienting the business, exiting unprofitable lines of business and focusing on the profitable ones. They researched successful aviation companies, and what they had done differently, which in most cases was to focus on one thing and excel at that. They also began determining what business jet customers wanted and weren't getting. It was there that the vision for the XO Jet business model began to take shape.

"The vision was to take the fractional model into the next generation," Kirsten says, "to do what the fractional providers did, and do it better. Why did you need to buy a quarter share? Why not buy hours, and if you committed over longer periods your hourly price went down? For shorter commitments you paid more per hour. It just made sense. XOJET also didn't try and be all things to all people, we wanted to be the best within the super mid-size aircraft space. We were also careful to develop rules for our customers where they couldn't game the system and where they were incentivized to do things that helped the company."

The rest, as they say, is history. Kirsten was a co-founder, board member and CFO of XOJET, which grew to be the third-largest business jet fleet operator in the U.S. before it was sold in the fall of 2018. XOJET featured an innovative jet sourcing model that was unique to the industry. As CFO, Kirsten oversaw financial and strategic initiatives, including capital raising and aircraft purchasing and financing for XOJET's 50+ aircraft. While there, Kirsten raised and structured more than $3 billion of equity and debt financing which included the first export credit agency pre-delivery payments financing in the business jet space, the first commercial style business jet leasing transaction by a major investment bank, and a Middle East sovereign government-financed equity and debt facility.

Kirsten stayed with XOJET until 2008. Soon after, she was recruited to serve as a senior executive for the Hawker Beechcraft Corporation (HBC), where she held the position of Vice President, Strategy, Structured Finance and Corporate Development. But even as she performed her duties for HBC, her mind for innovation was developing another vision for the finance side of the industry.

"I noticed there was a void in asset-based financing mechanisms," she says. "I also noticed it was extremely challenging for clients outside of the United States to get financing for aircraft. That was the genesis for AirFinance, which provides a new vision for aircraft financing."

In 2012, after leaving HBC, Kirsten teamed up with Tom Low, the former president of Cessna Finance Corporation's captive finance arm, to form AirFinance Leasing, LLC., a firm that specializes in the global financing of helicopters, business jets, simulators, and aerospace equipment. Since its creation, AirFinance has originated and approved more than $1 billion in aerospace financing. AirFinance has won numerous awards for innovation in aircraft finance, and Kristen herself was listed among the top 10 on the Corporate Jet Investor Power List in 2015.

But Kirsten's vision for aviation finance didn't stop there. She has also been active as an early stage technology investor, especially in aerospace technology companies and the emerging vertical takeoff and landing (VTOL), urban air mobility (UAM) and unmanned aerial vehicle (UAV) space.

"The technology is already available to fly vertically in urban areas without a pilot (i.e. unmanned)," Kirsten says. "We just need to develop the infrastructure to manage, organize and control those UAVs. I am so excited for what flight will look like in 20 years, it should be a radical transformation from how we do it today due to autonomy and electrification.

"My vision for our industry is to build on it and improve it," Kirsten continues. "It's about incremental change and moving it forward, hopefully in leaps and bounds. XOJET was about trying to make NetJets better. AirFinance is about fulfilling a voiding in the market around aircraft finance. We, as an industry, can't rest on our laurels. We must have the vision to see the future of the industry and find a way to get there" (Bartok, 2019).

Where Kirsten Bartok's vision is about the future of our industry, Lisa Swartzwelder's vision was focused on the present in her operation and the impact of catastrophic events on her colleagues.

LISA SWARTZWELDER

Lisa Swartzwelder is the Director of Shuttle

Operations and Flight Administration for a large retail corporation based in Ohio. She grew up under the approach path of a small airport in northeastern Ohio and fell in love with aviation at an early age. Her father spent time on an aircraft carrier while he was in the Navy, and both he and her mother encouraged Lisa to pursue a career in aviation.

"I come from good stock," Lisa says. "I have a lot of positive and nurturing memories from them. They were always telling me I could do anything."

Lisa graduated from the Ohio State University, with an Aviation Major in Human Factors. She also attained her private pilot certificate. Executive Jet Aviation (now NetJets) hired her out of college as second shift dispatcher, but that ended about 18 months later when the company fell on hard times in the early 1990s. Lisa decided to shop the Port Columbus airport for a follow-on job. It wasn't long before she found a dispatcher position with her current employer, the flight department for a large retail chain. She's been there ever since.

In 2001, Lisa was promoted to her current position, where she is responsible for all aspects of her company's corporate shuttle program. Lisa has over 20 years of leadership experience.

Lisa's vision for her current position started with her boss's encouragement and a business plan she co-wrote for the corporate shuttle program. After attaining an MBA from Franklin University, she had the opportunity to execute the startup of the company's first scheduled service with a large cabin aircraft. Lisa attributes a successful program launch in 2001 to teamwork within flight operations while establishing new cross functional relationships and bridging the flight operations closer to the brands and business units of the company. This collaboration empowered all stakeholders to rally behind the program with a common mission of creating a safe, efficient, and exceptional travel experience for employees. The goal was clear, to improve the quality of life and productivity for traveling associates to attract and retain the best talent. The shuttle continues to fly twice a day, five days per week, on a CRJ-200 carrying over 20,000 passengers annually.

But Lisa's vision didn't stop with the commencement of shuttle operations. She began to become concerned about how the company would react in the event of an accident.

"I was losing sleep at night," Lisa says. "Especially when I was thinking of large-cabin aircraft, filled with passengers. Don't get me wrong; we had a fantastic safety program. Still, when I looked at the safety continuum, I realized that we didn't have the same systematic plan or resources in place to take care of people in the event of an incident or accident. We needed a program that went beyond the standard flight department emergency action plan."

Lisa reached out to resources in the industry, and she found the Family Assistance Education and Research Foundation in Atlanta, Georgia[34],

---

34 More information about the Family Assistance Education and Research Foundation can be found at www.fafonline.org.

which specializes in providing research-based, people-focused emergency response to companies, employees, and families in the event of crises. She received training from the founder, Dr. Carolyn Coarsey, who had lost her fiancé in an airline crash in 1985. Lisa then went to the training center for Canada's WestJet airlines and took their Care Team initial training.

"After I had my training, it was time to talk to our HR," Lisa says. "I worked with them and our leadership team to build our own Care Team program. That was in 2005. Now Care Teams are deployed to support associates and their families when a crisis occurs during the scope of work. HR owns the program, and it has become a significant component of the company response model. We integrated the best of human service response into the company's global crisis response program. We also partner with the National Air Transportation Safety Board (NTSB) and Fireside Partners for training and expertise. We practice crisis calls (notification) to emergency contacts and Care Team operations at least once per year, and we don't just practice for aircraft accidents, we practice for other crises like mass shootings and natural disasters.

"One cool thing about the Care Team concept is that is has led to other things that are essential for our people," Lisa continues. "We train with Dr. Coarsey on QPR (Question, Persuade, and Refer). This training adds awareness about depression and how we can help each other in the workplace. We've managed to build a layer into our culture that says,

'It's okay to not be okay". We'll be there for you.' And provide resources that can help. It's another way to live our values as a people-centered organization" (Swartzwelder, 2019).

Ed Bolen, Brian Proctor, Kirsten Bartok Touw, and Lisa Swartzwelder have demonstrated the importance of vision in a leadership role. Whether that vision is about the industry or a segment of it, or an organization with a new mission, it is no less crucial. Vision provides a rallying mechanism for the people in an organization. It gives them an objective, and as the leaders in this chapter have demonstrated, it provides a means to define success.

THOUGHTS FOR LEADERS ON VISION

While finding a definition for leadership vision may be challenging, a search for ways to implement vision yields a multitude of results that run the gamut from sublime to the tedious. John Kotter's thoughts on the topic are among the most straightforward I've found. But before he tells us how to provide a vision, he gives us a diagram to show us why it's essential.

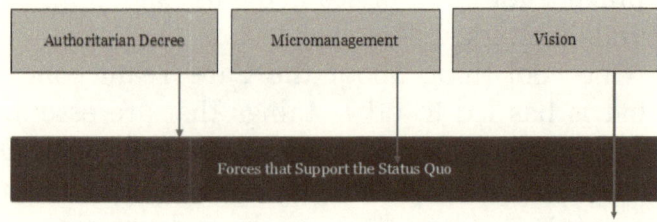

Figure 11. Breaking Through Resistance with

Vision (Kotter, 1996)

While Kotter's diagram shows the importance of Vision in leading change, it also emphasizes the importance of vision in guiding an organization and shows that a clear vision is more effective than other, less desirable forms of leadership. Kotter goes on to provide the characteristics of a compelling vision:

1. **Imaginable.** It conveys a picture of what the future will look like;
2. **Desirable.** It appeals to the long-term interests of employees, customers, stockholders, and others who have a stake in the enterprise;
3. **Feasible.** It comprises realistic, attainable goals;
4. **Focused.** It is clear enough to provide guidance in decision making;
5. **Flexible.** It is general enough to allow individual initiative and alternative responses in light of changing conditions; and
6. **Communicable.** It is easy to communicate; can be successfully fully explained within five minutes (Kotter, 1996, pp. 678-680).

A PERSONAL REFLECTION ON VISION

After twenty years in the Air Force, where the vision and mission of my service and the units I served in were clearly articulated, transitioning to the civilian world's version of vision was, and remains, a challenge for me. Often, the political correctness that seems to be infused with corporate communications can dilute the sense of purpose that useful vision can instill.

So, for this personal note, I'll resort to an anecdote from my USAF days. For one year, from September 1998 to September of 1999, I had the best job I've ever had in my professional career – I was the Operations Officer for a fighter squadron at Luke Air Force Base in Arizona. In the Air Force, the Operations Officer position is roughly equivalent to Chief Pilot, and I had responsibility for all operational aspects of a squadron with 50 pilots and support personnel, 28 jets, and about 7,100 flight hours annually. Interestingly, to put this into a business aviation perspective in an age/chronology context, I was 39 years old at the time.

Very shortly after I took over the position, Rob "Roo" Kesterson, my squadron commander and my boss, came into my office, shut the door, and sat down across from me.

"I have a vision for the squadron," he said. "I want us to be the best squadron on base."

I remember nodding in agreement. "I want that too," I said.

He shook his head at me. "You don't understand," he said. "When the ORI comes early next year, I want us to kick ass. I want us to beat every other squadron on the base."

I nodded again. ORI was an acronym that stood

for Operational Readiness Inspection. It was the most in-depth evaluation an Air Force unit could receive and would place us under a microscope for a week while inspecting officers from our parent command would look closely at our organization. Luke was home to the 56ᵗʰ Fighter Wing, which boasted eight F-16 squadrons and was the largest fighter wing in the world at the time. In a few words, Roo had provided a vision that met all of Kotter's tenets above, but it was a tall order.

Yet, we carried it out. In the following weeks and months, that vision was articulated, and the men and women of my squadron worked on tightening our procedures, scrubbing our documentation, executing our mission, and performing with excellence. Early in 1999, the inspection team arrived and looked us over. As luck would have it, a former colleague of mine who had been promoted to full colonel, was in charge of the team. About two weeks later, the inspection results were released. Not only was our squadron the top-rated squadron on the base, but we were also the top-rated squadron in all of Air Education and Training Command, across 11 bases, 23 wings and nearly 65,000 people.

And it was Roo's vision that got us there.

Great vision can be powerful. As leaders, we should never forget that.

PART II

CHAPTER NINE

HUMILITY

THE DEFINITION

Humility, like transparency, requires us to look at the basis of the word, the adjective form, rather than the noun form to get a sense of its definition. Since humility is the state of being humble, we'll look at that definition.

1. *Not proud or haughty: not arrogant or assertive*
2. *Reflecting, expressing, or offered in a spirit of deference or submission*
3. *Ranking low in a hierarchy or scale: insignificant, unpretentious, not costly or luxurious* (Merriam-Webster, 2019)

Like some of the other attributes we've discussed,

172

it's easy to find literature that discusses the importance of humility for leaders but challenging to find a precise definition for it in a leadership context. Perhaps a more explicit way to define humility from a leadership perspective can come from the application of the attribute. Jeff Hyman, a contributing writer for Forbes magazine, describes it this way:

> *Humble leaders understand that they are not the smartest person in every room. Nor do they need to be. They encourage people to speak up, respect differences of opinion, and champion the best ideas, regardless of whether they originate from a top executive or a production-line employee.*

> *When things go wrong, humble leaders admit to their mistakes and take responsibility. When things go right, they shine the spotlight on others* (Hyman, 2018).

Stephen Covey, in his ground-breaking work, The Seven Habits of Highly Effective People, gave the attribute of humility center stage in his call for personal change for leaders.

> *I have come to believe that humility is the mother of all virtues. Humility says we are not in control; principles are in control; therefore, we submit ourselves to principles, not our values* (Covey, 2013).

Jim Collins, in his classic book <u>Good to Great</u>, also credits humility as a key virtue of the CEOs who led companies that made the jump in performance that likened them to the title of his work.

We were surprised, shocked really, to discover the type of leadership required for turning a good company into a great one. Compared to high-profile leaders with big personalities who make headlines and become celebrities, the good-to-great leaders seem to have come from Mars. Self-effacing, quiet, reserved, even shy – these leaders are a paradoxical blend of personal humility and professional will. They are more like Lincoln or Socrates than Patton or Caesar (Collins, 2001, pp. 12-13).

THE RESEARCH

With the importance of humility for leaders apparent, the perspective gleaned from the research is somewhat perplexing. I used a portion of Hyman's description above to create the summary phrase to measure respondents' views on the importance of humility in the 2019 study.

Isn't afraid to admit errors or limitations.

I also used the respondents' 1-3 ranking to determine where humility fell in the overall list of attributes.

Overall Mean	5.97
Leaders Mean	6.00
Followers Mean	5.94
Levene's Test for Variance	$F = .084, p = .772$
Means Statistically Different?	No

Table 13. Respondent ratings on the importance of humility.

The results from Levene's test, as shown in Table 13, show that *Leaders* and *Followers* are aligned in their opinions about the importance of humility, but ranked it low in importance - 9th in the list of 15 attributes. Interestingly, the mean for the importance of humility was slightly higher for *Leaders* than *Followers*, although not statistically different. *Leaders* ranked humility as the number 9 attribute, while *Followers* ranked it as number 8.

THE LEADERS

JENNIFER GUTHRIE

Jennifer Guthrie is the President and CEO of In-Flight Crew Connections (IFCC), an aviation staffing company. Jennifer always wanted to have her own business, but it took her several years to achieve that dream.

After graduating from college with a degree in business administration, she returned to her hometown of Charlotte, North Carolina, where she started her career working for State Farm insurance. Over the next 15 years, she tried several side businesses and started a family. While the business activities weren't necessarily successful, they taught her several business and life lessons.

"In 2002, corporate flight departments in our region were struggling to find experienced and professional flight attendants," Jennifer says. "I co-founded In-Flight Crew Connections to fill that gap. We started a service to manage and train flight attendants."

Two years later, Jennifer went through a divorce and found herself a single mother who needed to support three children. During this period, she served as a company contract flight attendant and managed the company to support her family.

Since then, IFCC has expanded its range of services to include contract pilots and full-time recruiting services for all flight department personnel. In 2009, IFCC's gross revenue was $500,000. In 2019, that figure topped $19 million. IFCC has won multiple awards for the quality of the services it provides, and Jennifer herself has been recognized several times as a top small-business CEO. She has over 28 years of leadership experience.

Jennifer's entire business model is based on humility, and her leadership style follows suit.

"Humility is required to serve people," she says. "We do that every day in this company. Humility is required to listen to our clients, listen to what they want, and deliver to their expectations, not our own. We can't allow our personal pride to get in the way of serving our customers. But humility is also essential from an internal perspective as well as an external one. I need to be humble to serve the members of my team. My team members need to be humble to serve each other, to recognize the contributions and accomplishments of one another. Humility gives all of us the freedom to drive customer service, improve our processes, and get better results. Humility is the key to everything. I like what Larry Bossidy[35] said about it:

"The more you can contain your ego, the more realistic you are about your problems. You learn how to listen and admit that you don't know all the answers. You exhibit the attitude that you can learn from anyone at any time. Your pride doesn't get in the way of gathering the information you need to achieve the best results. It doesn't keep you from sharing the credit that needs to be shared. Humility allows you to acknowledge your mistakes.'

"We try to live that every day in the office and in our lives" (Guthrie, 2019).

Jennifer Guthrie's view of humility is about putting others before herself and serving her customers. Katherine Staton's view of humility is similar and has been forged in the highly charged environment

---

35 Lawrence "Larry" Bossidy is a former businessman and author of several books on business and leadership. He was also the former CEO of Honeywell International. You can find more information here: https://www.cnbc.com/larry-bossidy-profile/

of civil litigation.

KATHERINE STATON

Katherine Staton is an equity partner and chair of the aviation law practice at a major law firm in Dallas, Texas. Like some other leaders in this book, Katherine's career path in aviation was more incidental than intentional.

Katherine grew up in San Antonio, Texas, where her family went through alternating periods of both wealth and near poverty. She had to work to help support her family, so she developed a strong work ethic early on and learned the value of humility in service to others. She had dreams of becoming an attorney, so after attending St. Mary's University in San Antonio, she put herself through the prestigious law school at Southern Methodist University in Dallas. While at SMU, Katherine joined the law review of the Journal of Air Law & Commerce, not because she had an interest in aviation, but because it seemed to be the better law review journal to join.

When she graduated from SMU, Katherine clerked for an appellate judge in El Paso for a year before returning to San Antonio. When a local firm was searching for a Texas lawyer with aviation experience, her work on the Journal of Air Law & Commerce sealed the deal. She joined the firm in the early 1990's when not many women were practicing aviation law, and performed aviation plaintiff's work for about 8 years, traveling extensively throughout Latin America in support of her clients and their claims.

Eventually, Katherine knew plaintiff's work was not what would hold her interest, and she wanted to do aviation defense work. She joined a major Texas law firm and thanks to the expertise she had gained in plaintiff's work, she forged a specialized practice in aviation defense work. She has been involved with several high-profile cases including some well-known airline accidents. Katherine also does business aviation aircraft transaction work at her firm.

Katherine's take on humility is a unique spin on the quote attributed to C.S. Lewis in Chapter One. "Humility," Katherine says, "is how you behave when people who matter aren't watching. Humility is humbleness at its best." She goes on to explain. "Very early in my career, I learned how important it was to be humble and respectful. When I was clerking for the appellate judge, I saw this in action. All courts have a back office and when you argued in front of the court, the back office wasn't visible. In El Paso, attorneys would go to the administrative side, the back office, and treat the staff poorly. They would be verbose, narcissistic, and impatient with the staff. Then they would go argue their case, totally unaware that the administrative staff, including the briefing attorneys, would have access to the judge and would often tell him how the attorneys had comported themselves. Judges would get a sense of the attorney and that would impact how judge viewed them. That made a huge impression on me."

Later, when Katherine was a plaintiff's attorney, she had a chance to put that humility in action. One of her trials as a plaintiff's attorney was against an airline (the same airline she would represent as a defense attorney). While one of the airline's lawyer was abusive and demeaning, the airline's corporate representative was extremely nice and cordial (this representative sat at the counsel table for the airline during trial as the corporate representative, and she was the "face" of the airline to the jury). Katherine could have responded in kind to the airline's lawyer's behavior, but instead took the path of humility, arguing her case aggressively, but respectfully. At one point, she actually told the airline representative: "You're killing me! You're being too nice! The jury loves you! (as was true-the airline corporate representative was all those things)."

That humility came full circle, because several years later, when Katherine was sitting in that same airline's headquarters, this time as their defense attorney on a high-profile case, that same representative was in the room and commended Katherine for her words and demeanor in the prior case.

The humility to treat her opposing counsel with respect and empathy has played out in other situations.

"We had a case where plaintiff's counsel blew a deadline," Katherine says. "That could have been a death knell for the plaintiff's case. We could have moved for the case to be dismissed, but all I could think of was 'there but by the grace of God go I.' After getting approval from my client, I called the opposing counsel and offered the opportunity to resolve the case, and we did resolve it. We needed to do the right thing, and if I'm not prepared to administer grace (and thankfully my client was in the same camp to administer grace), I should expect none."

As aviation work has taught her about humility, there is unique area in her practice that has taught her even more. One specialized niche in her aviation work has been the defense of airlines in cases where a passenger has been sexually assaulted or molested by another passenger. The expertise she gained from this practice brought her to the attention of a local Catholic diocese when it was sued for alleged sexual misconduct by diocese personnel in the past.

"These are tough cases," Katherine says, "but the diocese is trying to do the right thing. When I work these cases, even though I'm working for the diocese, I try to put myself in the victim's place and approach them from a position of forgiveness and humility. Having the humility to say you're sorry can have an incredible impact."

Katherine's approach to this difficult work has made her the "go-to" attorney for cases like these, not only in the local diocese, but also across the entire state (Staton, 2021).

The same humility that Jennifer Guthrie practices in a company environment and Katherine Station practices in a legal one, Sean Lee manifests and in environment that is familiar to most of us – the corporate flight department.

SEAN LEE

Sean Lee is the Global Vice President of Global Operations and Workplace Services for a Fortune 100 company located in Atlanta, Georgia.

'There's never been a time in my life when I haven't been in aviation," Sean says. "My dad was an A&P in the Air Force, and my uncle did sheet metal work on naval aircraft. So, I always knew I'd wind up flying military aircraft, and going to the Air Force Academy was the perfect avenue to make that happen. I majored in Physics at the Academy and, based off of a medical condition, stuck around afterward to teach it. I was working on my Ph.D. in Physics, but then was medically cleared to fly, and I never looked back."

Sean entered U.S. Air Force Undergraduate Pilot Training and graduated to fly the KC-10 tanker. Eventually, he transitioned to VIP lift and flew the Air Force version of the Gulfstream G-V Sean's last position in the Air Force was the Chief of Standards for the 15th Wing's 15th Operations Group, where he was responsible for operational standards for a diverse fleet including the G-V, the Boeing BBJ, and C-17.

It was while he was flying the G-V that he first met pilots from his current company and decided to make the transition to business aviation. He stayed with that company for about three years and earned an MBA while he was there. Sean then pursued other opportunities with a company on the west coast and another in New England. He returned to his current company in 2018, initially as a general manager for aviation. He was promoted into his current position early last year. Now, he doesn't just lead the aviation function; he also leads a multi-networked team that includes real estate and facilities, corporate travel, aviation, meetings and events, and the company credit union.

"Leadership is about two things for me, setting clear expectations as a leader, and then understanding the expectations of those you lead," Sean says. "Every leader should be able to describe the things that are important to their vision of what great looks like."

For Sean, those expectations boil down to several items. "For me, leadership is about being humble; don't assume you know what the problems are. Listen, listen, and listen to understand. Be an active listener, and don't speak or skip to problem solving. Learn to focus on processes first, not the people. Make sure processes are sustainable and scalable. Becoming a good evaluator of talent by stressing autonomy, mastery, and purpose (AMP). Managing change around quick incremental change and monumental changes cautiously. And finally learning how not to be afraid to fail, by learning from your failure."

To learn about the expectations of his team members, Sean stresses an open communication approach. "I try to do a couple of one-on-one meetings with my team members every day. After we break the ice and catch up on what they've done, I have three standard questions that I ask."

"The first question I ask is, 'What do you need?' You'd be surprised how many people don't know how to answer that question, but it's essential to get them to think about that. The reason being, is that when a person is forced to describe their needs (physical or directional) in relation to being able to complete a job, they either have what they need, or they don't. If they acknowledge that their needs are met, then accountability of successful accomplishment of their job is transferred to them. If they state that their needs are not met, then they are forced to cogently describe what will allow them to be successful. Either way the leader can then level set expectations or gain powerful insight into organizational gaps" (Lee, 2021).

Leaders like Jennifer Guthrie, Katherine Staton, and Sean Lee show their humility in the way they view themselves and their successes. But humility can also be manifested through a leader's willingness to admit and discuss their mistakes. Tony Kern and Tom Cantabene are both bluntly honest about theirs.

As a prominent figure in the fields of human performance and safety, Tony Kern[36] could have chosen not to call attention to some of the mistakes he has made in the past. But that's not who Tony is. Instead, he points them out and uses them as teaching points.

In many of his presentations, Tony mentions an accident that has inspired him to pursue the improvement of human performance in the cockpit. When Tony was an instructor and evaluator pilot in the B-1B bomber at Dyess Air Force Base, Texas, one

---

[36] Tony's introduction and bio appear in Part II, Chapter Three.

of the crews he had trained was killed in a high-speed controlled flight into terrain (CFIT) accident while they were on a training mission. Tony takes responsibility for the deaths of that crew and considers it a personal failure that he didn't do more to prepare them for what they might encounter. When Tony discusses the accident, his language is blunt and harshly honest about what occurred. It is apparent that the incident still haunts him, but he doesn't distance himself from it; instead, he embraces it.

But there is another incident that haunts Tony.

When Tony was the Director of Aviation for the U.S. Forest Service, a contract operator was conducting fire tanker operations in a C-130A and suffered a fatal accident when the wings separated from the aircraft in flight.

"These aircraft were 40-50 years old," Tony says. "The government didn't inspect them, and the companies that operate them have financial reasons to continue flying them regardless of airworthiness. I had noticed that and documented it earlier, but now human lives had been lost. I ran my concerns up the chain of command, but I was told, 'this is the way we have always operated, and there is no indication of a problem across the fleet' and I let it drop.

"Then, 31 days later, the wings came off another aging military air tanker, this time in level flight, and three more people were dead. That's on me. I should have stopped the flying. A leader's first responsibility to his people is keeping them out of harm's way, and I failed to do that. I'll never make that mistake again. Scar tissue gives you the strength to make the hard calls" (Kern, 2019).

THOMAS CANTABENE

Tom Cantabene is the Aviation Manager for a vehicle company based in the southern U.S. He grew up watching airplanes flying into and out of Rochester International Airport when he and his soccer fellow players would eat ice cream at a shop across the road after their games.

When it was time for college, Tom went to the Florida Institute of Technology and received a B.S. degree in Aviation Management / Flight Technology. He also earned his ratings while he was at school. It was the early 1990s, a difficult era to gain flight time, so Tom performed flight instructor duties, worked odd jobs, and flew as much as he could to gain experience.

One fateful day, as Tom was walking across the ramp, the owner of a local charter company met him and recruited him to be a first officer on a Lear 35. Tom went right from piston-powered aircraft to jets and spent the next several few years flying Lear Jets for small operators and then eventually for Flexjet, rising through the ranks from first officer, captain, and Standards Captain. Tom was also fortunate to be selected as initial cadre for two new fleet types at Flexjet, the Learjet 45 and the Challenger 300.

In 1999, Tom transitioned from the line to the Bombardier Aerospace Training center located at the DFW airport as the first Learjet 45 Training Center Evaluator. He eventually performed the same duties for the Challenger 300. Flexjet's Chief Pilot position opened up, and Tom was invited to apply. In the face of some keen competition, Tom was selected, and at age 36, he was in charge of 450 pilots, based nationwide. Within his first year in the job, times changed at Flexjet, and the company went from hiring 30-40 pilots per year to furloughing them. During the next few years, Tom gained a valuable education through experience on the delicate arts of both hiring and firing people, skills which would become important as he moved on.

In 2013, Tom took a job as the Chief Pilot at his current company, working for a friend who was the Director of Aviation. Together, they tripled the fleet size from two aircraft to six in twelve months, expanding their capacity for domestic and international operations. Tom has over 12 years of leadership experience.

Like Tony Kern, Tom could have chosen to brush over some of the mistakes in his past as he rose to a position of leadership. But also like Tony, Tom has the humility to talk about them, even emphasize them to use them as teaching points.

"It was one of those days," Tom says, "one of those CRM[37] stories you read about. The whole chain of causation thing. We were about 5 seconds from being an oil slick on the ocean.

"Back when I was an FO in the Lear, this captain

---

37 CRM is Cockpit or Crew Resource Management, depending on what text you read. You can find a good discussion of it here: https://www.flightdeckfriend.com/ask-a-captain/what-is-crm/

and I had flown together for three long days, and we were exhausted. It didn't help that we were flying well into the night and getting on the wrong side of the clock. We were flying into one of the islands in the Caribbean, at night of course, and we lost hydraulic pressure. We put the flaps down, and the air load didn't sound right. Then we put the landing gear down and heard a thud. We recycled the gear, and nothing happened. I pulled out a checklist to start running different procedures, and the captain began tinkering with stuff in the cockpit. Neither one of us was flying the airplane – for a while. Then I looked up and noticed we were at 200 feet above the water. I told the captain to fly the airplane, and he climbed back up to a safe altitude.

"Eventually, we completed the checklists, got the airplane configured, and landed safely. But a few more seconds of inattention and it could have been disastrous. I talk about that story all the time. I'm not proud of it, but there's nothing like a brush with death to show you your limitations. And I want to make sure nothing like that ever happens on my watch with my people. I use that story to teach the importance of knowing our own limitations and how teamwork can overcome them" (Cantabene, 2019).

The leaders in this chapter have presented examples of some important aspects of leadership humility. Jennifer Guthrie showed us how a company can be built and operated with a sense of humility. Katherine Staton exhibited the importance of respect and humility in the often-confrontational world of litigation. Sean Lee showed us the importance of humility in dealing with his team members in the day-to-day operations in his organization. Tony Kern and Tom Cantabene showed us humility in their willingness to discuss their past mistakes.

Humility is something of a paradox. One might be tempted to make the argument that a leader who shows humility is also showing weakness, but the reverse is true. Leaders who demonstrate humility, convey strength and confidence both to their superiors and subordinates. A true leader recognizes his or her limitations and isn't afraid to admit them.

THOUGHTS FOR LEADERS ON HUMILITY

It's challenging to provide guidance on how to be humble. Like many other virtues that we, as leaders and human beings, are capable of, humility is essentially a choice that we all make on a daily basis. Or an hourly one. We can choose to be humble, or we can choose not to.

But I thought an interesting perspective might be what does humble leadership look like? Dan Cable, a professor of organizational behavior at the London Business school, writing in the Harvard Business Review, has an interesting perspective. He believes in the concept of servant-leadership, and in his mind, servant leadership is about humility. As he puts it:

To put it bluntly, servant-leaders have the humility, courage, and insight to admit that they can benefit from the expertise of others who have less power than them. They actively seek the ideas and unique contributions of the employees that they serve. This is how servant leaders create a culture of learning and an atmosphere that encourages followers to become the very best they can (Cable, 2018).

He goes on to list three guidelines to illustrate how humble leadership works:

1. **Ask how you can help employees do their own jobs better — then listen.** What it comes down to is this: employees who do the actual work of your organization often know better than you how to do a great job. Respecting their ideas and encouraging them to try new approaches to improve work, encourages employees to bring more of themselves to work. (Tom Cantabene provided an interesting perspective on listening. He said: "The ability to listen takes a long time to develop. It takes maturity. It takes eye contact. You can't think about what you're going to say next because if you do that, you're not really listening. Comprehend what someone is saying and answer later. Listening is a critical skill, and I'm not sure you ever master it (Cantabene, 2019).);

2. **Create low-risk spaces for employees to think of new ideas.** Sometimes the best way for leaders to serve employees — and their organization — is to create a low-risk space for employees to

experiment with their ideas. By doing so, leaders encourage employees to push on the boundaries of what they already know; and

3. **Be humble.** Leaders often do not see the true value of their charges, especially "lower-level" workers. But when leaders are humble, show respect, and ask how they can serve employees as they improve the organization, the outcomes can be outstanding. And perhaps even more important than better company results, servant leaders get to act like better human beings (Cable, 2018).

A PERSONAL REFLECTION ON HUMILITY

Sometimes, words about leadership and humility come from places you don't expect. In the course of writing this book, nearly every leader I interviewed mentioned the importance of humility and the lessons that he or she had learned from mistakes or failures. Having made more mistakes in leadership roles than I can count, I related to these expressions of humility, and I guess they keyed my mind to notice things in places I may have overlooked in the past.

I have a home gym, and I usually have the TV on in the background while I push the iron around. Today's feature was a movie called "The Core" from 2003. (You can catch the background here: The Core - IMDB.) I've seen it before, multiple times, but a particular scene caught my attention like I was seeing it for the first time. The scene takes place in a simulator for a unique ship that is going to tunnel into the center of the earth. Major Rebecca Childs (Hilary Swank), a NASA astronaut, is trying to "fly" the ship and crashes the simulator for the second time that day. The ship's commanding officer, Commander Iverson (Bruce Greenwood), who was Childs' commander on a previous space shuttle mission, talks to her about it. This is a part of an ongoing dialogue that has occurred between the two of them.

Iverson: You can practice all you like. It doesn't mean you're ready to sit in that seat.

Childs: So, you keep reminding me, sir.

Iverson: You know, I doubt you're even going to listen to this, but I'm going to give it a shot. Being a leader isn't about ability. It's about responsibility.

Childs: Got it, sir.

Iverson: No, you don't, Beck. I mean, you're not just responsible for making good decisions. You have to be responsible for the bad ones. You've got to be ready to make the shitty call.

Childs: What makes you think I'm not?

Iverson: Because you're so good! You haven't met anything you couldn't beat. I mean, hell, you were the one who figured out how to save the shuttle (a reference to one of the opening scenes of the movie). You made me, you made the rest of NASA just look like an ass. It's just that you're used to winning...and you're not really a leader until you've lost.

The words of this scene ring true with the leaders I've spoken to as they ring true with my own experience. You can't lead well until you've lost, made mistakes, dealt with the responsibility and the consequences, learned the appropriate lessons, and moved on. You can't be a true leader without some scars. And you can't be a true leader without the humility that comes from losing. No leader wants to lose, but true leaders don't fear losing. And they're honest enough to admit when they do.

CHAPTER TEN

SELFLESSNESS

THE DEFINITION

To find the definition of selflessness, we have to dig a little. Selflessness is the state of being unselfish, and unselfish is the opposite of selfish. So, perhaps the place to start is the definition of selfish.

1. *Concerned excessively or exclusively with oneself: seeking or concentrating on one's own advantage, pleasure, or well-being without regard for others*
2. *Arising from concern with one's own welfare or advantage in disregard of others a selfish act* (Merriam-Webster, 2019)

Logically then, it would follow that selflessness

is a state opposite the definitions above. Where leadership is concerned, Dr. Jo Ann Lyon provides us a closer look at that contrast.

"Selfless leadership" is ethically leading others in the achievement of assigned goals and the greater good for the benefit of all others before oneself. "Self-centered leadership" is leading others in the achievement of assigned goals using ways and means that maximize the personal recognition and benefit of the leader over the institution and all others.

These leadership approaches are polar opposites in their focus, goals, strategies, ways, and means. Selfless leaders focus externally on enabling and achieving the success of the organization and people before their own personal success. In any endeavor, these leaders first ask themselves and their teams, "What's the right thing to do here?" and then, "How best can we do it?" Accomplishing the goal or mission and doing it right becomes the team's guiding and unifying focus. This type of selfless leadership grants freedom to every team member to take necessary action and removes all potential paralysis and doubt in the face of danger, risk, and opposition. Ultimately, selfless leaders leave lasting and positive institutional accomplishments. They shape lives by their leadership, and they earn an honored and emulated reputation going into the future (Vincent, 2015).

Colonel Eric Kail, Ph.D., Course Director of Military Leadership at the U.S. Military Academy at West Point, regards selflessness as a critical component of servant-based leadership.

One of the best leaders I've had the privilege to follow once told me: "To lead is to serve; nothing more, nothing less." His first concern was for how he could help those doing the most critical work of the day. He suffered no fools either, and yet he was not the focus of my accountability as a subordinate leader. Together we served those we led, and he always made clear that those following us deserve our very best (Kail, 2011).

THE RESEARCH

Analysis of the perspective of leaders and followers on the trait of selflessness provided mixed results. For the 2019 study, I used a phrase to describe selflessness that I thought captured the essence of the thoughts above.

It's about the team, not themselves.

I also used the respondents' 1-3 ranking to determine where humility fell in the overall list of attributes.

Overall Mean	5.86
Leaders Mean	5.89
Followers Mean	5.84
Levene's Test for Variance	$F = 5.954, p = .015$
Means Statistically Different?	<u>Yes</u>

Table 14. Respondent ratings on the importance of selflessness.

Even though the mean responses from *Leaders* and *Followers* are close numerically in Table 14, Levene's Test shows that from a statistics perspective, the means are statistically different. *Followers* rated selflessness lower in importance than *Leaders*, yet in the rankings, *Followers* rated selflessness 9th in the list of 15 attributes, and *Leaders* ranked it 11th. The means indicated one disparity between the *Leaders* and *Followers*, and the 1 -3 rankings indicated the opposite. This is a curious paradox.

THE LEADERS

There are many ways that leaders can display selflessness. Perhaps the most dramatic examples occur when they are willing to stand up to those above, even to the point of risking their employment. As we saw in Chapter 1, Milt Hobbs risked his own job for the sake of one of his helicopter pilots when his CEO wanted to fire the pilot for canceling a flight due to weather (Hobbs, 2019). Milt didn't lose his job on that occasion, but John Rambo[38] did when he fought for better compensation for his pilots – placing their needs above his own (Rambo, 2019).

A leader can also show selflessness in the act of mentoring and developing subordinates. Nearly everyone I interviewed for this book talked about leaders who had mentored them and prepared them for the positions they attained or the people they were mentoring or both. Kevin Nichols[39] probably summed it up best with a quote that he keeps on his phone:

"The mark of a true leader is not how many followers you have; it's how many leaders you create[40]" (Nichols, 2019).

Kellie Rittenhouse[41] urged one of her people to apply for a lead flight attendant job even though that person would be the youngest applicant for the position.

"Even though she was the youngest, she was also

---

[38] John's introduction and bio appear in Part II, Chapter Six.

[39] Kevin's introduction and bio appear in Part II, Chapter Seven.

[40] This quote has been attributed to Mahatma Gandhi, but I couldn't find any documentation to that effect. Similar quotes have come from Tom Peters and Roy T. Bennett.

[41] Kellie's introduction and bio appear in Part II, Chapter Three.

the most qualified," Kellie says. "I helped her prep for the interview, and she got the job. Then after she got it, when she had questions, she'd come to me for help, and I was happy to be there for her."

But Kellie's efforts didn't stop with one person.

"When I was Chairman of the NBAA Schedulers and Dispatchers Committee, I chose another one of my younger people to come to one of our meetings and give a presentation. She later became chair of that committee.

"I like nudging people," Kellie says. "I want to mentor people, bring them along. In my mind, part of success as a leader is seeing someone else succeed" (Rittenhouse, 2019).

Like Kellie, Jamie Stone likes to develop people for their own success.

JAMES STONE, CAM

Jamie Stone is the former Director of Aviation for an insurance company located in the southeastern U.S. He has since transitioned to be the Director of Aviation for a major health care insurance provider. Jamie always had an interest in aviation and wanted to fly. His father was a mechanic for American Airlines during Jamie's childhood. While his dad didn't really like flying, he had travel benefits that came with his position, and Jamie enjoyed it when they flew on family trips.

When Jamie entered high school, the aviation job market was on the downturn. His father knew several mechanics with aviation ratings who were waiting for jobs, so he recommended that Jamie consider other options. Jamie pursued his other passion, music, instead and received a full college scholarship through it.

About two years into college, the aviation job market began to recover, and Jamie transitioned to the University of Oklahoma and began flight training there. Almost simultaneously, he was hired by Southwest Airlines as a cargo operations agent at Will Rogers World Airport in Oklahoma City. It was his first aviation job.

Jamie went on to complete his aviation ratings at the University of Oklahoma, and then worked as a CFI after graduation to build his flying time. Ten months later, he interviewed at ExpressJet, then Continental Express Airlines, and was hired in July of 2000. Jamie flew a turboprop Embraer Brasilia there, followed by the Embraer regional jet. But after 9/11 occurred, he decided to look outside of the airlines.

Jamie applied for a position with ConocoPhillips in Houston, Texas, and was hired to fly a Falcon 50EX in 2003. Over the next three years, he was checked out in the Gulfstream G-IVSP, the G-550, and the company's shuttle aircraft, an Embraer 135, as well. When the opportunity arose to move to Bartlesville, Oklahoma, and perform shuttle duties exclusively, Jamie took it.

"I was going to fly four or five times a week and be home every night," he says. "And my whole family was from Oklahoma, so it seemed like the perfect fit."

In short order, Jamie was promoted to Manager of Standardization and Training for the shuttle and then became the Chief Pilot and Director of

Operations under 14 C.F.R. part 125. After a few years in that position, another internal opportunity became available in Alaska. The company had a 737 shuttle based in Anchorage and used it to transport workers to the North Slope and back.

"I was presented with an opportunity to come out of the leadership role and get a recharge," Jamie says. "The whole time I was in Alaska, all I did was fly. We moved approximately 300,000 people a year between PANC and the North Slope. I got to enjoy life for a while."

In 2016, Jamie returned to the continental U.S., left ConocoPhillips, and took a Chief Pilot position for an air medical transport company with nine fixed-wing aircraft, seven helicopters, and eight bases. About five months into his tenure, the Director of Operations, resigned and Jamie moved up into that position. After a year there, in a 24/7 operation that ran at a non-stop, hectic pace, Jamie was recruited for his former job. He has over 14 years of leadership experience.

"One of the best parts of being a leader is developing people and watching them succeed," Jamie says. "In one of my previous jobs, there was this young guy who wanted to meet me for lunch and pick my brain about corporate aviation. He seemed very knowledgeable and competent, but he was also very humble. He asked my advice about what he should do. He already had a flying job, but I told him he should concentrate on finishing his degree since he only had a few credit-hours remaining.

"The guy took my advice. The next time a position came open in my organization, I hired him. Once he came to work for us, I began to groom him for increased responsibility, and it paid off because when I left that job, he succeeded me. Later, when a Director of Aviation job came open for a well-known flight department, I recommended him for the job, and he was hired there as well" (Stone, 2019).

As Kellie and Jamie have shown, selflessness can be demonstrated in developing others, but it can also be more personal. Tom Cantabene[42] believes in empathy as an act of selflessness, as an act of service to his people.

"You have to know your personnel on a personal level," Tom says. "You have to know more about them than their job description or duties. You have to be able to interact with them on a personal basis, not just as superior and subordinate. That kind of interaction gives the employee a sense of belonging, and it helps you understand them. You can know what they're going through so you can serve them better. Knowing your people on a personal level is huge when something goes wrong in their lives. It provides a good perspective when things aren't the norm. Individual people and individual situations require individual responses and decisions. To put yourself in their shoes, you have to get yourself out of the way" (Cantabene, 2019).

As we saw from the definition section of this chapter, selflessness can mean serving others.

---

[42] Tom's introduction and bio can be found in Part II, Chapter Nine.

Sometimes that service can be personal. Dan Wolfe[43] has been a foster parent for 25 years, performing an act of service for children with difficult circumstances (Wolfe, 2019). Selflessness can also be demonstrated by service to an industry. Ed Bolen's[44] work with the NBAA has shown that. So has the work of one of his protégés, Shelly Simi.

SHELLY SIMI

Shelly Simi is the former President and CEO of the National Association of State Aviation Officials (NASAO). She has since expanded her roles in the workforce arena with a startup she founded called New Heights and is coordinating efforts to increase the pipeline for aviation industry personnel.

Shelly grew up with a passion for aviation. She lived 75 miles south of Memphis, Tennessee, where she could watch crop dusters perform their low altitude maneuvers over nearby farm fields and see FedEx jets flying overhead. After a flight with a female instructor at age 10, Shelly decided that was what she wanted to do. She eventually went to Delta State University, where she was only the second female in the flight program. Shelly pursued a major in commercial aviation management with a minor in flight operations. Through a mentor in the program,

---

43 Dan's introduction and bio appear in Part II, Chapter Two.

44 I have not found the original source document for this quote although it has been widely attributed to Powell.

she was hired as an intern for FedEx, where she performed duties as a flight coordinator and fuel dispatcher controller.

"I provided flight plans and data to 727 and DC-10 pilots," Shelly says. "Then I'd debrief them after their flights. I also worked in the weather shop and did fuel controller duties. It started as a six-month internship, but I ended up staying there for a year and a half."

When she graduated, the same mentor that helped her get the job at FedEx, made some phone calls on her behalf. She sent resumes to NBAA, GAMA, and Delta Airlines. GAMA called her back. Ed Stimpson, the founder of GAMA, hired her to be his executive assistant. Six months later, Shelly became assistant to GAMA's Director of Communications. In the 15 years that followed, she worked her way up the ranks to Manager, Director and then Vice President of Communications.

After a brief break to start a family, Shelly started her own communications company. Her largest client was Adam Aircraft, and the company eventually hired her to be its public relations and industry affairs counsel. After three and a half years though, the bottom fell out for Adam as a result of the 2008 U.S. financial crisis, and the company went bankrupt.

Jeppesen hired her then, to perform the same functions out of its Washington, D.C. office, as Manager of Communications and Industry Relations. Shelly performed so well in that position that Boeing, Jeppesen's parent company, attempted to entice her to move to Seattle to run its Global Services Division.

Wanting to remain in the D.C. area, she joined Aurora Flight Sciences as Director of Corporate Communications and Public Affairs. The company specialized in VTOL aircraft, unmanned flying electric aircraft, and systems for robotic first officer under a contract for the Defense Advanced Research Projects Agency (DARPA). After three and half years with the company, she received a call from Ed Bolen, whom she had worked for at GAMA.

"Would you like to run the National Association of State Aviation Officials?" he asked.

"I thought about it for a bit," Shelly says. "I learned a lot at Aurora. But after 3.5 years, I was ready to re-join the association world."

Shelly's efforts to serve the industry continued beyond her position at NASAO and into her startup, New Heights.

"I have a passion for our industry," Shelly says. "Aviation teachers or counselors who knew about aviation were scarce when I was growing up. Our industry needs funding from Congress for the states to provide more aviation instruction to young people and get them excited about aviation. Starting in middle school and taking them all the way into aviation careers. We're even looking at funding for ab initio type programs while partnering with the FAA with a focus on each region to ensure this national effort is a success."

Shelly has been in leadership positions since 1996. She's also a founding board member of Women in Aviation, International (WAI).

Shelly's attitude towards selflessness and service

is a product of the mentorship she's experienced.

"I've been very fortunate to have some incredible mentors," she says. "I still reach out to them for advice and solutions to issues I encounter, and they're always there for me. I'm always eager to mentor others as well, especially young women."

Like Tom Cantabene, Shelly believes in the power of empathy as a tool of service to her people and her organization as well as to achieve her own goals.

"I try to listen to others, see things from their perspective, and find the best way to get to a solution. If things get heated in a conversation, it's a sure sign that someone's ego is getting in the way, and they're not trying to understand the other person or the underlying need."

"For example," Shelly continues, "when I was working with Aurora, there was a particular member of the media who was difficult, even a bit hostile towards our company. I was in charge of communications, yet he seemed to have his own agenda and wasn't receptive to the facts and current status of a program that I was trying to provide. I could have taken that personally. But I didn't do that. Instead, I tried to put myself in his shoes. He obviously didn't see things from our perspective. What could I do to fix that? So, we brought the guy in for lunch with some of our young engineers, and they told him stories about our company and our project from their perspective. It provided the context for the material that I'd already given him, and he understood what we were working to achieve. With a little empathy, we won him over."

The leaders I've cited here aren't the only ones

I interviewed who exhibited selfless behavior in their stories, just the ones who provided examples that were the most illustrative. Yet, as I spoke with every leader in this book, there was an interesting phenomenon that I observed.

Often, in the media, we see people who perform heroic acts interviewed. To a person, they don't see their actions as brave, just doing what was right in that situation.

Selfless leaders are the same way. They don't see their acts as selfless. It comes naturally to them. It's who they are.

THOUGHTS FOR LEADERS ON SELFLESSNESS

Is it possible to become selfless if one is not? That's probably a question more appropriate to a self-help book than a leadership one. But a starting place might be to identify whether or not one is selfless. According to Inc. magazine's Michael Schneider, there are five questions we, as leaders, can ask ourselves to determine if we are, in fact, selfless.

1. **Do we take the initiative to serve others?** It's counterintuitive to some, but leaders who want to gain credibility have to relinquish control and share power. They need to empower employees to take ownership. Or as Simon Sinek says:

   The true price of leadership is the willingness to place the needs of others above your own. Great leaders truly care about those they are privileged to lead and understand that the true cost of the leadership privilege comes at the expense of self-interest.

2. **Are we flexible and view interruptions as opportunities?** The consequences of being open and approachable are that we will be approached for guidance, often at times that are inconvenient. Showing annoyance or frustration will discourage our people from coming to us;

3. **Are we cheerful givers?** *We need to give of our time, our guidance, our expertise, even our recommendations on behalf of others, with no expectation of return;*

4. **Do we use words to encourage rather than criticize?** *We need to understand the weight our words carry. The saying "it's not personal, it's just business" is not reality. If we plant words of doubt by being overly critical, we shouldn't be surprised when employees become insecure. We need to provide feedback in a way that instills a growth-minded mindset in our people and lets them know we're in it together; and*

5. **Do we balance speaking with listening?** *Our employees can tell when we're not paying attention to them, or worse, interrupting them with unhelpful information. We need to concentrate on*

*what our people are saying to us and not
let our prior biases impact what we're
hearing (Schneider, 2017).*

A PERSONAL REFLECTION ON SELFLESSNESS

The selfless behavior I've seen in the actions of the leaders in this book has given me great hope for our industry. Sadly, I haven't seen much of it in the leadership of the organizations I've been a part of during my business aviation career. But admittedly, my perspective on selflessness, like any member of the military, past or present, is held to a somewhat lofty standard.

When I think of the true meaning of the word, selfless, my mind goes back to a classmate of mine from the Air Force Academy, Steve Phillis.

There's a well-known verse from the Bible from the Book of John:

*Greater love has no one than this, that one lay
down his life for his friends (John 15:13,
NASB).*

Steve Phillis exemplified that on February 15, 1991.

Steve, a graduate of the Air Force's prestigious Fighter Weapons School, was leading a two-ship flight of A-10s looking for ground targets in northwest Iraq. His wingman was a young lieutenant named Rob

Sweet. They found a truck convoy, and after verifying that the convoy was hostile, they rolled in and began to expend ordnance. During one of their passes on the convoy, Sweet's aircraft was hit by ground fire, and he was forced to eject. Steve Phillis radioed the report of his wingman's ejection into the flight's controlling agency to begin a search and rescue operation to retrieve his wingman.

But then he noticed that Iraqi ground troops were closing in on Sweet's location. Steve didn't hesitate. He rolled in on the Iraqis multiple times and strafed them with the A-10's 30mm cannon. On one of these passes, Steve's jet was struck by a SA-13 surface-to-air missile. The explosion from the weapon is thought to have rendered him unconscious because his aircraft impacted the ground shortly thereafter with no attempt by Steve to eject. He was 30 years old.

Often, it is in the moments where we make unconscious choices that our true natures are manifested. Steve Phyllis could have orbited, he could have waited for more aircraft to arrive, or he could have been more conservative in his choice of weapons or tactics. Instead, thinking only of his wingman's fate at the hands of the Iraqis and not thinking of himself, he immediately attacked and lost his life in defense of his wingman.

Like the leaders in this book, Steve's first, instinctive thought was not for himself; it was for others. Would that we could all do the same.

PART II

CHAPTER ELEVEN

PASSION

THE DEFINITION

There are several definitions for the word passion when we consult the dictionary. Probably the ones most applicable to the discussion for this chapter are the following:

1. *Intense, driving, or overmastering feeling of conviction*
2. *A strong liking or desire for or devotion to some activity, object or concept* (Merriam-Webster, 2019)

Passion, by definition, is an emotion, but

211

something Dan Wolfe[45] said when I interviewed him resonated with me.

"There's a fine line between passion and emotion from a leadership perspective," he said. "Your people will follow the passion, but emotion will turn them against you. But," and I could hear him laugh when he said this, "if you're not on the edge, how do you know where it is?" (Wolfe, 2019)

What does passion look like from a leadership perspective? Randy Grieser, CEO, author, and speaker, believes that passion is a "profoundly positive feeling for something that is deeply and personally meaningful" (Greiser, 2019). He goes on to say:

Passion is about vision, and also contains energy, excitement, and enthusiasm.

Passion inspires others to join and identify with your vision. No one has ever been inspired by a leader who is not passionate. Passion – and alternatively, the lack of passion – is contagious. If you want to have a passionate, inspired workforce, it begins with you: the leader (Greiser, 2019).

Steve Moore, the president of Missio Nexus, believes that a leader's passion is critical to success.

---

45 Dan's introduction and bio can be found in Part II, Chapter Two.

He believes that passions are "like self-interests on steroids" (Moore, 2019). Like Dan Wolfe, he understands the line between passion and emotion:

Self-aware people actively seek to bridle their passions and constructively channel their inner currents of desire. Passions are like threads of inner concern that when woven together tightly form a rope strong enough to support your dreams (Moore, 2019).

He goes on to discuss two reasons why passion is essential for leaders.

First, your passion as a leader is one piece of the self-awareness puzzle that will enable you to focus your energies on the causes that resonate with the core of who you are. In addition to your personality, natural talents, and gifts, you need to understand and tap into your passions. Second, as a leader, you will need to help others understand their passions so you can place members of your team in areas of responsibility that contain what I call "passionators," intrinsic motivational forces that flow from inner passion (Moore, 2019).

THE RESEARCH

Analysis of the perspective of leaders and followers on the trait of passion provided separated, but consistent results. I used a simple phrase to encapsulate the notion of passion for the 2019 Study that captures the discussion above.

Cares about what we do.

I also used the respondents' 1-3 ranking to determine where passion fell in the overall list of attributes.

Overall Mean	5.71
Leaders Mean	5.79
Followers Mean	5.63
Levene's Test for Variance	$F = 7.876, p = .005$
Means Statistically Different?	Yes

Table 15. Respondent ratings on the importance of passion.

The mean responses from *Leaders* and *Followers* are separated in Table 15, and the results of Levene's Test confirm that difference. *Leaders* rated the importance of passion higher than *Followers*. The rankings echo that orientation. *Leaders* ranked passion as the number 10 trait, and *Followers* ranked it as 12th.

THE LEADERS

DAN DROHAN

Dan Drohan is the founder and CEO of Solairus Aviation, one of the world's largest aircraft management companies. Dan's story, and the story of Solairus, is one born from a passion for aviation and our industry.[46]

"I was always into airplanes as a kid," Dan said. "I had cockpit posters everywhere in my room, I was an early adopter MS Flight Simulator nut and I built remote-controlled aircraft. I even used to play in the cockpit of an aircraft that had crashed near my house. I was the only member of my family who was into airplanes. In 1984, when I had just turned twelve, my father passed away. So that my older siblings and mom could deal with my father's passing, a family friend offered to take me to the local airport for something to do to get me out of everyone's hair. He dropped me off one Saturday morning and I remember sitting down on a bench and spending the entire day watching the planes come and go. I was completely mesmerized by it. The next day, he took me to the airport again, but this time, as I sat there that second morning, a guy approached me and told me that if I washed and waxed his car, he'd give me a ride in his

---

[46] Full disclosure, Dan and I are friends. We were both part of the JetDirect debacle that occurred in the late 2000s, although we saw it from different perspectives.

airplane. I spent the whole day cleaning that car, and that afternoon we went out in a Super Decathlon and did aerobatics. I was hooked - and honestly I have never looked back!"

Dan started working at the airport the next weekend and spent the next five or six years working for the flight school, refurbishment and bi-plane ride operator at the field, spending his weekends during the school year and seven days a week during the summer. He spent plenty of time flying, but his enthusiasm went beyond building flight hours. In those early years, Dan got his first look at the inner workings of an aviation business. That early exposure and experience helped develop and channel his passion and entrepreneurial spirit into what would eventually become Solairus.

After completing high school, Dan attended the University of New Mexico. "College wasn't a good fit for me," Dan says candidly. "After one semester, I returned home and announced to my family that i was going to pursue aviation full-time, a decision that was not so wildly popular at the time!" After taking a few months to complete his instrument, commercial and multi-engine ratings, he convinced his family to partner with him on a 1970 Beechcraft Baron. Dan refurbished the aircraft and used it to launch an air-tour business, conducting sightseeing flights over the Bay Area and wine country. Sunset Aviation, the early predecessor of Solairus, was officially born in 1992. The one-aircraft operation eventually evolved into Part 135 charter, and soon clients were coming to Sunset with 400 series Cessnas to manage. Over the next 15 years, the company took on Beechcraft King Airs, Cessna CJs, Citations, Beechjets, and Hawkers and built a solid regional presence with 25 aircraft at four bases: Santa Rosa, Concord, Sacramento, and the home base in Novato.

In 2005, Dan was approached by JetDirect to acquire Sunset. JetDirect was amassing a national air charter and management brand by "rolling-up" regional carriers into one big operation. Sunset completed the sale to JetDirect in June of 2007. Though JetDirect ultimately failed just two short years later, Dan has no regrets about selling to the larger conglomerate. "I wanted to be part of something bigger, and I knew even then that scale was critical to success in this industry" Dan says. "I wanted my team who worked with me at Sunset to be part of the experience of building it."

When JetDirect collapsed in 2009, Dan's passion and persistence pushed him forward. Though he and his team attempted to recover the remnants of Sunset from JetDirect, they were ultimately unsuccessful in doing so and were forced to launch a new company from scratch. Knowing that building the right team would be critical to success in the midst of a downturn, he approached the Jake Cartwright[47] , the for-

---

47 Jake Cartwright, a former commercial pilot and marine aviator, led TAG Aviation USA during its heyday in the early 2000s. He was admired and respected by many in the business aviation industry. The NBAA has named a leadership scholarship in his honor.

mer president and CEO of TAG Aviation USA, to be a partner in the new firm. "If I hadn't met Jake and been exposed to TAG as part of the JetDirect debacle, there would be no Solairus today," Dan says. "We believe at Solairus that windshields are bigger than rearview mirrors for a reason, and our story became somewhat akin to the "aviation phoenix" rising out of the ashes. We felt that if we could create a new platform that looked and performed something like TAG, which had also been wrapped-up in the JetDirect debacle, that clients would come to us as something of a lifeboat. Jake was pivotal in creating that and I am very proud to have been able to work with him so closely for those years."

But Dan knew that starting from square one wouldn't be easy. "We recognized that we needed to refresh and take the original TAG management model a step further. We needed to add entrepreneurialism as a core value and go top to bottom to meld the two approaches. Today, there is a lot about Solairus that looks like TAG did, but I think we are nimbler and more entrepreneurial, though we have grown to twice the size. That is purely a function of the people, the timing of when we started and the journey of how we got here – not to suggest one approach was better than the other. One thing is for sure though, we've always been willing as a team to work incredibly hard to win at Solairus. And we keep our minds open to the possibility that just because something worked yesterday, it doesn't mean that it will work today or tomorrow. Hubris is a fatal flaw in this business, and we are always working to evolve and improve."

The same passion that fueled Dan in the evolution of Solairus extends to his leadership style and his high regard for his team members. "At the end of the day, my real true passion is for the people that have made this organization what it is, they are true Aviation people. It's in my DNA and I'm a self-admitted airplane head, so I love airplane people. I focus intently on the human element of our business. At Solairus we believe that it is critically important to arm people with the right tools, resources and assets and then take the most important step, which is the one backwards to get out of their way. 99% of the time, people will outperform your expectations if you have set them clearly, armed them with what they need and then get out of the way. Our entire business model is built on this concept. We win as an organization when the individuals who make up the team win as people. We can never be only as strong as one person."

Dan sums up his entire journey as a "passion pursuit with no grand plan". From a one-aircraft, one-person operation in 1992 to a complex operation with over 265 aircraft, 1600 personnel, and 70 operating locations today, Dan's passion has built a business that provides a valuable service to hundreds of clients, employs nearly two thousand people, and manifests a standard of operations that sets a high standard for our industry. Dan's passion provides a real-life illustration of Moore's words above and shows how critical passion can be for not only the success of a leader, but also the success of an entire organization. (Drohan, 2021)

LUCILLE FISHER

Lucille Fisher is the founder of Quality Resources, LLC., one of the most widely respected providers of aviation documentation in the industry. Like Dan Drohan, Lucille built a business based on passion.

Lucille didn't start her professional life with aviation as a focus. She began working in manufacturing, building equipment for nuclear power plants. One of her mentors told her to get an education, so she began to attend college courses at night. Eventually, she moved to Cleveland, Ohio, to finish her undergraduate studies and worked for a prototype company that was a subcontractor for McDonnell Douglas' guided missile division.

But then, her boyfriend, who was the Chief Pilot for a regional aircraft operator, asked her to write tests for his airline. Lucille agreed and became intrigued with aviation. She took a job as a flight scheduler for a bank holding company but was recruited by a fractional operator for a customer service position. Thanks to her interest in aviation, she changed jobs. She moved up the ranks of that company quickly, rising to Director of Owner Services, then Director of the Operations Center, and finally, Director of Standards and Training.

Lucille's expertise got her noticed in the industry, and she was hired by another fractional operator and then by a 14 C.F.R. Part 121 operator. She rose to the rank Vice-President in the 121 operation and noticed something startling along the way: she was good at standards and publications, a task that no one else wanted to do.

In 2002, she started Quality Resources, a company that provides standards and publications for operators. She's been there ever since.

"You have to love what you do," Lucille says. "I mean, who would voluntarily be in a business where you live in regulations and documents unless they loved it? Over my years in aviation, I developed a passion for standards, guidance, and compliance. I developed a passion for documents that convey the information our industry needs to do the right thing. I'm so fortunate. I get to do something I believe in, something I care about and something I love."

But Lucille doesn't just focus on her own passion. She also tries to bring out the passions of her people.

"As a leader, I try to help my people find their frisbees, their passions. The thing that motivates them, the thing they value and think is important. Then, I appeal to that, and it keeps my people grounded and satisfied. It keeps them with me."

But Lucille is quick to point out that she does other things to stoke the fires of her employees' passion for their jobs.

"We're great at celebrating birthdays here," she says. "Maybe not always on the day, but we make a big fuss about it. We go to the Capital Grille for lunch. One year, we actually did an Alaskan Cruise for the group."

Lucille has another mechanism to bring out passion in her people.

"I make my team members read books," she says. "It makes them think. It helps them to find their frisbee, build their professional knowledge, and makes them better people. The top three books on the list are <u>How to Win Friends and Influence People</u>[48], <u>Don't Take the Last Donut</u>[49], and <u>Who Thought this was a Good Idea</u>?[50]" (Fisher, 2019)

THOUGHTS FOR LEADERS ON PASSION

The examples of Dan Drohan and Lucille Fisher illustrated the importance of passion, both to leaders and their personnel. But what does passion look like to the rest of us? Leadership expert Michelle Ray believes that passionate leaders lead with "heart and soul" (Ray, 2019). She offers twelve characteristics of a passionate leader, characteristics that she says will distinguish passionate leaders from those who are not.

1. **Passionate leaders rise above naysayers.** They seek solutions rather than problems, critique instead of criticize, and look for the good in every situation;
2. **Passionate leaders have a profound**

---

[48] Carnegie, D. <u>How to Win Friends and Influence People</u>. New York, Simon and Schuster, 1936.

[49] Bowman, J. <u>Don't Take the Last Donut</u>. Franklin Lakes, NJ, Career Press, 2009.

[50] Mastromonaco, A. <u>Who Thought This Was a Good Idea</u>? New York, Hachette Book Group, 2017.

understanding of people. They are open-minded, appreciate differences, and respect divergent opinions;

3. **Passionate leaders are outstanding communicators.** They listen with the intent to genuinely understand, rather than to advance their own agenda;

4. **Passionate leaders have clarity of vision.** They are future-focused and have the capacity to engage others to realize their goals;

5. **Passionate leaders see opportunity in adversity.** They recognize that failure is part of success, and embrace challenges;

6. **Passionate leaders are fueled by positive energy.** They surround themselves with like-minded people and are enriched by collaborative relationships;

7. **Passionate leaders have compassion.** They give for the sake of giving, expecting nothing in return;

8. **Passionate leaders are resourceful.** They recognize potential and intuitively utilize others' strengths, rather than try to be all things to all people;

9. **Passionate leaders anticipate rather than react.** They are free thinkers and do not subscribe to the "herd" mentality;

10. **Passionate leaders take action.** They are risk-takers, execute ideas, and do not dawdle or dwell in the past;

11. **Passionate leaders are lifelong**

   learners. They remain teachable, aware, and tuned into key trends; and

12. **Passionate leaders believe in themselves.** They trust their gut instinct, do not take criticism personally, and are undaunted by obstacles at work, in business, or in life (Ray, 2019).

A PERSONAL REFLECTION ON PASSION (OR HOW NOT TO)

Passion can be powerful. But it can also be destructive and intimidating. One of the things I am very passionate about is the need for Upset Prevention and Recovery Training (UPRT) for business aviation pilots. As the air transportation industry continues to grow and airline traffic increases, we in the business aviation world face an ever-increasing likelihood that we can inadvertently fly into the wake vortices of a big jet and find ourselves sideways, upside down or worse[51]. Sometimes, inattention or unusual circumstances at high altitude can result in a loss of control situation as well, as the crew of Air France Flight 447 tragically demonstrated in 2009[52]. If

---

[51] One of the worst/best examples of this sort of encounter can be found here: https://ops.group/blog/airbus-380-flips-cl604-full-report-is-now-published/

[52] Numerous articles and even a book have been written about this accident. One of the best accounts I have read can be found here: https://www.popularmechanics.com/flight/a3115/what-really-happened-aboard-air-france-447-6611877/

either of these situations occurs and the flight crew is unable to deal with it, catastrophic aircraft damage and loss of life may follow.

As a former fighter pilot, I have flown with steep angles of bank, or been upside down, usually with g on the aircraft, more times than I can count. But to a civilian pilot who is trained in the normal track and has spent no time performing acrobatics, non-level flight attitudes present a hostile, alien environment. UPRT provides a safe, predictable course of instruction to teach pilots who have not been in a severe unusual attitude situation, how to recognize the signs of a severe attitude as it develops, prevent it if possible, and provide the tools to recover from those attitudes when they do occur. The FAA has mandated this training for airline pilots, and every accepted standard of business jet operations has listed it as a best practice for business jet pilots.

In a previous life as a Director of Aviation, my passion for this training led me to make it a mandatory part of our department's training program. I vetted several UPRT providers and settled on one located in California. The initial training syllabus consisted of one ride in a business jet and two rides in a subsonic jet trainer, equipped with ejection seats and instructed by pilots who had flight test experience. My pilots were directed to attend the initial course as soon as feasible after they completed their type ratings in the aircraft we operated. I asked the UPRT vendor to develop recurrent training syllabi because I believed that UPRT, like aircraft training, required regular practice. I even worked with the provider to validate a supersonic upset course because our aircraft flew well inside the transonic flight regime.

Most of the pilots who worked in my department loved the training. I heard comments like "the coolest thing I've ever done in an airplane" multiple times. But some of the pilots didn't like it, and a few were even intimidated by it. My counter to this reluctance and apprehension should have been empathy, communication, and explanation. But my passion got in the way, and maybe, as Dan Wolfe would have it, my emotion did as well. I was so convinced of the need for the training and so focused on my perception of the righteousness of it, that I lost sight of the human element.

How dare anyone challenge this! I thought.

I talked, even shouted (via email), when I should have listened, and pushed where I should have been more flexible and understanding. In spite of the fact that pilots are typically a homogenous group from a psychological perspective, we all have our differences, and my passion for the cause led me to lose sight of that.

But I learned a valuable lesson in this episode that Lucille Fisher's story above reinforces. Our passion as leaders only becomes the passion of our people when we encourage it to grow in them. Not when we ram it down their throats.

PART II

————— **CHAPTER TWELVE** —————

COURAGE

THE DEFINITION

The dictionary's definition of courage is quite direct and concise:

Mental or moral strength to venture, persevere, and withstand danger, fear, or difficulty (Merriam-Webster, 2019).

Bill George, a senior fellow at the Harvard Business School and former CEO, cites a definition of courage as "the quality of mind and spirit that enables a person to face difficulty, danger, pain, etc., without fear" (2017). He goes on to say that "Courage is the quality that distinguishes great leaders from excellent managers" (George, 2017). George characterizes courageous leaders as those who are willing to take risks and make bold decisions. Leadership guru John C. Maxwell agrees:

Whenever you see significant progress in an organization, you know that the leader made courageous decisions. A leadership position doesn't give a person courage, but courage can give him a leadership position (Maxwell, 1999, p. 40).

But for this book, we're going to limit the discussion of leadership courage to one particular aspect – the willingness to deal with difficult personnel in the leader's organization and to terminate them if required. In his book, <u>Taking Charge</u>, Perry Smith doesn't mention courage directly as one of his twenty fundamentals for leaders, but he does make a point to provide this one:

Leaders Must be Willing to Remove People for Cause. The leader is responsible for ensuring that the mission is accomplished. Inhibitors to this task, such as the continued presence of ineffective subordinates, drain the organization and its capable leaders of the time, energy, and attention needed to accomplish the mission. In such circumstances, leaders have a responsibility to the organization to remove those who stand in the way of success (Smith, 1986, p. 8).

THE RESEARCH

I used a condensed version of Smith's discussion to encapsulate the idea of courage for the 2019 study.

Isn't afraid to discipline/terminate non-performers or toxic individuals.

I also used the respondents' 1-3 ranking to determine where courage fell in the overall list of attributes.

Overall Mean	5.73
Leaders Mean	5.77
Followers Mean	5.67
Levene's Test for Variance	$F = 5.176, p = .023$
Means Statistically Different?	<u>Yes</u>

Table 16. Respondent ratings on the importance of courage.

The mean responses from *Leaders* and *Followers* are separated in Table 16, and the results of Levene's Test confirm that difference. *Leaders* rated the importance of courage higher than *Followers*. The rankings, however, reversed that orientation. *Leaders* ranked courage as the number 12 trait and *Followers* ranked it as 11th.

THE LEADERS

The subject of leadership courage generated one of the most memorable discussions I experienced during the interview process for this book. I was interviewing Bob Ranck[53] and getting the details on his background. He related a story that occurred when he was an Air Officer Commanding (AOC) at the Air Force Academy, and he flew a cross-country sortie in a T-41C with the Superintendent of the Academy at the time, Lieutenant General Bradley Hosmer[54].

"So, there I was," Bob says, "a newly-pinned-on major, and I get to share a cockpit with a three-star general for a couple of hours. All I could think of was what I could learn about leadership from this guy's experience. I was determined to pick his brain. We launched, leveled-off, and when the radio and workload calmed down, I clicked the mic on the intercom and asked him a question.

"'General,' I asked, 'what's the single greatest lesson you learned about leadership in all your years of doing it?'

"I'll never forget his answer. He didn't hesitate even a moment. He turned to me in the cockpit and said, 'I never fired people soon enough'" (Ranck,

---

53 Bob's introduction and bio appear in Part II, Chapter One

54 General Hosmer was Superintendent of the Air Force Academy from 1991 to 1994. He was a member of the Academy's first class, the Class of 1959 and the first academy graduate to return as superintendent.

2019).

There was a time in my career where a remark like that would have stunned me. But given some of the positions I've had and some of the personnel I've dealt with, I can only agree with the General's remarks. Most of the leaders I interviewed for this book discussed dealing with difficult employees and the actions required. Jerry Aiken's story was perhaps the most memorable.

JERRY AIKEN

Jerry Aiken is the former Director of Aviation for a prominent oil family in Texas. He has since retired. Jerry grew up in Africa as the son of a minister/missionary who worked in the Congo. He went to boarding school while he was there and traveled to and from school on a Cessna 185, flown by a missionary air service.

"That's when I fell in love with aviation," Jerry says. "The pilot guy was my hero."

When Jerry graduated from high school, he wanted to fly for the U.S. military but was rejected because his vision wasn't up to military standards. He decided he wanted to be a float pilot, so he got an A & P Certificate, moved to Alaska, and spent three years there, flying and maintaining floatplanes. It was both a professionally and personally fulfilling time for Jerry. He logged his first 1,000 hours in Alaska and married his wife, who was from California, toward the end of his time there.

When a real estate developer in Northern California offered him a job in the Golden State, Jerry decided it was time to make a change. He and his new wife moved to the Bay Area of California, and Jerry got his introduction to the world of turbine engines. Over the next few years, he flew an Aerostar, a Lear 35, a Hawker 800, and a Falcon 50. It was an enjoyable job for Jerry, but it ended when the developer went bankrupt in the early 1990s. Jerry took that opportunity to go back to college and get a Bachelor of Science degree in management. He also performed contract pilot services for AMI jet charter, which operated several aircraft locally.

After about 18 months of flying as a daily contractor, Jerry was hired into a full-time position by the Bechtel Corporation, where he worked for three years. In 1996, he took his first management position when he was appointed as the Chief Pilot of the Nextel Corporation's flight department, which was based in Reston, Virginia, and operated five aircraft. Jerry worked his way up to Director of Aviation for the department, but in 2002, after the dot com stocks crashed, Jerry found he was burnt out. He moved to the Dallas-Fort Worth area of Texas to attend Dallas Theological Seminary.

Jerry's aviation hiatus lasted less than two years. In 2004, he was recruited to build a new flight department for Nextel International. He helped to acquire three aircraft, a Falcon 2000EX, an early Falcon 7X and Falcon 900 EX. The department operated at a 600-hour per year pace for ten years, but Nextel International went bankrupt in 2014, and the department closed. In the process of winding down Nextel's operation, Jerry managed to find a job for every member of his team, but not for himself.

But he wasn't out of work for long. Jerry worked with a well-known personnel and recruiting firm, and in 2015, the firm placed him in his former position. Jerry has over 23 years of leadership experience.

Jerry's story of leadership courage began in a past leadership position when he had to fire his Chief Pilot, who was also a close personal friend.

"That incident was profoundly impactful to me," Jerry says. "I lost a good friend. But he was having an intimate relationship with a direct report/subordinate. The termination went down within 24 hours from the time I notified HR. I would have kept him in another role if I could have, but I wasn't permitted that option."

Having the courage not only terminate a critical team member but also one whom he knew well, developed muscles in Jerry that prepared him well for a later leadership position.

"They had some tremendous problems in this one department when they hired me," Jerry says. "They wanted me to fix them. I didn't even meet with the department team until after I was hired. When I got in there, I saw there was a toxic culture in place. Everyone thought they were in charge. The pilots were a backstabbing and arrogant bunch. They thought that everyone should be able to fly like Chuck Yeager and those who didn't shouldn't be there. I had to change that culture."

But the change took time. Over the course of the next four years, Jerry worked through the issues with each member of his department. He was able to resolve those issues with some of his personnel, but most of them were not willing to buy into the direction that he was taking the department.

"Unless you change the people, you're not going to get the culture change you need," Jerry says. "And if the people won't change, you have to have the courage to get rid of them."

Four years later, 75% of the team had turned over. Some were released just before Jerry arrived, some had medical disqualifications, some were retired equitably, but Jerry terminated three team members because they weren't a good fit for the company or the department. With the support of his boss, who was the vice-president of HR, Jerry was able to make the changes he needed to turn the culture of the department around.

"It took about two to three years before I enjoyed coming to work," Jerry says. "Even then, there were still a few issues. I had one last guy whose attitude I couldn't change, and I had to let him go as well. But even though we were terminating him, I still tried to help him by getting him a 737-type rating. I still tried to take care of him."

Jerry's thoughts on leadership courage reflect the journey he has taken as a leader. And the price he has paid.

"When people tell me they want to lead, the first question I ask them is 'why?'" Jerry says. "Why do you want to be a leader? Because leadership comes with a high cost. You need to have the courage to pay that cost. If you don't have that courage, you don't have what it takes to lead."

But that's not all there is to courage as far as Jerry is concerned.

"Courage isn't one dimensional," Jerry says. "It also means you have to have the willingness to fail. And you have to have the willingness to go outside your comfort zone, sometimes way outside your comfort zone" (Aiken, 2019).

Jerry Aiken wasn't alone in the demonstration of courage through personnel change. Jad Donaldson[55] has had to show similar courage. When he took over the Harley-Davidson flight department, its culture was one of autonomy and isolation from the company. Like Jerry, it took Jad several years to improve the department's culture and get it to a place where the department was focused on supporting the company, not just flying airplanes. Also, like Jerry, Jad had to have the courage to remove several toxic individuals to achieve the objective. When Jad managed the get the department to a state of cultural equilibrium, seven out of ten of the original staff were no longer there (Donaldson, 2019).

MICHAEL MCKENZIE

Michael McKenzie has also had to take decisive action on the people front on multiple occasions. He is the Director of Aviation for a high-net-worth individual located in the Bay Area of California.

---

55 Jad's stories have been used throughout this book but the most applicable story to this topic appears in Part II, Chapter Seven. Jad's introduction and bio appear in Part II, Chapter Four.

Mike grew up in the San Fernando Valley in California. His next-door neighbor was a helicopter pilot who flew for a local news station. The neighbor's wife was a tour guide for the airports in the Los Angeles area. Shortly after he graduated from high school, Mike witnessed an air-rescue operation where a helicopter landed right in front of him.

"I thought that was the coolest thing ever," Mike says. "I wanted to get my rotary-wing license. But the people I knew told me that I should get a fixed-wing rating instead. That wasn't the direction I wanted to go."

Mike joined the Army and attended flight school at Fort Rucker, Alabama. After serving on active duty for a few years, he continued his service with California Army National Guard, often flying firefighters to remote areas around the state. Mike also became a helicopter platoon leader and operations officer, managing 20 pilots, 40 enlisted personnel, and operating eight aircraft.

While he was flying with the Guard, he also tried to find work in civilian aviation while he completed his bachelor's degree. He took a job cleaning aircraft at Tenet Healthcare, and one day while he was at work, the CEO, who was a World War II veteran, saw Mike's Army gear and informed Mike's boss: "I want to make this guy a fixed-wing pilot!" The company funded Mike's commercial and multi-engine ratings in fixed wing aircraft and began to use him to fly company aircraft. Mike started in the Falcon 10 and transitioned through several aircraft as the years went by, eventually flying the Gulfstream G-IV and advancing to Chief Pilot of the department.

In 2001, Mike was hired by a wealthy individual in the San Jose area to build a flight department, and he has been there ever since. Mike leads a department of 3 Gulfstream aircraft, based in two cities. He has over 22 years of leadership experience.

Mike's leadership journey, both in the military and the civilian worlds, has taught him the importance of swift action when he has encountered bad actors in the organizations he has led.

"In one of my past jobs, the department was extremely dysfunctional, partially because the leadership wouldn't deal with toxic people," Mike says. "It taught me a lot about what not to do. You have to get rid of toxic people right away," he says. "You can't wait. You have to have the courage to act. And you have to act quickly. Three times when I've been in leadership positions and had toxic people on my team, I got them out of there as fast as I possibly could. One toxic person can infect an entire team. Multiple toxic people can cause disaster. No one likes firing someone, but if you're going to be a leader, you have to have the guts to do it sometimes" (McKenzie, 2019).

While Jerry Aiken, Jad Donaldson, and Mike McKenzie had to deal with multiple terminations, Jamie Stone, Greg Adams, and Ken Francomano only had to deal with one. But that didn't make the process easier or require less courage.

The scenario Jamie Stone[56] encountered occurred

---

[56] Jamie's introduction and bio can be found in Part II, Chapter Ten.

very shortly after a new employee joined his department and emphasized the importance of the hiring process.

"One of the most important parts of leadership is dealing with the selection of new employees, the hiring process," Jamie says. "I'm a believer in something Jim Collins said when it comes to building a team. You get the right people on the bus and in the right seats.[57] I also made a commitment to my team that I wouldn't let HR issues go undealt with. And we had an issue. We had a new team member who didn't perform. We tried to coach and develop this person, but our efforts didn't work. We had to let him go. At first, HR didn't want to support that move, but I told them I'm not going to fly this guy, so you'll be paying a captain salary to someone who won't be earning it. That got their attention, and they came to understand the risks involved. We got him terminated shortly after that. I didn't enjoy it, but it had to be done" (Stone, 2019).

KENNETH FRANCOMANO

Ken Francomano, the Director of Aviation for a high net worth individual in the New England area, had a similar situation. He had to have the courage to deal with it as well.

Ken's career with aviation took root when he was a teenager. The family's next-door neighbor was a 747

---

57 (Collins, 2001).

captain for an air freight company, and he frequently took Ken out to the airport. Ken looked into getting his pilot's license, but for various reasons, decided not to pursue it at that time. Instead, he went to Rollins College to play golf. But when he returned home after his freshman year, the girl next door was taking flight lessons. That got Ken hooked. During the summer, he began flight training and soloed. When he graduated from college with a business and economics degree, he already had his commercial license.

After a few jobs flying small aircraft, Ken wound up at the Phillip Morris flight department. He worked there for 20 years and always wanted to move up into a management position, but no openings were available.

Ken eventually moved on to Yum Brands and took a job as a G-550 captain at Yum's Louisville base. Two months after he arrived, Ken's boss asked him to move to Dallas and take over Yum's Dallas operation. Ken was there for five years, but continued conflicts with his boss, the Director of Aviation, drove him away. Ken was hired as Director of Aviation at Heinz in Pennsylvania, but one year after he started, in 2013, Heinz was sold, and the department was shut down. Ken considered moving back to New York and working as a contract pilot, but then his current position became available, and he's been there ever since. Ken has over 12 years of leadership experience.

Ken defines himself as a leader who fights for his team, and that includes having the courage to deal with subordinates who have attitude problems.

"If I say I'm going to do something, I do it," Ken

says. "I'm genuine with my people, and in return, they trust me. That trust requires me to have the courage to do the right thing personnel-wise when I have to.

"For example," Ken continues, "when I got to Heinz, I replaced a previous director who tried to do everything and took credit for all of it. When I got there, I created training and standards positions, even a fuel position, and I gave my people responsibility. The turnaround in morale was fantastic; people felt like they were part of the team. I did the same thing at Yum and my current job.

"But a bad actor can spoil it all. I had a line captain who had a bad attitude. He was highly qualified and highly experienced, but he didn't want to be a team player. As a leader, you have to walk the talk. If you say morale and teamwork are important to you. and you have someone who doesn't play well with others, you have to have the courage to do something about it. In this case, I took action to get this guy out of our department" (Francomano, 2019).

GREG ADAMS

Greg Adams, the Director of Flight Operations for a company based in Chicago, also had a problematic employee situation to deal with, but in his case, the employee wasn't a pilot but a technician, who was also his Director of Maintenance.

Greg doesn't remember a time when he wasn't fascinated with airplanes. Initially he thought he wanted to go to college to study aeronautical engineering, but he decided to go the pilot route instead. Greg attended Purdue University, graduated, and then performed instructor duties.

When he acquired enough time, Greg transitioned to a regional airline, then went on to a major airline, Northwest, where he flew the Boeing 727. But after 9/11, Greg was furloughed. He had three business aviation job offers in the post 9/11 timeframe, and all of them were bad. He picked the least objectionable one, and his career in business aviation began.

Initially, Greg flew for a corporate jet airline, but that operation went bankrupt. He then worked for a charter company, and after nine months, it went out of business. Greg moved to a startup charter operator at the airport in Aurora, Illinois, and worked his way through the ranks to become Chief Pilot. After three years, Greg's current employer hired him as Chief Pilot for a one-aircraft operation flying a Hawker 800 at the Chicago Midway airport. Since 2007, the operation has expanded. Today, Greg is in charge of a fleet of five aircraft, including G-550s, and leads 31 people. Greg has over 14 years of leadership experience.

Greg takes his leadership cues from the example set by Southwest Airlines' Herb Kelleher, an aviation leadership icon.

"My people are my customers," he says. "I treat them like customers. I treat them well. I've worked enough cruddy jobs and I don't want to be that type of boss. I staff appropriately, plan appropriately, and try to offer my people the best quality of life I can. People are the most important aspect of the operation.

"But," Greg continues, "to take care of my

people, I need to make tough decisions from time to time. Seven or eight years ago, I had an issue with an employee, my Director of Maintenance. He was fine with one Hawker to look after, but when the department expanded to multiple aircraft, he couldn't keep up. I gave him multiple opportunities to improve, counseled him, tried to develop him, but nothing worked. Eventually, I had to have the courage to let him go. My other employees respected that. They respect leaders who can make the tough decisions" (Adams, 2019).

It's probably safe to argue that none of the leaders cited in this chapter wanted to either encounter or deal with the personnel issues they experienced in their organizations. But when they faced dysfunctional culture, toxic actors, or non-performing personnel, they rose to the challenge and took the necessary action. They terminated the people responsible, and in every case, they gleaned positive results. They gained the respect of their employees, and they improved their organizations.

THOUGHTS FOR LEADERS ON COURAGE

Since we've chosen to define leadership courage within the bounds of personnel action, the actions seem relatively straightforward – deal with toxic people. But the decision process to take that kind of action may be more difficult. Leadership expert and keynote speaker Galen Emanuele offers some succinct guidance.

First, when it comes to the decision about whether

to terminate a person, the leader needs to ask himself or herself one simple question:

Knowing everything you know now about how they show up and perform their job, would you hire them again? (Emanuele, 2017)

If the answer to that question is no, Emanuele recommends terminating that person immediately. He goes to depict what can occur if a problem person is not terminated. Warning – the direct quotes contain some explicit language.

1. **Poor Morale**. (People will hate coming to work.) The biggest sign that there is a toxic individual in a group is an overall loss of morale. One toxic individual can infect others around him or her with negative words or attitudes, and that can lead to employees feeling a sense of dread as they come to the workplace;

2. **Good People Leave**. (High turnover). A leader can lose his or her best people by refusing to fire the worst ones. The longer toxic people stay in place, the more damage they can do. If you don't get rid of the bad apples, you're essentially paying someone to slowly ruin your organization;

3. **Performance Tanks: Poor Culture and the Rise of Unethical Behavior.** (Assholes Breed Other Assholes). As Dr. Cameron Sepah,

a Professor of Psychiatry, put it:

The biggest mistake that I see companies make is that they will retain competent assholes because they are seen as critical to the company or difficult to replace. However, by doing so, they not only passively reinforce the competent asshole's behavior by tolerating and promoting them, but they implicitly send the message to the rest of the company that you can basically get away with murder so long as leadership believes you to be indispensable. You can imagine what kind of culture this creates over time.

As leaders, we need to realize that what we allow, we endorse. If the consequences of poor behavior and performance become acceptable, productivity and morale go downhill. In short, misery loves company and assholes breed other assholes; and

4. **All the Hires That Could Have Been (What You're Missing Out On).** Think of the many qualified, high-performing people with better attitudes who could step into the position in question and excel. Don't miss out on exciting talent you have hired just because you're too afraid to hurt someone's feelings by letting them go (Emanuele, 2017).

While removing toxic individuals is essential, it should be done with dignity and compassion. As leaders, courageous leaders, we still need to remember our humanity and treat even toxic personnel with the consideration they are due as co-workers and fellow human beings.

A PERSONAL NOTE ON COURAGE (OR HOW NOT TO)

In my business aviation leadership career, I've had to terminate two people and remove one from a leadership position for failure to perform. The first two were performed in a timely fashion. The third one was not.

The terminations were line pilots who couldn't perform their flight duties. Without going into details about the events, there wasn't much development that could be done to improve the lack of performance, so I collected the documentation required, worked with my human resources team, and processed the terminations in as delicate and compassionate a manner as I could.

The removal situation was a different matter. In a previous job, I hired a Chief Pilot who came with a fantastic resume and glowing recommendations. He had a winning personality, a dynamic presence, and was a talented aviator.

But he had no courage. He couldn't make the hard calls with his people. He wouldn't confront them when counseling or discipline was needed; he couldn't be the "bad guy" when it was required.

As the department expanded, his unwillingness

to take personnel action, especially with one pilot who became particularly toxic, negatively affected the morale of the pilot corps and allowed factions to develop. I diagnosed the situation early, counseled him frequently, and even worked with our HR personnel to get him an executive coach to improve his leadership ability. Eventually, I realized that he needed to be replaced, and I went to my boss, the Senior Vice President of HR, to discuss it.

I was prohibited from taking action.

To this day, I'm not sure why. The easy answer would be because there were diversity issues involved, but I think the real answer is that he was so darn likable that my boss didn't understand why he wasn't effective as a leader. Her take on the situation was that I obviously wasn't working hard enough to develop him.

The situation was allowed to continue, and morale continued to deteriorate. The flying schedule was intense, and I had the opportunity to fly with all the other pilots and get their take on the situation. I learned, over time, that the reports I was receiving about pilot thoughts and morale were widely different depending on whether I spoke to the Chief Pilot or the pilots themselves. It became apparent that swift action needed to be taken. I went back to my boss and pleaded my case to remove the CP from his position.

Again, I was denied permission to take action.

About a month later, the company made a change to its headquarters organization structure, and the flight department fell under a different executive, also a female, but much more no-nonsense. Shortly thereafter, one of our most dedicated pilots resigned, and during his exit interview, he identified the Chief Pilot's action, or lack of action, as the cause for his departure.

This time, leadership listened. The CEO actually told me. "You were right. We should have let you take care of this a year ago."

I removed the Chief Pilot from his position, but the damage that had been created was extensive. It would take months to recover, during which more turnover would occur.

All the leaders I have mentioned in this chapter had the support of their HR personnel in the actions they took, and that made a huge difference to their success. I was not so fortunate. But I don't place the blame on HR or the executives above me. The responsibility was mine alone. There were several lessons learned.

First, hiring is all-important, and perhaps the most important thing we do in a leadership role. Many of the leaders I interviewed for this book discussed the importance of their hiring process. Candace Covington said something that resonated with me: "Be relentless in hiring practices" (Covington, 2019). I didn't do that when I hired my Chief Pilot. Instead, I allowed myself to be hurried, and I listened to the recommendations of friends rather than do the research I should have done. As I discovered subsequently and to my chagrin, my Chief Pilot's track record in leadership roles was not favorable. He would have been great as a senior captain or line pilot role, but not as a leader.

Second, there are some people who can't be developed. Contrary to the idealistic human resources perspective, some people will never be leaders, not necessarily because they can't be, but because they simply choose not to be. All the development and coaching available will not make someone a leader if they choose not to lead.

Third, there are times when human resources personnel can become a barrier to success rather than a facilitator of it. It seems that the larger companies become, the more regimented their HR procedures grow, and the less agility is allowed to the leadership of individual departments. A CEO who isn't afraid to take on the HR complex can fix that, but those are few and far between.

Fourth, there is no replacement for courage. I've never been afraid of professional confrontation, and I've never been afraid to state what I think. I'm obviously not afraid to fire people. But in this instance, I could have taken action earlier in the growth phase of our department, threatened resignation, or done something more drastic to remove an ineffective individual and allow the healing process in the department to begin sooner. But I didn't, and I'm not the one who paid the real price. My people did.

While courage doesn't appear in the top rankings in the survey research I performed and have provided with this book, much of the industry and scholarly literature I've encountered makes the argument that courage is the most important attribute a leader can have.

I tend to agree.

PART II

CHAPTER THIRTEEN

ENGAGEMENT

THE DEFINITION

Engagement can mean many things. The word can generate images of diamond rings and suitors on bended knee. As a former fighter pilot, when I think of engagement, I think of air-to-air combat with another aircraft. Each dogfight was called an engagement. But the definition we're looking for in the context of this book is right in the middle of the dictionary's list.

The act of engaging, the state of being engaged; emotional involvement or commitment (Merriam-Webster, 2019).

If we drill down on the words above and place them in a leadership context, we find a similar definition.

Holly Seaton, an executive coach for Flashpoint Leadership Consulting, says that "Employee engagement is the positive emotional connection an employee has to their work and their workplace" (2018). She goes to say:

> *In short, engaged employees care about their work, are committed to their organizations, and want to give more than is required or expected.*

> *More than simply satisfaction, employee engagement is a positive connection to the work employees do and a belief in the goals, purpose, and mission of that work. Employees (and remote employees) want to feel pride, satisfaction, recognition, and support, but more than that, they want to believe that their work matters, that they contribute, and that it resonates with their values (Seaton, 2018).*

THE RESEARCH

For the 2019 study, I used a definition that focused on the personal relationship between leaders and their people, a relationship that I believe generates the engagement behavior defined above.

> *Knows who I am and cares about me as a person.*

I also used the respondents' 1-3 ranking to

determine where courage fell in the overall list of attributes.

Overall Mean	5.24
Leaders Mean	5.36
Followers Mean	5.11
Levene's Test for Variance	$F = 2.798, p = .095$
Means Statistically Different?	No

Table 17. Respondent ratings on the importance of engagement.

While mean responses from *Leaders* and *Followers* seem to be separated somewhat in Table 17, the results of Levene's Test indicate that statistically, the means are not different. Also, *Leaders* and *Followers* ranked engagement 13th out of the 15 traits I asked them about.

THE LEADERS

Nearly every leader I interviewed mentioned engagement as an element of their leadership style. During my research for this book, I encountered indications of engagement from a most unexpected source: General George S. Patton Jr., arguably the best Army Commander in our history as a nation. Those who are familiar with Patton's accomplishments, but not the man himself, will typically portray him as a tyrannical and pedantic leader. I've read two biographies of the man, but neither was a personal account. <u>General Patton's Principles for Life & Leadership</u> was written by Porter Williamson, a fellow soldier who knew the general well and worked alongside him. Williamson's description of how the men felt about their service with Patton provides an exemplary description of what engagement should feel like to subordinates. In the quotes below, the underlines for emphasis come directly from the text.

I served <u>with</u> General George S. Patton, Jr. No man served under Gen. Patton; he was always serving <u>with</u> us.

General Patton possessed an unprecedented ability to inspire and motivate the men under his command. During the war, when his troops were asked who they were with, they would simply holler, "We're Georgie's boys." Years after the war, veterans would holler with pride, "I was with Patton."

That was all that needed to be said. Few commanders in history have generated such loyalty and devotion among the men they commanded (Williamson, 2009).

When leaders engage, they create the loyalty and devotion that Williamson describes. These are traits that Sheryl Barden, the president and CEO of Aviation Personnel International (API), knows well.

SHERYL BARDEN

Sheryl got into aviation because her mother, the legendary Janice Barden[58], was in aviation. Janice founded API in 1971, when Sheryl was in 2nd grade and at that time, having a mother who was also a professional was a rarity. Sheryl was involved in the business for as long as she can remember. She retrieved the mail and ran errands for her mother, worked for the business during the summer, and even interviewed candidates when she was older.

But when she graduated from college, Sheryl took a different path. She became a sales and marketing professional, spending 12 years in the paper packaging industry and seven years in the forest products industry. Without being aware of it at the time, her work in corporate America was preparing her for her role in API.

In 2001, she returned to her mother's business, just as the internet was coming into its own as a tool for employers and job seekers. The industry hiatus after 9/11 allowed her some time to get her feet wet and learn the business from a leadership perspective. That brief era also made her realize that her company needed a "bag of tricks," tools, and a strategy, to deal with the downtimes in aviation. She developed an

---

58 Janice K. Barden founded API in 1971. She contributed to the business aviation industry for over 60 years and was the recipient of numerous honors and awards. She passed away in 2016.

out-placement product to serve clients during those downturns, a service which API has been able to use multiple times since that time when companies have closed or downsized flight departments for various reasons.

Today, Sheryl is perhaps the most widely recognized voice in the industry on aviation personnel matters. She is chairperson of the NBAA Advisory Council and a member of the NBAA Board of Directors. She has over 30 years of leadership experience.

"For me, engagement starts with grace," Sheryl says. "'There but for the grace of God go I' is a mantra for me. It's the first line in our company values statement. I treat my employees and my customers the way I want to be treated. It is my goal to always treat people with grace. That inspires loyalty.

"I'm also very quick to admit mistakes and apologize for them. Humility, rather than ego, can bring people together. Two years ago, when we were doing annual reviews, I asked my team to review me. I wanted their feedback. I brought in an outside facilitator so my team would be honest, and I received feedback that was direct and candid. I didn't complain about it, and I didn't contest it. I implemented it. When people see that their input makes a difference, that engages them.

Sheryl's generous attitude towards work-life balance is an additional element of her desire to engage her employees. "Life is to be lived, not worked" appears on API's corporate values statement, and Sheryl makes sure her employees do their share of the 'living' part of that statement.

"A couple of years ago, I had an employee who

previously worked at a very rigid company. During her second year at API, she asked to have Halloween afternoon off to spend it with her kids, getting them ready to go out trick or treating. I gave it to her. It meant so much to her as she had never had that opportunity before. Now I close the office at noon on Halloween every year. It's become a tradition. About a year later, I had two employees who were getting married, and they were worried about how much vacation time they'd take and how long they could be away. I did away with vacation. I let my folks take what they need when they need it.

"All of this comes down to the same thing," Sheryl concludes, "if you treat people well and if they have a passion for what they do, they'll stay engaged" (Barden, 2019).

Sheryl's theory of engagement starts with taking care of her people. Wendy Langen approaches it the same way.

WENDY LANGEN

Wendy Langen is the Executive Director of Aviation for a wealthy family in the Pacific northwest, and her journey to that position was a unique one.

Wendy was born and raised in Seattle, Washington and would spend summers on her great grandparents' farm, on the south end of Boeing Field, and watch the jets fly overhead. Her great aunt worked as a carpenter for Boeing and the fortunes of her mother's café rose and fell with the successes of the company. Many of her cousins and uncles worked at Boeing as well.

When Wendy was attending the University of Washington, she worked in a hotel in downtown Seattle that rented office space to the Rainier Bank. As Wendy worked her way through different jobs in the hotel, she would run into the bank President from time to time when he was in town. He was impressed by her work ethic and repeatedly asked what she wanted to do when she grew up. Eventually, he told her that he was involved with a new flight operation, and he wanted her to help with that project. Before she knew it, Wendy was recruited to work for a helicopter manufacturer and flight school, a job she had never considered.

Interestingly, her father, who was a teacher and who had served in Vietnam, never talked about his service until Wendy began working with helicopters. Then, he began to discuss his Vietnam War experience and a new bond formed between the two of them.

Wendy's duties extended to fixed-wing aircraft, where she assisted in the certification and Part 135 management of a Challenger 604 and a Lear 35, scheduling of aircraft and crew, and quoting charters. She stayed at that job for four years and enjoyed it.

In 1997, Wendy took a job with a Fortune 500 company located in the Seattle Area. Eventually, she found a position in the company's flight department. Initially, her responsibilities were administrative. She managed the budget and resources for the department and processed payroll. She grew into a program manager function where she oversaw the fractional shares used by the department. In 2008, she was promoted to the director position, and she's been there since. Wendy has 18 years of leadership experience.

"Engagement is about people," Wendy says. "And it's about the team. I actively shun the use of the pronouns 'I' and 'me' when I speak to my team. I say, 'us' and 'we.' I take the spotlight off of the individual and put it on the team or *us*. When it comes to the mission and goals of the department, I focus on the employee's personal needs and get to the goals and missions from there."

Wendy's actions reinforce her words. Her department's organizational chart is flat, making all managers peers and thus removing the barriers between those who fly and those who don't.

"Our experience shows how an unconventional org chart can provide better engagement," Wendy says. "It allows everyone to have a voice and for all voices to be heard. It helps us value one another better.

"Engagement isn't just between employees and leadership or employees and the company," Wendy continues. "It's about people engaging each other as well. I worked with the architects for our office space to ensure it was a place that fosters engagement. I wanted it to be a welcoming environment. Most people here don't get above the clouds and see the sun on a rainy day, so I wanted the office to be a place where people could enjoy working."

When asked what she regards as the most critical element of engagement, Wendy's response is nearly instantaneous.

"Communication," she says, "without a doubt. If you're open to listening to your folks, there's no limit to what they can do. I communicate with them continuously. They know about the challenges we face, and we work together to find solutions.

"One of the biggest problems we faced early on," Wendy continues, "was the growth of employees and their subsequent desire to leave the department and move on. But we faced it head-on and had frank conversations about what people wanted to do and where they wanted to go. We came up with a plan to increase responsibilities and roles in the department, and that helped. When you treat people like a team, it develops the individual, and the leader gets educated in the process. It makes us all better, and it keeps everyone engaged" (Langen, 2019).

Greg Adams[59] believes his use of Herb Kelleher's leadership philosophy – treating his people as customers – helps to keep them engaged.

"It's common sense," Greg says. "I just make an effort to find out what's important to my team, things like staffing levels, days off, vacation days, and I find ways to give them what they want. Like when the airlines started poaching our people, I went to crew members and asked them what was important to them. They told me retirement was important, so that's what got fixed first.

"Another thing I do," Greg continues, "is I get people in the right jobs and give them ownership. I get out of the way, and I don't micromanage them. I don't look over their shoulders. I allow them to make

---

59   Greg's introduction and bio appear in Part II, Chapter Twelve.

mistakes, and I don't second guess them.

"I preach that people are the most important thing in the department," Greg concludes, "and me engaging them like they're my customers keeps them engaged as well" (Adams, 2019).

Like Sheryl, Wendy, and Greg, Marcela White[60] is also very focused on the engagement of her team. She believes that engagement starts with understanding and empathy for her people.

"They need to see me alongside them," she says. "I don't ask anyone to do something that I wouldn't do, whether that is accounting, administering, cleaning aircraft, whatever it takes. I felt like I needed to understand the jobs my folks do. I worked as a cabin attendant, so I could see what life was like on the road and see my employees in an informal environment. I got my private pilot's license so I could understand the piloting side of the business better. I felt I needed to understand the challenges of all of my employees, so I could be more empathetic and understand their challenges better" (White, 2019).

Engagement can be a powerful force inside organizations like the leaders above have demonstrated. John Rosanvallon's use of engagement goes further.

JOHN ROSANVALLON

John Rosanvallon is the former President and CEO

---

[60] Marcela's introduction and bio appear in Part II, Chapter Four.

of Dassault Falcon Jet, a wholly-owned subsidiary of Dassault Aviation, a public French corporation which celebrated its centennial in 2016. John has had a storied career in aviation that can't be captured in adequate detail here, but elements of his journey are very instructive.

Like others in this book, John ended up in the aviation industry almost by accident. He grew up in a provincial mid-size city in France. No one in his family was involved in aerospace. His initial plan was a career in business and finance, and he attended the prestigious Hautes Études Commerciales (HEC), an elite French business school. In 1975, after his one year of mandatory military service, John interviewed with Dassault Aviation and was hired. Initially, he was assigned to coordinate Falcon activities between the company's Paris headquarters and the Falcon subsidiary in Teterboro. At that time, the unit was a joint venture between Pan American World Airways and Dassault Aviation, known as Falcon Jet Corporation. He was the third person of a three-person team. But then, in 1979, when the U.S. Coast Guard signed a contract to purchase 40 Falcon aircraft, John was transferred to the United States as Assistant to the President of Falcon Jet. Or in his words:

"I was the French guy embedded in our U.S. operation," he says. "Mostly on the finance side. I'm sure they initially thought I was spying on them."

Although the contract was financially and technically challenging, the Coast Guard operation was a huge success for Dassault, and John was promoted to Vice President of Finance. In 1984, John was transferred back to France, where he assumed the position of Executive Vice President of Sogitec, a Dassault subsidiary specializing in flight simulation. John retained close ties with the Falcon Jet business in his new position, and in 1989, John rejoined Falcon Jet as the Vice President of Sales and Marketing, based in Paris.

In 1994, John moved back to the U.S., and in 1996, he was promoted to President of Dassault Falcon Jet. He became the CEO in 2003 and became a U.S. citizen in 2017. His current title is Special Senior Advisor to the CEO and Chairman of Dassault Aviation. John has been named a Living Legend of Aviation, and he has nearly 40 years of leadership experience.

Since the majority of Dassault stock is owned by the Dassault Family, the company considers its employees and customers as part of the family as well. The company's values and culture emphasize that family relationship. The company even hosts a breakfast every year at NBAA BACE called the Falcon Family Breakfast and welcomes employees and customers, both current and former, to the event. John engages both his personnel and his customers through that family relationship.

For his subordinates, John uses informal meetings to break down the barriers of communication.

"I'm a social guy," John says. "And I'm an open guy and a good listener. One of the things I do is schedule regular lunches with my direct reports. We get out of the building for 90 minutes and have an open dialogue away from the pressures of the office. They have my sole attention for that time, and they know I'll listen to them."

But John's concern for his employees goes beyond his direct reports. In early 2019, Falcon Jet's demonstration pilot corps was suffering from severe personnel attrition. John retained Aviation Personnel International, Sheryl's Barden's firm, to do a full retention analysis and compensation study to see what the company could do to engage its pilot force at a higher level. I worked with Sheryl on that analysis. It was quite extensive. I interviewed every pilot on the demonstration and flight test teams. Their feelings about their compensation notwithstanding, every one of them expressed intense commitment to the brand, the products, and the company. That level of commitment reflects well on John's leadership and style of engagement with that area of the company.

The engagement John offers his personnel extends to his customers as well.

"I'm a people person, so I reach out," John says. "Fifty percent of my daily activities are customer-related. About half of our customers are big companies; the others are entrepreneurs, so the guy paying is more directly involved. I establish personal relationships with them. For example, Elon Musk had Falcons and bought a new one. After he looked at the way we did business, he invited me to tour his facility in LA. We established a relationship with Richard Santulli and delivered 60 planes to NetJets. We even sold him one for his personal use. That kind of thing only happens with personal engagement."

But the engagement doesn't stop with customers, it takes in the industry as well.

"Some of our salespeople saw consultants and management companies as obstacles," John says. "I saw them as members of the family. We needed to embrace them and include them. One of the things we do is the Aviation Professionals Conference. We're in our 22nd year of it. People from all over the industry attend. It helps us keep our customer perspective and helps us to engage our customers and the industry that supports them."

John's engagement even extends to an international level. In 2019, he received the AsBAA[61] Business Aviation Leader of the Year / Icon of Aviation Award.

"I'm a bi-cultural guy," John says. "By staying engaged with both the U.S. and French sides of the company, I've tried to help combine the best talents of our bi-cultural company. Dassault Aviation in France is well known for its excellent engineering, and the U.S. side has been leading the development of a customer service culture, which has allowed us to become number one in customer satisfaction in both the 2019 AIN and ProPilot surveys" (Rosanvallon, 2019).

The stories in this chapter have shown us that a leader's style of engagement can be as unique as the leaders themselves. Yet, while the variable elements of a leader's personality certainly play a role in the engagement equation, some constants are present as well: communication, empathy, and perhaps most importantly, the willingness to treat employees as

---

[61] The AsBAA is the Asian Business Aviation Association, the Asian equivalent of the U.S. NBAA.

people, rather than objects or tools.

THOUGHTS FOR LEADERS ON ENGAGEMENT

In 2015, Gallup published a survey on the level of engagement of employees in their workplace for the two years prior. The results were surprising.

U.S. Employee Engagement, 2013 vs. 2014

% Employees	2013	2014
Engaged	29.6	31.5
Not engaged	51.5	51.0
Actively disengaged	18.8	17.5

GALLUP

Figure 12. Gallup levels of employee engagement. (Adkins, 2015)

In the several job fields listed in the survey, managers had the highest engagement percentages for 2014, 38.4%, and transportation workers[62] had one of the lowest, 25.4%. Furthermore, the millennial generation was the least engaged of the generations polled, 28.9% versus 32.2% for Generation X, and 32.7% for Baby Boomers. (Adkins, 2015).

---

62   The term "transportation workers" typically includes personnel in the aviation industry. The U.S. Bureau of Labor Statistics specifically includes pilots in this category.

None of these numbers demonstrate a favorable trend for the American workforce in general and our industry in particular. So, in spite of the efforts of the leaders quoted above, substantial numbers of the workforce remain unengaged. What can we, as leaders, do to improve that? Glenn Llopus, a leadership consultant and contributor to Forbes magazine, provides six things leaders can do to engage their personnel in an article that is probably one of the best I've seen on the subject.

1. **Stop Unknowingly Creating Tension.** Leaders unknowingly create tension with their employees when they encourage their employees to mimic their behavior, to be clones of the leader, rather than being themselves. Leaders also create tension by not taking the time to engage with their employees. When a subordinate feels their leader doesn't care about him or her personally, or isn't honest about abilities or career progression, the subordinate can become bitter, distrustful or worse, toxic;

2. **Detect the most positive capabilities in people.** Job descriptions are important, but leaders need to have the flexibility to make work enjoyable and let employees find their passion at their jobs;

3. **Empower to discover potential.** Leaders need to let their people "run with the ball." A leader will never know what an employee is capable of accomplishing until

that employee is empowered to discover his or her potential;

4. **Put them in a position of influence.** When leadership, managerial or project management positions become available, leaders should put their subordinates in them and see how they perform, both for the good of the organization and the development of the employee;

5. **Share your success to build their momentum.** In a team environment, leaders share the success of the organization with their subordinates, showing them how their efforts contributed to that success. When leaders realize personal success as a result of the team's efforts, they should share that as well; and

6. **Be consistent and have their backs.** True leaders take care of their people and are consistent with them. That doesn't mean being perpetually lenient, but it does mean being understanding, empathetic, and present (Llopis, 2015).

A PERSONAL REFLECTION ON ENGAGEMENT

In 2009, after nearly a decade in the charter/management side of business aviation, I was hired to be the Chief Pilot for a Fortune 100 telecommunications company with a Part 91 operation based in the Midwest. The competition for the position was fierce, and I was fortunate to be chosen for the job from a field of some 200 candidates. Little did I know what I was in for.

The Chief Pilot position had been vacant for several months after the previous occupant had been encouraged to take early retirement due to some age-related performance issues. The Director of Aviation, my boss, had only been in his position for a year and had been responsible for the departure of my predecessor. I became the instant "new guy" and supervisor in a department with five other pilots, all of whom had at least ten years of tenure with the company. Three of the pilots were in their early sixties.

Almost from the moment I moved into the Chief Pilot's office, I could sense an atmosphere of tension and distrust emanating from the pilot corps. At first, I was puzzled. We had no history; they hadn't seen me in action, so why the skepticism? In response, I did what I had done since I was a young captain in the Air Force in a new organization, I kept my eyes and ears open and my mouth shut. I didn't try to change anything. I didn't make it a point to espouse my opinions. I just flew, and I watched, and I listened.

In time, the reasons for pilots' distrust became clear. The previous Chief Pilot had acted as interim director and was denied the job when my boss was hired. Then, when the former Chief Pilot was essentially terminated, and the hiring process for his replacement began, none of the pilots had been considered for the position because my boss perceived that none of them had the ability. With the age-related context of the previous Chief Pilot's departure, the pilots perceived that I was the director's "boy," and maybe even his "ax man," and I would be targeting the older pilots in the group for termination and replacement.

I had to take a deep breath and step back when I finally understood my predicament. Breaking through the pilots' defenses, engaging them, and winning their support would be no easy task.

The first thing I did was sit down with each of the five pilots and try to understand who they were, their place in the department, and their goals and aspirations. I spoke as little as I could during the conversation, and made it about them, not about me.

The second thing I did was something my predecessor never considered. I took over the scheduling function for the pilots, and took steps to equalize their workdays, weekend/holiday flying days, and nights on the road. As part of that, I put myself into the scheduling rotation and made sure the director flew a fair share of sorties that were compatible with his position. I also made sure there was no favoritism where the trips and the pilots were concerned, me included. We all flew our fair share of the 'good trips' and the bad ones. As part of that process, I let the pilots schedule hard days off when they needed them and made the schedule work around them. I accommodated vacations and training dates and did my best to equalize the load. At the end of every month, I sent the pilot group a copy of my tracking spreadsheet so they could see how the load was distributed. In a period of a few months, complaints about the schedule ceased.

The next thing I did involved our manual suite. The department's operations manual was outdated and not in compliance with the IS-BAO. I rewrote the manual with multiple inputs, including the old manual, and sent it out to the group for their edits and comments. I told them I wanted it to look the way they wanted it to look, with the only caveat that it had to be IS-BAO compatible. The process took several months, but every member of the department had a say in the manual's format and content.

Throughout these processes, I also did the most important thing I could; I flew alongside them on the line. I stayed proficient in the jet, ate my fair share of nights on the road, performed my share of pre-flights and cabin cleanups, and most importantly, when we were alone at FL 410, I listened to what they had to say.

The result was that gradually, over time, I won their engagement and their trust, a trust that was severely tested when one of the older pilots began to manifest cognitive performance issues. Our IS-BAO Stage I audit was coming up in the next few months, so I put all of our pilots, including myself and my boss, through a benign LOFT[63] scenario. The itinerary required the pilots to make a few changes to their departure and arrival game plans and deal with an abnormal procedure in flight. Everyone passed

---

63 Line-oriented Flight Training – essentially a flight between two typical airports that mimics a normal sortie in length and tasks.

with flying colors, except the pilot in question. His mind couldn't keep up with even a mildly changing scenario. I took him off the flying schedule, and after two subsequent failed LOFT rides with practice sims in between, we terminated him with as generous a severance package as the company could muster.

Through that process, I kept the trust and engagement with the other pilots. In fact, there was a collective sigh of relief when the pilot in question left the building for the final time. What I learned is similar to what the leaders above have shared. Engagement is a multi-faceted animal. It's part listening, part sharing, part empowering, and being authentic, but most of all, to Sheryl's words above, it's about being human with your people. It's about treating them the way you want to be treated. In short, it's about grace.

PART II

CHAPTER FOURTEEN

DECISIVENESS

THE DEFINITION

Decisiveness is the noun form of the word, decisive, an adjective. The definition of decisive is straightforward, as we might expect.

1. *Having the power or quality of deciding*
2. *Resolute, determined*
3. *unmistakable, unquestionable* (Merriam-Webster, 2019)

Decisiveness, therefore, is the state of being decisive, i.e., willing to make a decision. But what does that look like from a leadership perspective? This definition, on an obscure website sponsored by The Four Corners Character Council, captures it better than anything else I found:

Decisiveness is the ability to cut quickly to the heart of a matter. It involves getting to the fundamental issues and making a clear, concrete call. Decisiveness knows what facts are important to consider in making a decision, knowing the right decision to make and taking responsibility to see that decision through to completion (The Character Council, 2012).

Why is decisiveness necessary for a leader? Perhaps for no other reason than it keeps the organization in motion, executing its mission. As Perry Smith puts it:

...a leader must be decisive. Institutions and organizations need decisions...A non-decision is itself a decision and should be recognized for what it is (Smith, 1986, p. 13).

An often-cited quote, frequently attributed to President Theodore Roosevelt captures the importance of decisiveness this way:

In any moment of decision, the best thing you can do is the right thing, the next best thing is the wrong thing, and the worst thing you can do is nothing (Brainyquote, 2019)[64].

---

64 According to the Theodore Roosevelt Center, while this quote is often attributed to the President, there is no documentation to substantiate that he actually said it. See www. theodorerooseveltcener.org for more.

In an article in the Harvard Business Review, published in May-June of 2017, four researchers presented the results of what they called <u>The CEO Genome Study</u>, a 10-year analysis to identify the specific attributes that differentiate high-performing CEOs. To perform the study, the researchers tapped into a database with 17,000 assessments of C-suite executives, including 2,000 CEOs. In the study, the researchers identified four behaviors that set high-performing CEOs apart, and the first one on the list is: "deciding with speed and conviction" (Botelho, E.L., Powell, K.R., Kincaid, S., Wang, D., 2017). Their discussion of the attribute of decisiveness echoes the quote attributed to Roosevelt.

Legends about CEOs who always seem to know exactly how to steer their companies to wild success seem to abound in business. But we discovered that high-performing CEOs do not necessarily stand out for making great decisions all the time; rather, they stand out for being more decisive. They make decisions earlier, faster, and with greater conviction. They do so consistently—even amid ambiguity, with incomplete information, and in unfamiliar domains. In our data, people who were described as "decisive" were 12 times more likely to be high-performing CEOs (Botelho, E.L., Powell, K.R., Kincaid, S., Wang, D., 2017).

THE RESEARCH

For the 2019 study, I used a definition for decisiveness that captured the essence of the words above:

Isn't afraid to make a decision.

I also used the respondents' 1-3 ranking to determine where decisiveness fell in the overall list of attributes.

Overall Mean	5.80
Leaders Mean	5.85
Followers Mean	5.76
Levene's Test for Variance	$F = .200, p = .655$
Means Statistically Different?	No

Table 18. Respondent ratings on the importance of decisiveness.

The results in Table 18 would seem to indicate that *Leaders* and *Followers* were aligned on the importance of decisiveness. Of interest here, is that while *Leaders* and *Followers* both ranked decisiveness as 14th of 15 attributes, the mean values of the importance ratings for the attributes, when sorted from high to low, moved the ranking from 14th up to 9th.

THE LEADERS

Just as leadership and organizational culture are two sides of the same coin, decisiveness and courage manifest the same orientation. When a leader has courage, he or she is not afraid to make decisions. Correspondingly, when a leader is decisive, it is often because he or she has the courage to take action. We have already seen several stories of decisiveness and courage, but they are useful to review for emphasis.

Jerry Aiken[65] and Jad Donaldson[66] took over dysfunctional organizations and had to be decisive in their actions to remove toxic individuals and achieve the cultural change that was necessary (Aiken, 2019) (Donaldson, 2019). Mike McKenzie had to remove three toxic employees from multiple organizations in his career to maintain the culture he worked to attain (McKenzie, 2019). Ken Francomano and Greg Adams took the same action, but with one individual (Francomano, 2019) (Adams, 2019). Both Mike and Ken had to be decisive in those actions. Jamie Stone[67]

---

[65] Jerry, Mike, Ken and Greg's introductions and bios appear in Part II, Chapter Twelve. See that chapter for more in-depth discussions.

[66] Jad's introduction and bio appears in Part II, Chapter Four. See Chapter Four and Chapter Twelve for a more in-depth discussion.

[67] Jamie's introduction and bio appears in Part II, Chapter Ten. See Chapter Twelve for a more in-depth discussion.

had to be decisive in the removal of an underperforming individual in spite of the initial resistance he received from his HR personnel (Stone, 2019). In every case, the actions of these leaders were courageous, but they were also decisive, and as Smith (1986) would have it, those decisions kept the organizations moving along.

Like the leaders above, Tripp Riedel had to be decisive and courageous as he implemented a cultural change in his organization as well. But in his case, the organization was one he returned to as a leader after leaving several years earlier to pursue other opportunities.

ALEXANDER "TRIPP" REIDEL

Tripp Riedel is the Vice President of Aviation for a major oil company. He became interested in aviation as a child and had his first airplane ride at age 12 with his parents. But at the time, he didn't consider aviation as a career path.

After he graduated from high school, Tripp drifted from job to job for a period of time, unsure of what he wanted to do. One of his bosses took him for another airplane ride, and Tripp realized that aviation presented a career opportunity. He enrolled in an aviation college, but when he graduated, during the 1980s, airlines were furloughing pilots instead of hiring them. Tripp worked as a line service technician and performed flight instructor duties. He even formed his own non-aviation business, a freight company, and ran it for five years while he performed flight instruction on the side.

Eventually, Tripp was recruited to run the flight school where he worked, and it was while he was working that job that he was initially hired by the oil company as a pipeline patrol pilot. He worked his way up to captain of their jet aircraft, but a lack of opportunities for further advancement led him to seek employment outside the oil company to manage aircraft. He returned to the oil company three years ago as Director of Aviation. Tripp has over 20 years of leadership experience.

When Tripp returned to the department, he found a situation similar to the one that both Jerry Aiken and Jad Donaldson encountered – a dysfunctional organization.

"The department was in meltdown mode," Tripp says. "The former aviation director had been fired, and there was a lot of internal strife. An internal audit had been conducted, and the leadership of the company thought the department was unsafe. The wanted me, as an outside guy but also a former inside guy, to come back and help to fix the place. It wasn't going to be easy. These guys didn't even have a flight operations manual. They were operating like a bunch of cowboys.

"So, there were decisions to be made. I led them into IS-BAO compliant operations, and we developed a manual that provided the right guidance for our organization. There were big safety changes that had to be instituted. It's taken me three years of non-stop decisions, hammering away at the new culture, one decision at a time, one person at a time, trying to instill a values system, and strong safety culture. IS-BAO provided the processes and helped us get things on paper, but it was a difficult and sometimes frustrating struggle. In the end, it was worth it. Today, I'd rate our flight department as one of the top ten in the world" (Riedel, 2019).

Decisiveness can be linked to integrity as well as courage. When a leader has committed to a high level of integrity, he or she can be decisive when they encounter situations that would compromise that integrity. Don Hitch[68] was decisive in his dealings with an account that pushed him for a safety waiver, and he was also decisive in his actions when JetDirect wasn't paying its bills (Hitch, 2019). Milt Hobbs was decisive in the stand he took against a former CEO that wanted to fire one of Milt's captains for making a safety call (Hobbs, 2019).

Decisiveness can also correspond with credibility, for it is a leader's willingness to make a decision that makes them credible to their subordinates. Stephanie Chung[69] faced two decisions in her career requiring swift, decisive responses that reinforced her credibility as a leader.

"When I was with Bombardier," she recalls, "I had a situation when one of my sales directors gave a bad cost of ownership estimate to a potential owner. It was off by $300,000. The client was going to hold us to it. The President of the company took me into his

---

[68] Don and Milt's introductions and bios appear in Part II, Chapter One. See Chapter One for more in-depth discussions.

[69] Stephanie's introduction and bio appear in Part II, Chapter Five.

office and asked me how it happened. Stephanie had researched how the error occurred before the meeting, and she knew the answer, an assistant for the sales director, had made the error.

"'Who did it? the President demanded."

In an instant, Stephanie had to decide how to handle the situation, but her credibility gave her the answer immediately.

"As far as you're concerned, I did," she replied.

"When you're in charge, you take responsibility," Stephanie says. "I wasn't going to give up my sales director or his assistant."

She had another situation where decisiveness was required when one of her salespeople was on vacation, and a request for proposal (RFP) came through from a sales lead that person had developed. Stephanie ran with the deal, pushed it through the approval process, and got it closed. When the substantial commission from the sale was paid, Stephanie had a decision to make about where it would go. Without hesitation, she insisted that the salesperson who developed the lead be paid, not her. The CFO refused to give the commission to that person because that person wasn't around when the deal closed, and Stephanie had performed the work.

"That doesn't matter," Stephanie insisted. "RFPs were that person's specialty, and they opened the door. I just made the decision because he wasn't here at the time, and I would have had to push it through anyway. The commission belongs to him."

The finance people resisted, but eventually, Stephanie prevailed, and the salesperson was paid.

Her decisiveness made the difference (Chung, 2019).

Sometimes, vision can drive decisiveness. Ed Bolen[70] demonstrated that when Hurricane Katrina ravaged New Orleans, Louisiana, the planned site for the 2005 NBAA BACE. The NBAA didn't have much time to adapt to the situation. It was Ed Bolen's vision for the event that generated the decisiveness required to lead his team through the process of securing Orlando as an alternate site for the convention and saving the event that year (Bolen, 2019).

Selflessness can fuel decisiveness, as Kevin Nichols[71] demonstrated when a flood event threated Conagra Aviation's base of operations at Eppley Airfield in Omaha, Nebraska. In 2011, 65 feet of snow melted in the Rocky Mountains. The resulting runoff generated 200,000 cubic feet of water per minute on the Missouri River and overwhelmed the dams upriver from the airport. The water level rose to within two feet of the top of the levee that protected the airport from the raging river, but the levee held. The senior leadership of Conagra summoned Kevin to a meeting to discuss options for the flight department; the memories of the 1993 St. Louis flood still somewhat fresh in his mind.

"When I met with them, I realized they didn't want me to ask them what to do," Kevin recalls. "They wanted me to tell them. To recommend a plan."

Kevin took decisive action. Thinking of his team

---

70 Ed's introduction, bio and a more in-depth discussion of this event appear in Part II, Chapter Eight.

71 Kevin's introduction and bio appear in Part II, Chapter Seven.

before himself, he ordered an immediate evacuation of the department's hangar at Eppley Field to the Council Bluffs airport, across the river and inland. With the help of Conagra's real estate team, Kevin moved all the furniture and supplies to offsite storage. He moved the maintenance support equipment to Council Bluffs, along with all but one of the department's aircraft. Kevin and his managerial staff kept the remaining jet at the hangar at Eppley, along with minimal office supplies, and a supply of life preservers. They operated the aircraft at Eppley along with pilots on a standby rotation until the threat of the flood passed (Nichols, 2019).

Engagement can push leaders to be decisive. Greg Adams encountered a situation in which an extended duty day would have pushed his people too hard. Shortly after one of his jets took off from Miami International Airport bound for White Plains, New York, the lead passenger informed the captain of the aircraft that he'd need to travel to Buenos Aires, Argentina the following evening. The captain phoned Greg with the news, and Greg and his schedulers began to work on a plan to make it happen. By the time the jet landed at White Plains, Greg had a plan, but he also had a dilemma. The crew would need to do some substantial planning for the trip, and they couldn't do the planning and get the rest they needed to perform their duties. As soon as Greg realized this, he made a decision. He called the lead passenger and informed him that they couldn't support the trip.

"It was the right thing to do," Greg says. "I told him we'd be working the crew too hard and couldn't do the trip. The principal was actually thankful. He was glad I wasn't a 'yes man'" (Adams, 2019).

All of these leaders faced different situations and scenarios and were decisive in their actions. While the circumstances and timelines varied, each was placed in a position where a decision or decisions were required, and rather than delay and consider, they acted. Sometimes swiftly, but always confidently, relying on their experience, their knowledge, and their core values.

THOUGHTS FOR LEADERS ON DECISIVENESS

There are few environments more physically and mentally challenging that the cockpit of a high-performance fighter in the act of aerial combat. The pilot has to assimilate information from multiple sources, process that information, decide on a course of action and implement that action, often many times over, while under g and possibly under fire. The amount of decisions required in a short period of time is staggering. It was in this environment that Air Force Colonel John Boyd[72] developed a concept of

---

[72] I cannot do justice to the background or contributions of John Boyd in this venue. He wasn't just a fighter pilot; he was an intellectual and a philosopher whose work has gleaned worldwide respect and admiration. If you Google, Colonel John Boyd or OODA, hundreds of thousands of hits will be generated. Probably the best work on his life and contributions is Robert Coram's <u>John Boyd: The Fighter Pilot Who Changed the Art of War</u>. (New York: Little Brown and Company, 2002).

decision-making that has become pervasive in both military and civilian thinking alike – the OODA loop. OODA stands for observe, orient, decide, act, and it a process that seems simple, yet is incredibly nuanced. It can offer leaders a framework to make decisions in their organizations.

The OODA loop has been described and explained in countless articles and publications, and a detailed explanation of it is not possible here. Instead, I'll try to synthesize the descriptions of what I've read with my own experiences in the air and attempt to provide a depiction of the model that may help my fellow leaders in their own decision processes.

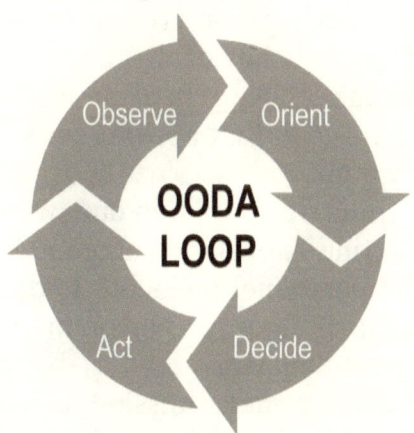

Figure 13. The OODA Loop.

STEP 1 – OBSERVE

Observation is about collecting information. It is the "what" phase of the process.

When I arrive at the endgame of an intercept

in a fighter, the visual merge, meeting a potentially hostile aircraft, I have situational awareness that has been conveyed by a radar controller and additional awareness that has been provided by on-board sensors and my own eyes, but I still have to watch the situation develop. I have to identify the other aircraft, I have to assess its energy state, and most importantly, I have to watch its nose position vis-à-vis my flight path. Is he maintaining course, or is he turning towards me? In this case, let's say that his nose is aggressively tracking in my direction.

Similarly, in a leadership role, we often can arrive at our own "merges" with individuals or issues in our organizations. Perhaps we are informed of another incident of poor behavior by a potentially toxic employee, or one of the users of our aircraft wants us to perform a mission that appears to be outside our normal operations.

The first thing we do is build our awareness of the issue by collecting information about it. What are the details of the personnel incident? Is there a logical explanation for it? Does the person in question have a history of poor behavior?

What does the new mission element entail? When will it need to be performed? We collect all the information we possibly can so that we can make the best decision.

How much information is required? According to General Colin Powell, enough so that we have at least a 40% chance of being right, but not more than 70% chance. Once we get in that realm, we are to trust our gut. If we think we have less than a 40% chance of being right, making the decision is irresponsible. If we have more than 70%, our waiting will cause us to act too late (Harari, 2002).

STEP 2 – ORIENT

This step is probably the most important one in the loop. It is the "why" phase of the process. It is here we analyze the information we've collected and visualize an end state for the situation we've encountered. Detailed explanations of the OODA loop discuss the importance of genetic heritage, cultural traditions, and the analysis and synthesis of both new information and previous experiences.

After arriving at the merge, I see the bandit's nose tracking in my direction, and my onboard sensors indicate his radar is locked on to me. My analysis is that he is aware of me and is maneuvering against me. While the final end state of the situation would be for me to win the engagement, that's too far ahead to think at the moment. The end state I have to visualize is the place in space where I can stay in an offensive position and maintain my energy.

As leaders, we need to evaluate the information we have collected and be mindful of our own biases and predispositions as we do so.

What could be the motivation of the latest incident of the individual's poor behavior? Is the individual stirring up trouble, or does he or she have a legitimate complaint and perhaps is not expressing it appropriately?

Is the new mission element within the performance

capability of the aircraft? Does the crew have the necessary experience and training?

Notice that there is no mention of feelings or emotions in this stage. While as human beings, our emotions can invariably work their way into anything we do, when it comes to a decision process, particularly one that may occur in the heat of aerial or organizational battle, we must maintain our objectivity to make the best possible decision.

STEP 3 – DECIDE

This is the phase in which possible courses of action are evaluated, and one or more is chosen. It is the "how" phase of the process.

As I see the bandit coming my way, I have several choices for counter-maneuvers. I can pull the nose of my aircraft towards the bandit's to deny him turning room, I can maintain my energy by staying co-altitude with him, or I can spend or gain energy by going vertically upwards or downwards. During the observe phase, I identified his aircraft as one that doesn't perform as well as mine, so I have the option of putting my aircraft into a flight regime that the bandit cannot match. I consider various maneuvers and opt to go into a pure vertical climb.

In a leadership role, I evaluate different courses of action for the individual. Is verbal counseling appropriate? Is a written warning necessary? Should termination be considered? Given the details, perhaps we choose verbal counseling as the course of action.

For the mission element, we ascertain that it is

within the performance envelope of the aircraft and doesn't violate safety guidelines, but currently, no crew members are trained for it. The course of action we decide upon is to pursue the necessary training and plan to execute the mission element.

STEP 4 - ACT

In this phase, we execute the course of action we decided upon. A decision without action is no decision at all, and as we have seen above, no decision is perceived by subordinates as a decision in itself.

In the aerial combat scenario, I pull my nose into an aggressive vertical climb, mindful of my opponent's nose position and the possibility that he might launch an infrared guided missile against my aircraft.

In the personnel scenario, we conduct a counseling session. We get a full understanding of the employee's attitude and actions and, if appropriate, sternly warn him or her about the consequences of repeating the action in question.

In the mission element scenario, we accomplish the required training and ensure we are ready to perform the task in question when directed to do so.

STEP 5/1 - OBSERVE

Now we are back to the observe phase, the "what" of the process; only this time, we are observing the effectiveness of our action in the situation.

Is the bandit's nose tracking up towards mine?

Can he match my performance? Or is he separating from the fight?

Does the counseling session sink in for the employee in question? Does it modify his or her behavior?

Once the training for the mission element has been accomplished, can we maintain currency? Will the weather allow us to perform it when the time comes?

The loop can be repeated multiple times, depending on the situation, but eventually, an end state will be reached. In aerial combat, typically, one aircraft wins, and the other loses. In leadership, the desired end state is for the organization to win, either through bringing a potentially toxic person back into the fold or ejecting them from the organization; or adding an additional mission element to the organization's portfolio of capability. As leaders, the more acquainted we are with this loop and the better we execute it, the more decisive we can be.

A PERSONAL REFLECTION ON DECISIVENESS

In the fall of 1989, I attended the A-10 Fighter Weapons Instructor Course at Nellis Air Force Base, Nevada. It was a four-month course of instruction that provided a Ph.D. in A-10 employment and is probably the most challenging thing I've ever done in my life. The culmination of the course was a two-week large force employment exercise where scores of outside aircraft were flown in and the students from the various schools at the time, the F-15, F-16,

A-10, F-111, are tested on what they've learned in an environment that is next thing to actual combat. To call it demanding would be an understatement of epic proportions.

I was one of five pilots in my A-10 class, and since only air-to-ground pilots could be in charge of the mission-package, two of us were designated to be mission commanders for the "blue" force. Dar Kemp, a fellow A-10 pilot from RAF Alconbury, had the helm on day three of the war. I was mission commander on day four.

The mission commander is responsible for the entire conduct of that day's battle. He has to understand the target array, build a game plan to strike all the targets and deconflict aircraft on and off target, coordinate air refueling, air-to-air fighter support, electronic warfare support, and develop his own game plan to get his four-ship formation to its own target and attack it with survivable tactics. On the day in question, the mission commander leads a strike package of 50+ aircraft into simulated battle.

I didn't fly on the day my fellow Hawg-driver, Dar Kemp, conducted his mission, because I was planning mine for the following day. But as I began to coordinate the elements of mission preparation, one of the pilots from the B-52 wing that was supporting the exercise cornered me.

"Your buddy got us shot down again today," he said without preamble.

"What?" I asked.

"We were shot down again. You bozos keep sending us in with the main package, and because they're all faster than we are, they get to the target area first and are coming off target by the time we get there. Then Red Air pounces on us and shoots us like fish in a barrel."

I was nodding as he spoke. The B-52 flew at about 350 knots, and all the other aircraft, with the exception of the A-10, flew at 480 on the ingress and 540 on the final attack run. The A-10's slower speed didn't hurt us as much as it hurt the B-52s or "Buffs" as we used to call them, because we attacked targets on the forward edge of the battle area, where the mock armies made contact, while the Buffs had to penetrate deep into enemy territory to drop their payload.

The B-52 pilot put his finger into my chest. "I'm flying in your package tomorrow. I don't want to die, even if it is simulated. You need to come up with a different plan."

Three hours later, I was on a small stage in front of a room full of representatives from all the different aircraft that I'd be commanding the following day. I had decided on the game plan, but I wasn't anxious to share it. I turned on the overhead projector (no computers with PowerPoint back then) and began to go through the lineup of aircraft that would be participating to ensure the appropriate personnel were present. They were. Now it was time for me to reveal my game plan. I put up a series of slides that showed the terrain under the Nellis airspace for orientation purposes since we were flying low altitude "Cold War" tactics for the mission. Each slide had the callsigns of the various flights in my package and the timeline for their departure from "Student Gap," which was the starting point for the westward ingress to the target area. I had the group's attention with the first slide, which showed the B-52 as the first aircraft through the gap. We, the A-10s, were next, and the fast-movers followed after making one 360-degree turn in the orbit area.

The pilots in the room were incredulous. Many were laughing.

"That's crazy," they said. "Red Air will jump on that Buff as soon as it gets through the Gap!"

I shrugged. "Maybe," I said. "But if Red Air commits on the Buff, our Blue Air will kill them early, and the rest of the strike package will get through without being touched. And if they don't commit until the main package arrives, it will be a standard battle, only by the time they tangle with the main package, the Buff will be off-target."

The room was quieter now as the group considered what I had said. After another fifteen minutes of discussion, the briefing ended, and we went back to our individual planning rooms. The B-52 pilot I had met previously cornered me as I left the room. He was nodding.

"Gutsy call," he said. "I hope it doesn't get us killed."

"Me too," I replied.

Fast forward 24 hours – the strike was successful, and the B-52 lived. And I drank for free at the Officer's club the following Friday night.

The moral of the story? Sometimes being decisive requires the courage to think "out of the box" and then stick by your decision when challenged. I was a 30-year-old captain at the time, and I had to stand up to a room full of senior captains, majors, and lieutenant colonels when I made that pitch. They had more experience than I did and had every reason to believe the plan would fail. They were skeptical, but they were willing to be led and attempt a new way to accomplish the mission. Why? For one reason only. Because I was decisive about it.

One of the primary functions of a leader is to make decisions. When we have the courage, integrity, credibility, vision, and selflessness to be decisive, as the leaders in this chapter have demonstrated, we serve our people and our organizations better. And if leadership is about nothing else, it is about service.

PART II

--------- CHAPTER FIFTEEN ---------

DETERMINATION

THE DEFINITION

The many dictionary definitions of the word determination run a full gamut of meaning across several different fields, including law, philosophy, and biology. The definition most applicable to this discussion appears in the middle of the list.

Firm or fixed intention to achieve a desired end (Merriam-Webster, 2019).

I discovered after I wrote the survey and analyzed the results that my understanding of determination confounded the definitions of both determination and persistence. I had always thought the two were synonymous, but that is not the case. While determination is about intention, persistence is about action:

Continuing or inclined to <u>persist</u> in a course
(Merriam-Webster, 2019).

I realized then that I had been influenced by a quote from former President Calvin Coolidge that I encountered years ago and have related to my children on many occasions.

Nothing in this world can take the place of persistence. Talent will not: nothing is more common than unsuccessful men with talent. Genius will not; unrewarded genius is almost a proverb. Education will not: the world is full of educated derelicts. Persistence and determination alone are omnipotent (Brainyquote, Calvin Coolidge Quotes, 2019).

I'm not alone in my identification of determination as the term to identify effective leaders, however. Peter Northhouse, Ph.D., a professor at Western Michigan University and author of the best-selling academic textbook on leadership in the world, identifies determination as one of five essential traits for top leaders (Northhouse, 2019). He defines it this way:

Determination is the desire to get the job done and includes characteristics such as initiative, persistence, dominance, and drive. People with determination are willing to assert themselves, are proactive, and have the capacity to persevere in the face of obstacles. Being determined includes showing dominance at times and in situations where followers need to be directed (Northhouse, 2019, p. 24).

THE RESEARCH

As I alluded to earlier, I chose a one-line definition for *determination* for the 2019 study that looks a lot more like persistence, but also captures Professor Northhouse's definition above:

Stays the course.

I also used the respondents' 1-3 ranking to determine where courage fell in the overall list of attributes.

Overall Mean	5.21
Leaders Mean	5.27
Followers Mean	5.14
Levene's Test for Variance	$F = .189, p = .664$
Means Statistically Different?	No

Table 19. Respondent ratings on the importance of determination.

The results in Table 19 indicate that *Leaders* and *Followers* were aligned on the importance of determination. The rankings of both groups confirm that. Both *Leaders* and *Followers* also rank determination as the 15th trait in importance out of the 15 provided in the list.

THE LEADERS

Determination, like decisiveness, does not occur in isolation. Dan Drohan's[73] passion to bring his company out of the ashes of the JetDirect debacle generated his determination to make Solairus the powerhouse that it is today (Drohan, 2021).

Kellie Rittenhouse[74] was determined to perform and succeed as she climbed the ranks in her organizations to eventually become a Director of Aviation.

"I've been called out by a few people," Kellie says, "who thought because I wasn't a pilot or a technician, that I didn't know what I was doing. Determination was important for me. I had to ignore that those kinds of people and comments, stay the course, and prove what I could do" (Rittenhouse, 2019).

David Davenport knows the importance of determination as well, although his take on it is

---

73 Dan's story appears in Part II, Chapter Eleven.

74 Kellie's introduction and bio appear in Part II, Chapter Three. An additional story about her appears in Part II, Chapter Ten.

slightly different.

DAVID DAVENPORT

Dave Davenport is the former CEO of FlightSafety International (FSI), perhaps the preeminent provider of business jet training in the world.

Dave attended the Air Force Academy[75] but only spent a short amount of time in the USAF after graduation. He was a first assignment instructor pilot in what was then Air Training Command, but then he left the Air Force to run a flight school in Florida. That venture led him to Flight Safety's West Palm Beach Learning Center in 1996. He became Center Sales Manager and then an Assistant Center Manager at the Palm Beach location. His experience there taught him how sales worked, and it also taught him about leadership.

"I learned that leadership is about trust," he says. "The more relationships you can build with the people in your organization, and the more trust you can build as part of those relationships, the more you can inspire people to follow you."

After a year in Palm Beach, Dave moved to Flight Safety's Academy at the Vero Beach Airport, where initial flight training was conducted for students from Europe to qualify them for the right seat of airliners.

---

75 Full disclosure, Dave and I were classmates from the Air Force Academy, although much to my chagrin, I didn't realize that until I interviewed him.

In 1999, Dave transitioned to Flight Safety's Atlanta Learning Center, where he served as Center Sales Manager and Assistant Center Manager until 2005 when he moved to the Savanah Learning Center to become the Center Manager there. Since FSI's Savannah Center is located next to Gulfstream's factory, it is the nerve center for all of Gulfstream Training at FSI centers all over the world. Dave oversaw those programs in addition to performing Center Manager duties.

In 2012, Dave was promoted to Vice Present of Operations and moved to FSI's headquarters in New York, where his duties included oversight of all of FSI's non-military training. In the fall of 2018, when Bruce Whitman, FSI's long-time CEO, passed away, Dave was promoted to Co-CEO of the company, with responsibility for the same areas. Shortly thereafter, he became sole CEO. Dave has over 33 years of leadership experience.

Dave's four years at the Air Force Academy taught him the meaning of determination, an attribute that has served him well at FSI.

"One of my mottos is don't ever quit," Dave says. "I preach that to my people. We'll always run into a snag or an obstacle. We need to realize that, accept it, and figure out a way to get things done anyway."

Dave's determination led to the development of FlightSafety's innovative advanced training program, or ATP, a groundbreaking program with four courses of instruction that goes far outside of the normal confines of typical aircraft training.

"The genesis of ATP was customer-driven," Dave

says. "And it was a function of our determination to do better for our them. FlightSafety has a seat on Gulfstream's advisory board, and twice a year, customers would give feedback on Gulfstream's products. I would listen for any issues the customers had with training, and it became apparent that they wanted something more than the standard FAR 61.58[76] courses, especially after the Air France 447 accident[77]. Gulfstream had the aerodynamic data for aircraft when they departed controlled flight, so we programmed that into the simulators. That became the Upset Prevention and Recovery Training Course. It's a one sim ride program that teaches pilots to recognize, prevent, and recover from extreme and unusual attitudes. The FAA actually validated the model. Our customers asked for it, and we partnered with Gulfstream to make it happen. Once the course was ready, we invited our customers to try the course. They tried it, loved it, and wanted more.

---

[76] 14 CFR 61.58 requires annual pilot-in-command proficiency check rides for pilots of aircraft that require more than one crewmember or are turbojet powered. Non-commercial business aircraft recurrent courses are designed to satisfy the requirements of this regulation.

[77] See note 51.

"We had some data gathered from FOQA[78] programs that indicated we needed to develop a course that dealt with stabilized approaches," Dave continues. "That turned into the energy management course, another one-ride program where the pilots learn to manage their energy with more consistency so they can determine if they can hit stabilized approach criteria much further out than 1,000 or 500 feet on final approach.

"Then we looked at the rejected takeoff decision and developed the Rejected Takeoff Go/No-Go course. That course has eighteen takeoff scenarios where the crew has to make the go/no-go decision. We also developed a CRM advanced course for crews to explore human factors in a real-time environment.

"None of these courses would have happened without our determination to give our customers what they wanted," Dave concludes. "And they wouldn't have been successful without our customers' trust in that determination. These courses aren't cheap, but customers trust in us and the product we deliver."

Determination was a crucial factor in another critical area for FlightSafety, the G-650 program.

In 2011, FlightSafety had already spent several million dollars to build one G-650 simulator and was preparing to expend the funds to build a second. At the

---

78 FOQA is flight operations quality assurance. Flight departments that participate in a FOQA program gather information from special flight data recorders and analyze that data for trends that may be potentially dangerous.

time, the aircraft was still in the test phase, and FAA certification was destined for some time in the future. Then, on April 2, 2011, one of the test aircraft crashed in Roswell, New Mexico. At the time, Dave was in charge of all the Gulfstream training programs, and he had to make a choice, suspend construction of the second simulator in case the G-650 encountered an extended delay in certification, or continue building the simulator, in the expectation it would be required sooner rather than later.

"Gulfstream had over 200 firm orders for the aircraft and was going to have fifty aircraft ready to be delivered by the time the G-650 was certified," Dave says. "All the pilots for those aircraft couldn't be trained on one sim. We knew that, so we stayed the course and hoped for the best."

That decision was rewarded. After a minor certification delay, the G-650 was certified in September 2012. FlightSafety was ready to support it. Dave's determination to serve FlightSafety's customers paid off.

Like Dave Davenport, Bob Hobbi has customer-centric determination. But in Bob's case, his determination has led to the creation of a company that teaches other businesses to function more efficiently so they can serve their customers better.

BOB HOBBI

Bob Hobbi is the Founder, President, and CEO of ServiceElements International, Inc., a company that specializes in organizational and professional development.

Bob's aviation career started with FlightSafety International (FSI) shortly after he graduated from the University of Evansville, Indiana, with a degree in international business. After he moved to the New York City area with his wife, he wound up at FSI as a file clerk. We worked his way up through the ranks and several positions, and 15-16 years later, he became known as the company 'fixer.' Whenever a division of FSI ran into challenges, Bob was called in to find solutions. He restructured FSI's customer support and customer management, and merged functions like scheduling, contracting, billing and training records processing into one team as customer support. Additionally, he cross-trained people so anyone could help customers. He also became responsible for the overall pricing structure of the company's training products and programs.

Eventually, Bob was recruited by Honeywell to run an aerospace academy with eight training facilities which was responsible for training approximately 15,000 aviation professionals per year, from business and commercial aviation, the military, and the government, on all of Honeywell products avionics, accessories, engines. After working there for a few years, Bob had an epiphany. The industry was focused on technical training, but it expected its people to be leaders and customer service agents as well. And there was hardly any training for either.

"The industry seemed to believe, for example, that if someone was a good pilot or a good technician, they would somehow naturally be good at leading people, or fostering a service culture as well," Bob says. "That wasn't what I had seen. I knew the industry was going to be continually challenged, as it matured, with people issues, and there wasn't really a place they could go to get training in customer service and the core skills (soft skills) necessary to strategically interact with people. So, I founded ServiceElements to provide that option for the industry."

ServiceElements opened its doors in 2003, and Bob has been there ever since. He has over 30 years of leadership experience.

Bob's determination to help improve professionals and organizations has led him to focus on several areas as part of that process. Communication is an area that he is particularly keen on.

"Clarity of communication is something that I'm pretty militant about," Bob says. "I spend a lot of time in interviews and our coaching sessions, ensuring candidates and leaders understand the importance of 'over-communication.' That's more important today than ever. Technology has provided us with amazing tools and additional options or choices to do our work, jobs and providing services. But the other side of the coin has introduced us to more complexity in decision making. Technology provides more options which ultimately—creates flexibility. And flexibility is demanded and required by our users and customers. However, the result of this is a need or requirement for a much higher degree of communication. Organizations need to utilize specific and multi-dimensional communication that yields clarity. Information and direction are much more complex, and we have to ensure that robust communication takes place. We often need to unpack work and business activity to further clarify, not only the specific end result but the also the path to achieve it. Our teams need to consistently repeat the variety of goals and objectives. We need to be determined to communicate utilizing new techniques and paradigms and do it well. The old assumptions are no longer as valuable. In the past we could assume that experience and knowledge minimized the need for communication. The old "she or he knows what to do, that's why we hired them." This is no longer the case because of the continuous changes and the evolution of technology in our industry.

"Another communication challenge is that today's leadership struggles with many different means of communication, so many choices," Bob continues. "This, coupled with the fact that the speed of change is astronomical, and multi-layered, adds to the communication challenge. That's why we teach and advocate that today simplicity is the best form of sophistication. Leaders need to take complex things and make them simple, break them down, make them easier to fit today's requirement for faster comprehension of goals and objectives. That's one reason we instruct the 'new art of communication' in our leadership programs. We teach how to compose memos, send them, review them, how to brief them and bring them to life. We also teach leaders to understand the impact of those directives on various job functions and individuals, their personnel, and their customers."

Another issue ServiceElements targets is interpersonal dynamics, and the fact that those dynamics have also become more complex.

"We were working with an organization that had several hundred people in various jobs," Bob says. "There were lots of deep and established silos. We were there to improve their service culture, and we saw some obstacles in the organization. So, we had some sessions with no PowerPoint, no workbooks, just free-flow conversation. This is the new form of learning and communication. It requires patience and focus on "the people impact" of our day to day work lives.

"'What are the obstacles you see?' we would ask them. 'And what would you do to get rid of them, to mitigate them or to work around them?'

"People came up with hundreds of obstacles, from hiring to expense report processing. Eventually, it dawned on them that 70% of what they thought were obstacles were actually based on misperceptions or a lack of understanding of why things were being done certain ways. They didn't understand the purpose and benefits of those procedures and the impact on others. Communicating a more global picture is more effective and important so that individuals can understand the impact of what they do or what they are required to do. This type of activity can come across as a gripe session, and it can be seen as counter-productive because it becomes all about finger-pointing and excuses for not doing the job or delivering on expectations. Leaders have to have the patience to sift through this by staying with it and changing their communication requirements.

"This is where that determination to communicate and make them better comes into play," Bob says "We have to convince people and leaders to listen, put their egos aside, and focus on issues, not the blame. We should be able to coach our way through it. As a leader you should always want to know what's in the undercurrent in your organization and culture. If you don't, success will be hampered. In the modern era of organizations, sometimes our job is to unearth issues, perceptions and challenges. That is the only way to address them. You can't fix what you don't know. We were able to turn them around by focusing on the outcome and the improvement of the organization. Once leaders weren't defensive anymore, they focused on solutions."

Bob adds, "I recognize that people may view this discussion as a bunch of mumbo jumbo babble. But we have seen and experienced the positive outcomes, when leaders understand the new organizational challenges we face. It's not something ServiceElements alone is advocating, it is a shift we all face in the nature and the new structure of organizations. This is what we are facing and must adapt to. Our old ways are not going to be as helpful or productive. People issues are going to be more and more front and center. And enhanced communication will be the tools for us" (Hobbi, 2019).

We've seen some other examples of determination to deliver for customers in some of the stories from other leaders earlier in this book. Kirsten

Bartok[79] showed determination to better the fractional experience for aircraft owners in her role in the formation of XO Jet, and later, she showed determination to increase aircraft financing options for international buyers in the creation of her current company (Bartok, 2019).

Brian Proctor's[80] determination to serve customers in the brokerage and consulting business led to his creation of Mente Group and its 10-year climb to become one of the top brokerage and consulting firms in the U.S. He also demonstrated determination to improve the ethics and transparency of the brokerage business for aircraft buyers and sellers through his work as President of IADA (Proctor, 2019).

Some leaders have demonstrated determination to take care of their people. Bob Ranck[81] showed determination to hold one of his sergeants accountable for alcohol abuse when Bob was a squadron commander at Andrews Air Force Base. In fact, Bob's determination to hold the sergeant accountable saved the sergeant's career and perhaps even his life (Ranck, 2019).

Sonnie Bates also showed determination to take care of the people he supervised in the Air Force, but that determination translated into a larger concern

---

79 Kristen's introduction and bio appear in Part II, Chapter Eight.

80 Brian's introduction and bio appear in Part II, Chapter Eight.

81 Bob's introduction and bio appear in Part II, Chapter One.

as his career progressed. He became determined to improve safety in our industry.

SONNIE BATES, CAM

Sonnie Bates is the CEO of WYVERN, one of the most trusted business aviation auditing firms in the world. Like other leaders in this book, his display of the attribute under discussion is wrapped up in his life story.

Sonnie's love affair with aviation began when he saw the Air Force Thunderbirds perform as a child and decided the sky was where he wanted to be. That desire kept him on track through high school and away from bad influences. He joined the Air Force Reserve Officer Training Corps at the University of Cincinnati and studied math and science at Northern Kentucky University. Sonnie worked full-time to pay for flight lessons and college.

"I've always had a strong work ethic," Sonnie says. "You should earn your way in life."

After Sonnie was commissioned as an officer in the Air Force, he attended pilot training at Vance Air Force Base in Enid, Oklahoma. Sonnie finished near the top of his class and was fighter-attack-reconnaissance qualified. He was hand-picked by one of the squadron commanders at Vance to be an instructor pilot, and Sonnie spent his first tour of duty at Vance as an instructor pilot.

"I enjoyed it," Sonnie says. "The only thing better than flying is teaching someone else to fly. As an instructor pilot, my biggest area of emphasis was professionalism. We can all be like Thunderbird pilots if we brief, lead, and fly like they do."

When Sonnie's instructor tour ended, the Air Force was in the process of closing bases and reducing the force, so no fighter slots were available. Consequently, he transitioned to the C-5 Galaxy, the largest jet aircraft in the U.S. inventory, and was assigned to Dover Air Force Base. While at Dover, Sonnie's squadron commander advised him to accept a leadership opportunity to improve his chances for promotion to the rank of major. Sonnie accepted the challenge and volunteered to command the aerial port unit at Dover, the largest aerial port in the U.S. Department of Defense. He excelled in the position and was promoted to major.

Sonnie was subsequently assigned to Headquarters, Air Force Materials Command, to lead safety initiatives for the production and development of the Boeing C-17 aircraft. While there, he learned about safety and quality programs, and trained C-17 product teams to be system safety managers.

Sonnie returned to Dover Air Force Base just in time for mandatory anthrax inoculations. Having seen many of his fellow service members become seriously ill from the vaccine and witnessing his Wing Commander being reprimanded and forced to retire for halting the program to the dismay of Pentagon leadership, Sonnie refused to accept the vaccine and was forced to leave the Air Force.[82]

"It was a difficult time to be at Dover Air Force Base," Sonnie recalls. "Our top-ranking officer was fired by the Pentagon for standing up for the troops. I tried to make a difference the best way I knew how, but ultimately had to make a decision to be quiet and take the shot or speak the truth and refuse it. In my mind, I did the right thing. Together, with other Air Force officers, we petitioned the federal court system and halted the program so others would no longer be injured by a bad vaccine. Our effort was a success, but it cost me my Air Force career to accomplish it."

Sonnie recalls an early test of determination while he was teaching an experienced military pilot who was upgrading to instructor pilot. The trainee couldn't fly formation.

"The guy was a former U.S. Marine C-130 driver," Sonnie says. "He was having trouble flying formation in a small trainer aircraft because he was a former C-130 pilot and had become accustomed to the formation references for a larger aircraft. He couldn't bring himself to get close enough to the lead aircraft. I couldn't let him fail. I had to find the right thing to say or do to motivate him. Thinking of the U.S. Marines' virtues, I told him, 'This isn't optional. It

---

82 Mandatory anthrax vaccine injections were repeatedly challenged in all branches of the military. There were serious questions about the safety of the vaccine and the quality of its production. For more information, see: https://www.ncbi.nlm. nih.gov/pmc/articles/PMC1447151/

is your duty to get into formation.' And those words did the trick. He got into position, and he stayed there. That episode taught me a lot about the power of words. Leaders need to choose their words very carefully."

Sonnie's next test of determination came when he was the Commander of the aerial port squadron at Dover Air Force Base. When he took the position, he assumed responsibility for freight deliveries for the entire base and had 185 people working for him, 22 of whom were union civilians.

"There was a problem with household goods deliveries for the base," Sonnie says. "They were always delivered late. It wasn't sexy to unload aircraft and load trucks, so outbound airlift freight always got priority. Many families all over the U.S. were waiting for their household goods. The phones in the office were ringing off the hook with complaints. The Chief Master Sergeant in my office told me that late household goods were a problem every new captain in my job had to deal with. He told me I needed just to get used to it. It had always been this way and would never get better. The people in my unit blamed the trucking division. But that wasn't the right answer as far as I was concerned."

Sonnie decided to put a quality-driven process into place, and he selected an employee, we'll call him Bill, to run the process of household goods offloading and delivery. Bill picked three people he trusted to be on his team, and within three months, the problem was fixed.

"All it was really about was accountability," Sonnie

says. "Someone had to take ownership of the process, and someone in charge had to be determined enough to make it happen. After a while, Bill got the process working so well his team was almost getting bored. They found themselves with time to do some personal and professional development."

Sonnie's determination to improve safety in business aviation had its roots in the Air Force when he was working in the C-17 program office, but his experiences in his first two business aviation jobs cemented it.

Sonnie's first business aviation job had him flying a Gulfstream G-IV and chasing yachts all over the world.

"The Director of Aviation was not professional," Sonnie recalls. 'He'd say, you don't need a safety manual. You don't need an operations manual. Just do what I tell you and you will be safe.'

"Then, I was hired by a large insurance company in the northeast. One of our flight attendants had a safety concern about sitting in a jumpseat during takeoffs and landings. The department policy was that jumpseat stayed in the sideways configuration, but it was designed to be facing forward during these phases of flight. I presented her concerns to the Chief Pilot. His response was similar to the Director in my previous job. He said: 'You don't have a safety issue unless I tell you so.' The culture was so bad there that we were losing four pilots per year."

Sonnie reached his tolerance limit for this kind of management behavior and accepted an opportunity at CAE Simuflite to lead the Falcon 7X training program.

His experience there added to his determination to improve safety.

"I was given the opportunity to build the pilot training program for the new Falcon 7X aircraft," Sonnie says. "It was the best job I had since the Air Force. I was leading a cadre of highly skilled professionals. We video recorded scenarios in the flight simulator to show how CRM in the 7X should be. Our first effort was terrible! The second one wasn't much better. Subsequent recordings improved, but it took many tries to achieve excellence. That taught me a valuable lesson. When we perform, we are not aware of our errors. But when we take the opportunity to review our performance objectively, with others, with an open mind for seeking what is right versus who is right, we can achieve excellence."

Along the way, Sonnie decided to be an entrepreneur. He designed two courses: one to teach aviation industry personnel how to prepare for and pass the test for Certified Aviation Manager (CAM) and another course that prepared people to be safety managers, the Safety Leader Training Course. He implemented both through a small company that he created.

Sonnie also went on to become the Program Director of IS-BAO for the International Business Aviation Committee (IBAC).

"I enjoyed my time at IBAC," Sonnie says. "Promoting safety and quality in business aviation is very rewarding. I traveled all over the world teaching IS-BAO and preaching the 'gospel.'"

Sonnie was directly involved with IS-BAO for

nearly six years. During his tenure, not only did the IS-BAO program improve but also the International Standard for Business Aviation Handling (IS-BAH) was implemented. Sonnie's determination to improve safety was reflected on a global level. After leaving IBAC, that determination found a home at WYVERN.

"I feel like I'm at the right place, at the right time," Sonnie says. "I have an awesome team, and we elevate safety and security worldwide every day. Together, we make a difference" (Bates, 2019).

JO DAMATO, CAM

If there is one title for a female in today's professional environment that instantly conveys a profound sense of determination, it's the title of "working mom." Joanne "Jo" Damato[83] is NBAA's Senior Vice President for Education, Training, and Workforce Development and has worked in the business aviation industry for over 23 years. Most impressively, she has realized success within the NBAA while raising two sons and co-parenting all of their busy schedules with her husband, a major airline pilot. So it is only fitting that her story is included in

---

[83] Full disclosure, Jo and I work together on the NBAA's Business Aviation Management Committee (BAMC). We've known each other for many years but she took on oversight chores for the BAMC in 2018. She was one of the major sources of inspiration for the first edition of this book. It was my idea to include her in the second edition.

the second edition of this book.

Jo came from a non-aviation family. She had three older brothers who excelled in the same sports that she was trying to excel in, and by the ripe age of 8, she decided she wanted to do something different and be a pilot. But her journey into aviation really started when she was 15. She was given a bomber jacket for her birthday and inside the jacket were coupons for flight lessons.

"It was kind of comical in a way," Jo says. "I was going to a Catholic high school, and I wasn't old enough to drive in New Jersey so I had to be driven to flight training – in my school uniform - where I flew airplanes!"

When Jo graduated from high school, she attended the Florida Institute of Technology in Melbourne, Florida. She majored in Aviation Management and had every intention of joining the airlines. She performed flight instructor duties as an undergraduate, and after finishing school, she tried a few different jobs that didn't fit well, one of which was flying checks in the middle of the night.

"All of a sudden, there I was, one year out of college with 1,000 hours of flight time, and there were no airline opportunities available," Jo says. "I was handing out resumes left and right. I even applied to a charter sales position that my boyfriend (now her husband) heard about. That didn't work out, but a position as a dispatcher became available at Executive Jet Management, and I applied.

"The EJM job was really a period of transition for me," Jo continues. "I found I had an aptitude for project management and my aviation knowledge helped me connect with the pilots. Over two to three years, my life-long goal of flying airplanes turned into flying an office. I even handled EJM's first flight across the Atlantic!"

After eight months in dispatch, at the age of 23, Jo became director of pilot training for EJM. But after three years in the job and with her new husband domiciled in Orlando while she worked in Cincinnati, she had a decision to make. Fortunately, the NBAA came to the rescue.

"The NBAA created a position that read like my resume," Jo says. "I was hired as the NBAA's general aviation specialist onsite at the FAA Air Traffic Control System Command Center near Washington, D.C. It was a fantastic opportunity to build something. The job was an externally facing position where I'd have to go toe-to-toe with representatives from the airlines and haggle about the prioritization of traffic into places like New York on bad weather days.

"And this is where determination came into play," Jo continues. "We were making tactical and strategic decisions on a daily basis. Every day was negotiating. I did it for six years. I had to grow a very thick skin and stay focused on what I needed to do for our industry. I had to learn what worked and what didn't and keep the relationships I had established in place. And when we hired additional people, and I was promoted into a supervisory role as the senior manager of the GA desk, that determination became more critical. I was one person at a conference table representing business aviation versus eleven airline representatives. The airline reps push me hard. They tried to make me crack – sometimes for sport - but that was good too. I was forced to keep my emotions in check and use data and objectivity to prove my case. I needed to communicate well and with integrity.

After essentially building the NBAA's GA desk, Jo moved up through several roles to her current one. When asked about her proudest accomplishment in her career, Jo is quick to answer. "It's being able to put our sons' needs first while my husband and I balance our aggressive work schedules and our caregiver responsibilities all while doing my best as a business aviation professional," she says. "That takes a daily dose of determination. But's it's been worth it for my sons to see that anyone – mom or dad - can work hard towards meaningful goals and effect change." (Damato, 2021).

THOUGHTS FOR LEADERS ON DETERMINATION

There are many works and articles in the public domain that discuss the importance of determination for leaders but virtually none that provide a description or even an indication of what it looks like.

Stephen Covey, in his classic work The Seven Habits of Highly Effective People, equates determination with a leader's expression of independent will. That expression takes the form of what Covey deems Habit Three - Put First Things First (Covey, 2013). Covey argues that Habit Three is the product of the implementation of Habit One – Be Proactive, and Habit Two – Begin with the End in Mind. He goes on to say:

> *In addition to self-awareness and conscience, it is the fourth human endowment— independent will—that really makes effective self-management possible. It is the ability to make decisions and choices and to act in accordance with them. It is the ability to act rather than to be acted upon, to proactively carry out the program we have developed through the other three endowments.*
>
> *The human will is an amazing thing. Time after time, it has triumphed against unbelievable odds. The Helen Kellers of this world give dramatic evidence of the value, the power of the independent will* (Covey, 2013).

Where Covey is more esoteric, Jeff Haden, an author and contributing editor for Inc. magazine, is more concrete, although Haden's ideas parallel Covey's to an extent. Haden says that people who demonstrate determination and willpower display four essential qualities:

1. They delay gratification;
2. They withstand temptation;
3. They overcome fear to do what they need to do; and
4. They don't set priorities; they do the things they decide are most important (Haden, 2015).

To develop those qualities, Haden provides eight recommendations:

1. **Let your past inform your future – nothing more.** The past is valuable. Learn from your own mistakes and the mistakes of others. And then let it go. Consider it as training for you, not a definition of you;

2. **See your life – and future – as totally within your control.** There's a quote often credited to Ignatius: "Pray as if God will take care of all; act as if all is up to you." Most successful people do feel good luck played some role in their success. But they don't wait for good luck or worry about bad luck. They act as if success or failure is totally within their control. If they succeed, they caused it. If they fail, they caused it;

3. **Learn to ignore the things you can have no control over.** Mental strength is like muscle strength -- no one has an unlimited supply. Don't waste your power on things you can't control. Do what you can do. Be your own change--but don't try to make everyone else change;

4. **Don't resent but instead** *celebrate* **the success of others.** Success is not a zero-sum game. Resentment consumes a considerable amount of mental energy -- energy that is better applied elsewhere. Create and celebrate awesomeness,

wherever you find it, and in time you'll find even more of it in yourself;

5. **Never stoop to complaining, criticizing, or whining.** Your words have power, especially over you. Whining about your problems always makes you feel worse, not better. Don't talk about what's wrong. Talk about how you'll make things better, even if that conversation is only with yourself;

6. **Don't focus on others; only try to impress yourself.** Genuine relationships make you happier, and you'll only form genuine relationships when you stop trying to impress and start trying just to be yourself;

7. **Constantly revisit your long-term goals.** Think of moments when you are most likely to give in to impulses that take you farther away from your long-term goals. Then use tangible reminders of those long-term goals to interrupt the impulse and keep you on track; and

8. **Count your blessings.** Before you turn out the light every night, take a moment to quit worrying about what you don't have. Quit worrying about what others have that you don't. (Haden, 2015)

A PERSONAL REFLECTION ON DETERMINATION

There have been several times in my life when

determination was required to stay the course. My journey to the Air Force Academy started when I decided I wanted to go there at age 12. I didn't waiver on the path even when I was nominated but not appointed out of high school and had to do a year at the Academy Prep School before entering the Academy.

The four years at the Academy, as Dave Davenport, Bob Ranck, Jeff Lee, Glenn Gozales, and Sean Lee will confirm, is an exercise in determination and perseverance. From the moment a cadet enters the doors, until the day of graduation, there is non-stop stress. Class attrition is high. Our class entered with over 1,400 students. We graduated with just over 800. When my daughter was considering going to school there, she asked me what the most important key was to success there. I didn't hesitate with my response. "You have to want it," I said.

When I first arrived at the Academy, I planned to fly transport jets out of pilot training and go to the airlines as soon as possible. But then, in my junior year, I had a backseat ride in an RF-4 and saw my first F-16 demonstration. I decided I wanted to be a fighter pilot and fly the F-16. I graduated in 1982 but didn't get into the Viper until 1995. I also ended up spending 20 years in the Air Force.

After retiring from the USAF, I chose business aviation as a career and wanted to be a Corporate Director of Aviation. That journey took me 11 years. Along the way, I decided to become a Ph.D., and due to the demands of job and family, that process took six years.

Part II

My experiences are not unique. Every one of the leaders in this book has similar, if not greater, stories. Expressions of determination and persistence are not isolated events in the lives of those who manifest those traits but occur repeatedly. With each event, the 'muscles' required to exercise those traits become stronger, and the power of individual will grows greater. Look into the eyes of a determined leader, and you will see someone who has become that way over time, as a product of the path they took to get where they are and the choices they make to stay there.

—————— CONCLUSION ——————

(AND SOME MORE RESEARCH...)

THE IMPORTANCE OF TRAITS

Over the last few hundred pages or so, we have discussed fifteen leadership attributes or traits and examined definitions, manifestations, and implementations of them. But how important are they?

Recall that in the 2019 study, respondents were asked to rank their top three attributes in order of importance to them. After they provided those rankings, we asked them to answer the following question:

The leadership in my department manifests one or more of the top three leadership attributes I identified.

The responses took the form of a five-point Likert

scale where the choices were:

1. Strongly Disagree
2. Slightly Disagree
3. Neutral / Undecided
4. Slightly Agree
5. Strongly Agree

Their responses appear in Figure 14 below. The statistics appear in Table 20. Note that Levene's test for variance generated a high value of F with a very low probability of error, indicating that the mean responses of *Leaders* and *Followers* were statistically different. So, while the overall mean response lies somewhere between neutral and agree, *Leaders* were stronger in their belief that their top three traits were present than *Followers* were. This is a manifestation of misalignment between the two groups.

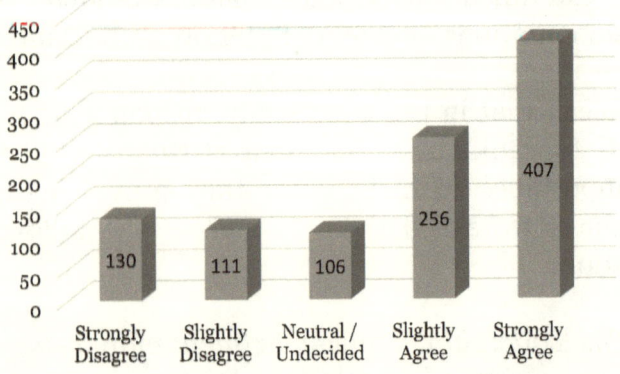

Figure 14. The leadership in my department manifests one or more of the top three leadership traits I identified.

Overall Mean	3.69
Leaders Mean	4.00
Followers Mean	3.4
Levene's Test for Variance	F = 28.602
	$p = .000$
Means Statistically Different?	<u>Yes</u>

Table 20. Statistics for the leadership in my department manifests one or more of the top three leadership traits I identified.

It is one thing to feel a certain way about leadership in one's organization. It is another to take action on it. To determine the likelihood of that action, we segregated the *Followers* in the population and correlated their answers to this question with their answers to an earlier question:

I am considering leaving my current organization.

In order to generate a positive slope for the manifestation of the traits with the consideration to depart, the results for consideration to depart question were reverse-coded so that agreeing with the question generated low values and disagreeing to it generated higher ones. The results from this correlation exercise show a positive relationship, as Figure 15 depicts.

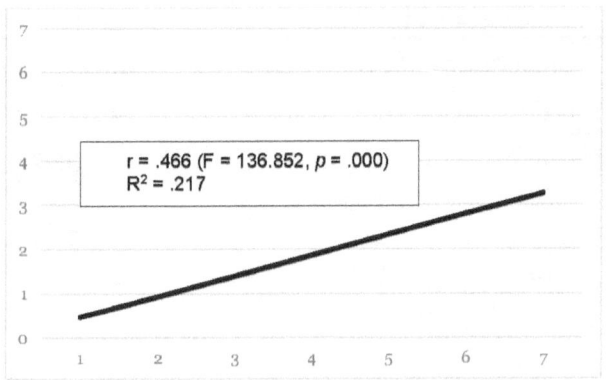

r = .466 (F = 136.852, p = .000)
R² = .217

Figure 15. Correlation of leadership trait manifestation to not considering departure from organization.

The small "r" is Pearson's correlation coefficient. It indicates that for a one-unit change in the manifestation of traits, there is a .466-unit change in the consideration not to leave the organization. In the statistics world, we call this a moderate degree of correlation. R^2 is an indication of the amount of change in the dependent variable (not considering leaving) that is explained by the independent variable (manifestation of traits). In this case, 22% of the variance in followers' decision not to leave is explained by the manifestation of desirable traits.

THE IMPORTANCE OF LEADERSHIP

For the next and final question in the study, we were more direct about the relationship between organizational leadership and personnel retention. We asked respondents to answer the following statement with the 5-point Likert scale above:

I am satisfied with the leadership of those who have the most effect on personnel retention in my department/account/company.

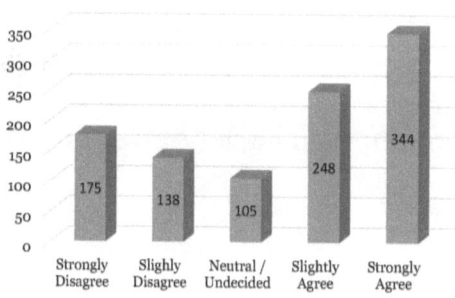

Figure 16. I am satisfied with the leadership of those who have the most effect on personnel retention in my department/account/ company.

Overall Mean	3.44
Leaders Mean	3.8
Followers Mean	3.1
Levene's Test for Variance	F = 16.163 p = .000
Means Statistically Different?	Yes

Table 21. Statistics for I am satisfied with the leadership of those who have the most effect on personnel retention in my department/ account/company.

The responses to this question show misalignment between *Leaders* and *Followers* since the means are statistically different, with a probability of error that is very low. Note that the *Followers* mean response approaches the *agree* level.

When we run a correlation in the *Followers* group between the answer to this question and the 'considering departing' question, with the answers to the latter reverse-coded as explained above, the results show an even higher degree of correlation.

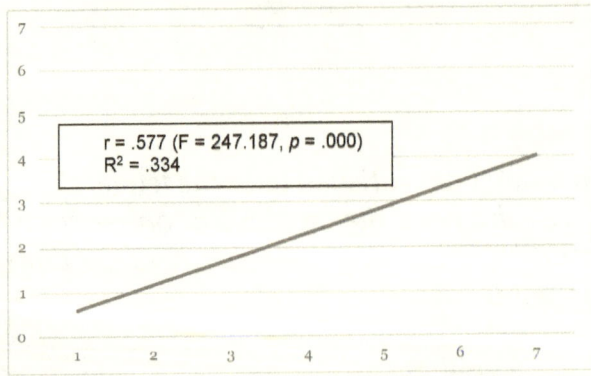

Figure 17. Correlation of satisfaction with leadership to not considering departure from organization.

Pearson's correlation coefficient indicates that for a one-unit change in followers' satisfaction with leadership, there is a .577-unit change in their consideration not to leave the organization. From a statistics perspective, this is a high degree of correlation. R^2 has increased to .334, indicating that precisely one-third of the variance in the decision not to leave is explained by satisfaction with leadership. Looking back at the model of retention we started this book with, the R^2 value for leadership satisfaction makes sense for while leadership can have an impact on both quality of life and compensation, its impact is most direct on the third leg of the stool, individual value.

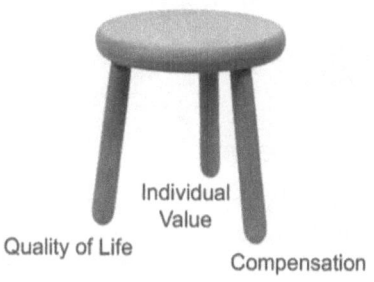

Figure 18. The Three-Legged Retention Stool.

FINAL THOUGHTS AND CONCLUSIONS

In the preceding pages, we've examined the retention issue and leadership's impact on that issue. We've delved into leadership traits and looked at some inspiring stories of leaders in our industry as they have manifested those traits in the day-to-day trenches of leadership. As the results for these last two study questions have shown, the expression of those traits by leaders correlates to whether followers consider leaving or staying with an organization. Further, we have seen that followers' satisfaction with leadership is a critical element in the retention equation.

But none of this is a surprise. Often, the result of

research is merely to add data to a discussion that previously was addressed only by opinion, and that is certainly the case here. Yet, with the examples and the data comes a distinct challenge.

As leaders, we need to remember that the traits we manifest have a direct impact on the people we lead. To succeed in our mission and earn the loyalty of our people, we must first:

- Lead with integrity;
- Lead by example;
- Communicate openly;
- Empower our people; and
- Be credible.

The research shows the importance of these traits, and the leaders we've seen have given us examples to follow in the manifestation of them. Together, they challenge us to improve ourselves, improve our leadership, and improve the lives of our people.

When I was in leadership positions in the Air Force, I would often hear junior officers lament their inability to make a difference in such a large organization. I would often tell them:

Don't worry about making a difference in the Air Force. Just make a difference where you are. Don't worry about making a difference to the entire wing, group, or even the squadron. Just make a difference in your flight and in the lives of your people. Just make your own little corner of the world better.

If we accept the challenge of excellence that the data and the leaders in this book have presented, we can all make our little corners of our organizations, our industry, and perhaps even our world, a little better.

As leaders, as human beings, this should be our highest calling and our constant objective. It should be our sacred duty.

REFERENCES

Adams, G. (2019, March 21). Leadership Book Discussion. (C. Broyhill, Interviewer)

Adkins, A. (2015, January 28). *Majority of U.S. Employees Not Engaged Despite Gains in 2014*. Retrieved from news. gallup.com: https://news.gallup.com/poll/181289/majority-employees-not-engaged-despite-gains-2014.aspx?utm_source=alert&utm_medium=email&utm_content=heading&utm_campaign=syndication

Agostino, R. (2019, May 17). Leadership Book Discussion. (C. Broyhill, Interviewer)

Aiken, J. (2019, April 17). Leadership Book Interview. (C. Broyhill, Interviewer)

Allgeier, S. (2009). *The Personal Credibility Factor, Kindle Edition*. Upper Saddle River, N.J.: FT Press.

AVM. (2019, May 15). *The State of the Shortage*. Retrieved from Aviation Maintenance Magazine: https://www.avm-mag.com/the-state-of-the-shortage/

Barden, S. (2019, June 13). Leadership Book Discussion. (C. Broyhil, Interviewer)

Bartok, K. (2019, August 22). Leadership Book Discussion. (C. Broyhill, Interviewer)

Bates, S. (2019, March 28). Leadership Book Interview. (C. Broyhill, Interviewer)

Blank, A. (2018, September 18). *3 Ways To Maintain Your Integrity In Difficult*

Workplace Situations. Retrieved from Forbes.com: https://www.forbes.com/sites/averyblank/2018/09/11/3-ways-to-maintain-your-integrity-in-difficult-workplace-situations/#4bf6f68c1a77

Boa, K., Buzzell, S., Perkins, B. (2007) Handbook to Leadership. Atlanta: Trinity House Publishers, Inc.

Boeing. (2019, October 26). *Pilot and Technician Outlook*. Retrieved from Boeing: https://www.boeing.com/commercial/market/pilot-technician-outlook/

Bolen, E. (2019, March 16). Leadership Book Discussion. (C. Broyhill, Interviewer)

Bolman, L. D. (2013). *Reframing Organizations, 5th Edition*. San Francisco: Jossey-Bass.

Botelho, E.L., Powell, K.R., Kincaid, S., Wang, D. (2017, May - June). *What Sets Successful CEOs Apart*. Retrieved from hbr.org: https://hbr.org/2017/05/what-sets-successful-ceos-apart

Brainyquote. (2019). *Calvin Coolidge Quotes*. Retrieved from brainyquote.com: https://www.brainyquote.com/quotes/calvin_coolidge_414555

Brainyquote. (2019). *Theodore Roosevelt Quotes*. Retrieved from Brainyquote.com: https://www.brainyquote.com/quotes/theodore_roosevelt_403358

Brearley, B. (2019). *You Lead By Example. What Mindset Are You Encouraging?* Retrieved from Thoughtfulleader.com: https://www.

thoughtfulleader.com/lead-by-example/

Business Insider. (2015, December 21). *11 quotes that show the great leadership of General George Patton*. Retrieved from Businessinsider.com: https://www. businessinsider.com/11-quotes-that-show-the-great-leadership-of-general-george-patton-2015-11

C.S. Lewis Foundation. (2019). *Living the Legacy of C.S. Lewis*. Retrieved from cslewis.org: http://www.cslewis.org/aboutus/faq/quotes-misattributed/

Cable, D. (2018, April 23). *How Humble Leadership Really Works*. Retrieved from hbr.org: https://hbr.org/2018/04/how-humble-leadership-really-works

Cantabene, T. (2019, April 17). Leadership Book Discussion. (C. Broyhill, Interviewer)

Chaney, M. (2019, April 11). Leadership Book Interview. (C. Broyhill, Interviewer)

Chung, S. (2019, May 22). Leadership Book Discussion. (C. Broyhill, Interviewer)

Collins, J. (2001). *Good to Great*. New York: Harper Collins.

Covey, S. (2013). *The Seven Habits of Highly Effective People - 25th Anniversary Edition for Kindle*. New York: Rosetta Books, LLC.

Covey, S.M.R. & Merrill, R.R. (2006). *The Speed of Trust, Kindle Edition*. New York: Free Press.

Covington, C. (2019, May 6). Leadership Book Discussion. (C. Broyhill, Interviewer)

Damato, J. (2021, October 26). Leadership Book

Discussion. (C. Broyhill, Interviewer)

Daum, K. (2013, September 30). *8 Tips for Empowering Employees*. Retrieved from Inc. com: https://www.inc.com/kevin-daum/8-tips-for-empowering-employees.html

Davenport, D. (2019, March 7). Leadership Book Discussion. (C. Broyhill, Interviewer)

De Pree, M. (2004). *Leadership is an Art*. New York: Doubleday.

DirectorX. (2019, March 22). Leadership Book Discussion. (C. Broyhill, Interviewer)

Donaldson, J. (2019, October 4). Leadership Book Discussion. (C. Broyhill, Interviewer)

Dornak, E. (2019, May 16). Leadership Book Diecussion. (C. Broyhill, Interviewer)

Drohan, D. (2021, November 16). Leadership Book Discussion. (C. Broyhill, Interviewer)

Duncan, T. (2019, March 18). Leadership Book Discussion. (C. Broyhill, Interviewer)

Eisenhower, D. D. (1954, May 12). *Quotes: Leadership and Organization*. Retrieved from www.dwightdeisenhower.com: https://www.dwightdeisenhower.com/190/Leadership-Organization

Emanuele, G. (2017, June 28). *Should You Fire Them? Hell, Yes!* Retrieved from shiftyes. com: https://www.shiftyes.com/blog/should-you-fire-them-hell-yes

Field, A. (2013). *Discovering Statistics Using IBM SPSS, 4th Edition*. Thousand Oaks, CA: Sage Publications, Inc.

Fisher, L. (2019, June 5). Leadership Book

Discussion. (C. Broyhill, Interviewer)

Francomano, K. (2019, July 23). Leadership Book
Discussion. (C. Broyhill, Interviewer)

George, B. (2017, April 24). Courage: The Defining
Characteristic Of Great Leaders. Retrieved
from Forbes.com: https://www.forbes.com/
sites/hbsworkingknowledge/2017/04/24/
courage-the-defining-characteristic-of-great-
leaders/#2979d6b811ca

Gleeson, B. (2013, April 23). *7 Simple Ways to
Lead by Example*. Retrieved from Inc.com:
https://www.inc.com/brent-gleeson/7-ways-
to-lead-by-example.html

Gonzales, G. (2021, December 22). Leadership Book
Discussion. (C. Broyhill, Interviewer)

Greenberg, C. (2015, May 28). *The Navy SEALs
Ethos: A Blueprint for Leadership*. Retrieved
from Fearless Leaders Group: http://
fearlessleadersgroup.com/blog/the-navy-
seals-ethos-a-blueprint-for-leadership/

Greiser, R. (2019). *Randy's Blog*. Retrieved
from theordinaryleader.com: https://
theordinaryleader.com/blog/why-passionate-
leadership-matters/

Guthrie, J. (2019, August 16). Leadership Book
Discussion. (C. Broyhill, Interviewer)

Haden, J. (2015, November 10). *8 Habits of
People With Amazing Determination and
Willpower*. Retrieved from Inc.com: https://
www.inc.com/jeff-haden/8-habits-of-
people-with-exceptional-determination-and-
willpower.html

Harari, O. (2002). *The Leadership Secrets of Colin Powell*. New York: McGraw-HIll.

Harari, O. (2003). *The Powell Principles: 24 Lessons from Colin Powell, a Legendary Leader*. New York: McGraw-Hill.

Hitch, D. (2019, March 12). Leadership Interview with Don Hitch. (C. Broyhill, Interviewer)

Hobbi, B. (2019, June 13). Leadership Book Discussion. (C. Broyhill, Interviewer)

Hobbs, M. (2019, August 12). Leadership Book Interview. (C. Broyhill, Interviewer)

Hyman, J. (2018, October 31). *Why Humble Leaders Make the Best Leaders*. Retrieved from Forbes.com: https://www.forbes. com/sites/jeffhyman/2018/10/31/ humility/#586cc8241c80

Kail, E. (2011, July 22). *Leadership character: The role of selflessness*. Retrieved from washingtonpost.com: https://www. washingtonpost.com/blogs/guest-insights/ post/leadership-character-the-role-of- selflessness/2011/04/04/gIQALaziTI_blog. html

Kern, T. (2019, September 2). Leadership Book Discussion. (C. Broyhill, Interviewer)

Korner, W. (2019, March 22). Leadership Book Interview. (C. Broyhill, Interviewer)

Kotter, J. (1996). *Leading Change, Kindle Edition*. Boston: Harvard Business School Press.

Kouzes, J.M. & Posner, B.Z. (2012). *The Leadership Challenge, 5th Edition*. San Francisco: Jossey-Bass.

Krejcie, R. V. (1970). Determining Sample Size for Research Activities. *Educational and Psychological Measurement, 30*, 607-610.

Langen, W. (2019, August 15). Leadership Book Discussion. (C. Broyhill, Interviewer)

Lee, J. (2019, March 21). Leadership Book Interview. (C. Broyhill, Interviewer)

Lee, S. (2021, December 20). Leadership Book Interview. (C. Broyhill, Interviewer)

Lipman, V. (2016, Feb 4). *The Best Managers - Always - Lead by Example*. Retrieved from Forbes.com: https://www.forbes.com/sites/victorlipman/2016/02/04/the-best-managers-always-lead-by-example/#455d1d55279d

Llopis, G. (2015, February 2). *6 Things Wise Leaders Do To Engage Their Employees*. Retrieved from Forbes.com: https://www.forbes.com/sites/glennllopis/2015/02/02/6-things-wise-leaders-do-to-engage-their-employees/#68230b9b7f5d

Maxwell, J. (1999). *21 Indispensible Qualities of a Leader*. Nashville: Thomas Nelson.

McCrimmon, M. (2019). *Vision and Leadership*. Retrieved from Leadersdirect.com: https://www.leadersdirect.com/vision-and-leadership

McKenzie, M. (2019, September 4). Leadership Book Discussion. (C. Broyhill, Interviewer)

Mclendon, K. (2019, August 22). Leadership Book Interview. (C. Broyhill, Interviewer)

Merriam-Webster. (2019). *Dictionary*. Retrieved

from Merriam Webster Online Dictionary: https://www.merriam-webster.com/dictionary

Mindtools. (2018). *Standing Up for Your People.* Retrieved from mindtools.com: https://www.mindtools.com/pages/article/standing-up-for-your-people.htm

Moore, S. (2019, February 10). *Passion and Leadership.* Retrieved from growingleaders.com: https://growingleaders.com/blog/passion-and-leadership/

Nichols, K. (2019, March 5). Leadership Book Discussion. (C. Broyhill, Interviewer)

Northhouse, P. (2019). *Leadership: Theory and Practice, 8th Edition.* Thousand Oaks, CA: Sage Publications, Inc.

NTSB. (2009, October 23). *Aircraft Accident Report, Controlled Flight Into Terrain, Korean Air Flight 801.* Retrieved from NTSB: https://www.ntsb.gov/investigations/AccidentReports/Reports/AAR0001.pdf

Olson, C. (2019, March 5). Leadership Book Interview. (C. Broyhill, Interviewer)

Orwin, J. (2019, March 5). Leadership Book Discussion. (C. Broyhill, Interviewer)

O'Toole, J. & Bennis, W. (2009, June). *A Culture of Candor.* Retrieved from Harvard Business Review: https://hbr.org/2009/06/a-culture-of-candor

Page, N. & Czuba, C.E. (1999, October). *Empowerment: What Is It?* Retrieved from Joe.org: https://www.joe.org/

joe/1999october/comm1.php/php

Palanski, M.E. & Yammarino, F.J. (2007, June). Integrity and Leadership: Clearing the Conceptual Confusion. *European Management Journal, 25,* 171-184.

Premack, R. (2018, September 5). *Airlines are 'desperate' for new pilots, and the shortage is contributing to canceled routes that are taking a toll on smaller cities.* Retrieved from Business Insider: https://www.businessinsider.com/airlines-pilot-shortage-cancelled-routes-2018-8

Proctor, B. (2019, June 5). Leadership Book Discussion. (C. Broyhill, Interviewer)

Prosinski, D. (2019, June 17). Leadership Book Interview. (C. Broyhill, Interviewer)

Rambo, J. (2019, March 11). Leadership Book Discussion. (C. Broyhill, Interviewer)

Ranck, J. (2019, May 3). Leadership Book Interview. (C. Broyhill, Interviewer)

Raskob, C. (2019, March 20). Leadership Book Discussion. (C. Broyhill, Interviewer)

Ray, M. (2019, May 24). *Passionate Leadership: 12 Key Traits That Distinguish the Best from the Rest.* Retrieved from michelleray.com: https://www.michelleray.com/passionate-leadership-12-key-traits-that-distinguish-the-best-from-the-rest/

Riedel, A. (2019, March 5). Leadership Book Discussion. (C. Broyhill, Interviewer)

Rittenhouse, K. (2019, March 25). Leadership Book Interview. (C. Broyhill, Interviewer)

Rosanvallon, J. (2019, April 14). Leadership Book Discussion. (C. Broyhill, Interviewer)

Scarlet, A. (2019). *9 Easy Ways To Build Credibility as a Leader*. Retrieved from Allbusiness.com: https://www.allbusiness.com/9-easy-ways-build-credibility-leader-19543-1.html

Schein, E. (2010). *Organizational Culture and Leadership, 4th Edition*. San Francisco: Jossey-Bass.

Schneider, M. (2017, November 30). *Selfless Leaders Can Answer 'Yes" to These 5 Questions*. Retrieved from Inc.com: https://www.inc.com/michael-schneider/selfless-leaders-can-answer-yes-to-these-5-questions.html

Seaton, H. (2018, February 27). *Leadership and Employee Engagement: 5 Strategies to Engage Employees in 2018*. Retrieved from Flashpointleadership.com: https://www.flashpointleadership.com/blog/leadership-and-employee-engagement

Segarra, J. (2019, August 12). Leadership Book Interview. (C. Broyhill, Interviewer)

Simi, S. (2019, August 2). Leadership Book Discussion. (C. Broyhill, Interviewer)

Smith, P. (1986). *Taking Charge: A Practical Guide for Leaders*. Washington, D.C.: National Defense University Press.

Stack, L. (2014, August 1). *The Real Test of a Manager? It's Successfully Fighting for Your Team*. Retrieved from TLNT.com: https://www.tlnt.com/the-real-test-of-a-manager-its-successfully-fighting-for-your-team/

Statistics How To. (2014, March 4). *Levene Test for Equality of Variances*. Retrieved from Statistics How To: https://www.statisticshowto.datasciencecentral.com/levene-test/

Staton, K. (2021, November 16). Leadership Book Interview. (C. Broyhill, Interviewer)

Stone, J. (2019, August 13). Leadership Book Discussion. (C. Broyhill, Interviewer)

Swartzwelder, L. (2019, September 20). Leadership Book Discussion. (C. Broyhill, Interviewer)

Team, M. T. (2018). *Standing Up for Your People*. Retrieved from mindtools.com: https://www.mindtools.com/pages/article/standing-up-for-your-people.htm

The Character Council. (2012, July 5). *Decisiveness vs. procrastination*. Retrieved from the-journal.com: https://the-journal.com/articles/7541

Vincent, M. (2015, March 25). *An excerpt from "The Selfless Leader:" Courage to Live and Lead Selflessly*. Retrieved from designgroupinternational.com: https://www.designgroupinternational.com/mark-l-vincent-blog/the-selfless-leader-excerpts-from-tim-hanifen

Visconti, G. (2019, March 25). Leadership Book Interview. (C. Broyhill, Interviewer)

White, M. (2019, October 4). Leadership Book Discussion. (C. Broyhill, Interviewer)

Williamson, P. (2009). *General Patton's Principles*

for Life and Leadership, Edition 5.1. Tucson, AZ: Management & Systems Consultants, Inc.

Wolfe, D. (2019, March 5). Leadership Book Interview. (C. Broyhill, Interviewer)

ABOUT THE AUTHOR

Christopher M. Broyhill, Ph.D., CAM

Dr. Chris Broyhill is an industry veteran with over 40 years in aviation. Graduating from the United States Air Force Academy in 1982, Chris served with distinction for over 20 years in the Air Force and flew multiple aircraft including the A-10 and F-16. Chris was an outstanding graduate of the USAF's prestigious Fighter Weapons School and held multiple leadership positions at the squadron and wing levels throughout his career.

Upon retirement from the USAF, Chris chose a career in business aviation that now spans over twenty years. He has flown multiple aircraft and served as a Chief Pilot and Director of Operations under 14 C.F.R. Part 135, and served as Chief Pilot and Director of Aviation for two Fortune 100 companies operating under 14 C.F.R. Part 91. Chris currently performs retention and compensation consulting services, and is the inventor and President/CEO of the AirComp Calculator™, business aviation's only online compensation analysis engine. Chris also performs pilot services in the Falcon 900EX and Falcon 7X.

Chris holds a B.S. in computer science from the Air Force Academy, an M.A. in National Security Studies from California State University at San Bernardino, and a Ph.D. in Aviation from Embry-Riddle Aeronautical University. He is an established author with six fiction novels, multiple aviation periodical articles, and a Ph.D. dissertation to his credit. Chris is currently working on his Certified Compensation Professional (CCP) credential to broaden his knowledge of compensation methodology.